FOR
JEAN Y. KEKES

The unexamined life is not worth living.

—Plato, *Apology*

THE
EXAMINED LIFE

THE
EXAMINED LIFE

JOHN KEKES

LEWISBURG
Bucknell University Press
LONDON AND TORONTO
Associated University Presses

*BJ
1012
.K4
1988*

Associated University Presses
440 Forsgate Drive
Cranbury, NJ 08512

Associated University Presses
25 Sicilian Avenue
London WC1A 2QH, England

Associated University Presses
P.O. Box 488, Port Credit
Mississauga, Ontario
Canada L5G 4M2

The paper used in this publication meets the requirements of the American National Standard for Permanence of Paper for Printed Library Materials Z39.48-1984.

Library of Congress Cataloging-in-Publication Data

Kekes, John.
  The examined life.

  Bibliography: p.
  Includes index.
  1. Ethics. 2. Life. I. Title.
BJ1012.K4 1988   171'.3   87-48006
ISBN 0-8387-5132-6 (alk. paper)

PRINTED IN THE UNITED STATES OF AMERICA

Contents

Preface   9
Acknowledgments   11

 1   An Approach to Good Lives   15
 2   The Limits of Self-Direction: Human Nature   31
 3   The Context of Self-Direction: Moral Tradition   45
 4   Self-Direction   62
 5   Ideals and Commitments   77
 6   Self-Control   95
 7   Self-Knowledge   114
 8   Moral Sensitivity   129
 9   Wisdom   145
10   Good Lives and Happiness   161
11   Good Lives and Justification   174

Notes   188
Works Cited   194
Index   199

Preface

This book is about good lives, about what they are, and how they can be achieved. In civilized societies, freedom, security, and wealth often coexist with deep and serious disquiet about good lives. People reflect on the conduct of their affairs, because they are naturally thoughtful, or because they face grief, injustice, disappointment, illness, or boredom, and they wonder about the point of it all, about how their lives could be improved, and about why and how they should face adversity. Moral philosophers ought to be able to give reasonable answers to these questions, and that is what I try to do here. My view is that good lives, in civilized contexts, depend on self-direction, and that the current malaise is the result of insufficient self-direction.

The book begins with a discussion of why some common answers to doubts about good lives carry no conviction, and it continues with a sketch of the answer I aim to develop. In the next two chapters, I discuss the influence of human nature and moral tradition on living good lives. The fourth chapter illustrates self-direction by considering the example of Montaigne, who lived a good life in circumstances no less difficult than our own. Good lives are directed toward the realization of ideals, and they are made possible by the development of character. The fifth chapter is an account of the nature and justification of ideals. Each of the next four chapters concentrates on a particular character trait that is essential to good lives: self-control, self-knowledge, moral sensitivity, and wisdom. The development of character required for good lives involves the development of these character traits, attributes that have traditionally been called "the virtues." The last two chapters examine the connection between good lives and happiness and the grounds upon which reasonable judgments about the goodness of lives can be based.

I approach the topic from the point of view of eudaimonism or virtue theory. This approach to moral questions derives its chief inspiration from Aristotle, although there are many ways in which my thinking is at odds with Aristotelian thought. Much of contemporary moral philosophy centers on disputes between and among the proponents of utilitarianism, Kantianism, contractarianism, and rights theories. There is little in this book about such disputes. I find much of contemporary moral philosophy uncongenial, because it does not address the questions I think are important.

The nature of good lives is, of course, a large question. The answers to large questions depend on answers to small questions. But the answers to small questions derive their importance from the light they shed on large questions. If the intellectual life of a subject is healthy, one can strike a balance between asking and answering large and small questions. I try to achieve this balance by occupying a middle ground between trafficking in generalities and engaging in technical disputes of interest only to specialists. My hope is that there is still in our culture a literate nonspecialist audience for philosophical reflection, the audience that philosophers had traditionally addressed before specialization overtook the subject. In any case, it is for such an audience that I have written.

Acknowledgments

This book has been long in the making. In the course of it, I received much help from philosophers who read and criticized various parts of the manuscript. I am very grateful to them for taking time away from their own work to help me to do mine. Listed alphabetically, they are: Max Black, Josiah Gould, T. E. Hill, Sr., Konstantin Kolenda, Wallace Matson, Lynne McFall, David Norton, and Nicholas Rescher. Hill and McFall read two versions of the whole manuscript and offered tough-minded yet sympathetic criticisms; I did my best to meet their criticisms, but regardless of my success in that effort, I am especially indebted to them.

I was also helped, in a different way, by several foundations whose enlightened and generous policy it is to give financial help to scholars in need of it. I was in need, and I was helped. I am grateful to the Rockefeller Foundation for a Humanities Fellowship and for a period of residency at Villa Serbelloni in Bellagio, whose director, Roberto Celli, made the occasion one of the most pleasant in my working life. The Earhart Foundation honored me with two fellowships; they freed me from teaching and administrative responsibilities when I sorely needed the time to think and to write; I thank the Earhart Foundation for their help and confidence. Over the past years, Liberty Fund has invited me to many friendly and intellectually stimulating conferences; several ideas and arguments in the book first saw the light of day in the course of these discussions. I am grateful for their hospitality, organization, and farsighted policy. I thank the Research Foundation of the State University of New York for several smaller grants. The College of Humanities and Fine Arts of my own university, the State University of New York at Albany, has been extremely generous in granting me leaves and in providing financial and administrative support and encouragement for my research; I gratefully acknowledge it.

Several chapters of the book began as journal articles. I am grateful for permission to use them. "The Informed Will and the Meaning of Life," *Philosophy and Phenomenological Research* 47

(1986): 75–90 is used in chapter 1; "Human Nature and Moral Theories," *Inquiry* 28 (1985): 231–45 is used in chapter 2; "Moral Tradition," *Philosophical Investigations* 8 (1985): 252–68 is used in chapter 3; "Freedom," *Pacific Philosophical Quarterly* 61 (1980): 368–83 is used in chapter 8; "Wisdom," *American Philosophical Quarterly* 20 (1983): 277–86 is used in chapter 9; and "Happiness," *Mind* 91 (1982): 71–82 is used in chapter 10. They have all been revised, some radically.

With deep gratitude, I dedicate this book to my wife, Jean Y. Kekes, whose love and help, through thick and thin, made it possible.

THE
EXAMINED LIFE

1
An Approach to Good Lives

The Problem

Let us begin by taking note of some basic facts of human nature. We are born, mature, age, and die; we feel pain and pleasure; we learn from the past and plan for the future; we use language, think, feel, remember, and imagine; we are conscious of ourselves; and we have hopes and fears. These are some of the ways in which we are alike. The ways in which we differ, our individuality, develop because of the varied historical, social, and personal contexts surrounding these facts. Whether we live a good life depends on how we cope with our common humanity and develop our individuality.

This process involves a constant struggle. From a birth we did not choose to a death we rarely desire, we are beset by endless problems. If we fail to solve them, we suffer. And what do we gain from success? No more than some pleasure, a brief sense of triumph, perhaps a little peace of mind. But these are only interludes of well-being, because the problems do not cease. So it is natural to ask why we should continue on this treadmill. After all, we can stop.

The tough-minded answer is that the question falsely suggests that we stand in need of reasons for continuing to live. The truth is that our nature impels us to carry on; we have wants and the capacity to satisfy them, and instinct and training dictate that we do so. We live as long as we can, as well as we can, and we do so because we are the kinds of organisms we are. It is nature, including our nature, that makes us struggle. To look for reasons beyond this is a misuse of the respite we occasionally enjoy from the difficult business of living.

This bleak view correctly depicts the past and present condition of the vast majority of people. People struggle because they are hungry, cold, and threatened, and they aim for comfort. Although one should have compassion for the multitudes living in this way, not all of us face such unrelenting adversity. Hundreds of millions are able to enjoy the benefits of civilization. For them, the primitive struggle is over. They have gained the comforts for which the less fortunate billions yearn. The point of the struggle in primitive contexts is to overcome obstacles to living. But what should we live for, once the obstacles are overcome? What should we do with our comfortable lives? About this, the tough-minded answer is silent.

Having a comfortable life does not mean that the struggle is over, only that it takes on less deadly forms. The threat is loss of prestige, status, or self-esteem; the danger is social and psychological. Nonetheless, these we also want to avoid. Why should we not say, then, that in primitive conditions our purpose is to attain comfort, while in civilized conditions, it is to protect and maximize the comfort we already have? We struggle to win such prizes as our society affords and to avoid being adversely judged by prevailing standards.

But this is superficial. No doubt, in civilized societies many are motivated in this way. However, in these contexts there is some freedom and opportunity to stand back and reflect. Much of this reflection is concentrated on the strategy and tactics of the struggle. Yet there is some energy left over that enables us to ponder life and our own lives. If we are reflective, we shall ask why we should spend our lives in whatever happens to be the socially accredited way. We know the standards by which success is judged; we know the rewards and costs of failure. If we are honest, we shall admit that we care about success and want to avoid failure. However, reflection may prompt us to ask whether we should care.

It may seem to us that the whole business we are caught up in is bogus. We see that children are indoctrinated, adolescents are goaded and guided, and adults are rewarded and punished by the vast, impersonal, ubiquitous mold into which civilized societies press their members. And we may ask why we should put up with it. Why should we care about the emblems of success and the stigma of failure? What does it really matter to us in the dark hours of a sleepless night what our neighbors, acquaintances, or colleagues think about us? They employ standards and judge according to them, but we have come to doubt these standards. Life will seem hollow to us if we reflect in this way and we shall rightly ask what would make it good.

Maybe nothing would. Maybe evolution has resulted in our capacity to ask questions about our condition, and in civilized societies some even have the opportunity to use this capacity. But it is folly to suppose that just because we can ask a question there is going to be an answer we like. There are plenty of useless things in nature, and perhaps this capacity is one of them. Maybe life just is, as black holes, electrons, mosquitoes, and hurricanes are. Each has an explanation in terms of antecedent conditions and physical regularities, but that is all.

One may meet this answer with despair or cynicism. Both are injurious. They poison the enjoyment there is in life by corrupting the innocent connection between a want and its satisfaction. There intrudes the incessant questions about the point of it all. Despair and cynicism cleave us into a natural self and a preying, harping, jeering, or self-pitying reflective self. Thus we are turned against ourselves. Reflection becomes an incitement to self-destruction. If this is the truth, the human prospect is bleak. It may be that we evolved a capacity and it will undo us.

It is not surprising, therefore, that many people of sturdy common sense simply ignore the question. They go on with the business of living, do as well as they can, enjoy the comforts they may, and prudently keep out of deep waters. However, this evasion is likely to be possible only for those who are successful in life. Typically, these are middle-class males in mid-career, with good prospects. The young, the old, the losers, and many women are left out. The young fortunately have the tendency to ask why they should follow their elder's mode of life; the old may look back and wonder whether it was worth it; many women whose lot it is to arrange for the support of their men's careers may question whether their ambition deserves support; and the failures and the poor may well ask, with various degrees of resentment, about the point of the race in which they have not done well. We cannot reasonably ignore the question, because it is persistently raised.

Nor is it reasonable to avoid putting it to ourselves, quite independently of external challenges. It is demeaning to find ourselves participating in a race, giving and getting hard knocks, obeying rules we have not made, and chasing goals said by others to be rewarding, without asking about its point. Is it not the very opposite of prudence and common sense to invest our lives in projects whose value we have not ascertained? Furthermore, there are exceptionally few lives so smooth as to be undisturbed by serious crises. Grief, ill health, social changes, injustice, lack of merited appreciation, and the flourishing of the undeserving are likely to interfere with even the most prudently lived lives. And

the questions and doubts they raise in oneself should have answers. So, it is neither possible, nor prudent to try to ignore the
question of what, if anything, makes life good.

The Solution: A First Approximation

The central idea I propose to advance and justify is that good
lives depend on doing what we want. However, no sooner is this
said than it must be qualified, for we may want to do foolish,
inconsistent, or immoral things; and they, of course, do not lead to
good lives. To indicate that qualifications are needed, I add that
we should do what we *reasonably* want to do. A large part of my
concern is to spell out what is implicit in this qualification.

Although qualifications are needed, they are nonetheless
qualifications. As I see it, the presumption is in favor of doing
what we want. Doing that is natural and expected; there is a prima
facie case for noninterference. This case can be, and often is,
defeated and the initial presumption is thereby overruled. But
unless it is, we should do what we want, and it is interference that
must be justified.

Good lives require that we shape our characters to suit the ways
of life we are pursuing and to pursue ways of life appropriate to
our characters and circumstances. Internal and external conditions need to be balanced and mutually adjusted. The world being
what it is, this adjustment usually requires shaping ourselves to fit
the world, rather than the other way around. This process of
shaping ourselves is *self-direction,* the means to good lives, and the
central part of the subject matter of this book.

The achievement of good lives, then, depends on doing what
we want to do, provided good reasons do not stand in the way.
Wanting should be understood quite generally to refer to all the
various kinds of physiological and psychological promptings to act
or to refrain from acting. Needs, drives, motives, decisions, desires, acts of will, inclinations, intentions, and the like, are all
instances of wanting. When we have a want, we are prompted to
satisfy it. However, this may not always result in action, for we may
decide to restrain ourselves, or our aim may be to avoid something.

The satisfaction of a want need not involve pleasure. We may
want to do our duty, commit suicide, punish ourselves, or make a
sacrifice for someone we love, and none of these is normally
pleasurable. So by the satisfaction of a want I mean that its object

is achieved, but not that we necessarily get a thrill out of it. We may, of course, but, then, we may not. Nor need the object we want be our own satisfaction. We may want to benefit or harm, or be polite, respectful, or hostile to others. Thus the satisfaction of wants need not be selfish. This requires emphasis, because wants and satisfactions are often taken to be intrinsically connected with selfishness and pleasure-seeking. But as I understand them, they need not be selfish or involve pleasure.

The simple view of good lives is that they satisfy all of our wants. If we see how this must be amended, we shall arrive at a more reasonable view. The first difficulty is that the simple view overlooks the objective worth of lives: we may satisfy all of our wants and be vicious or otherwise deplorable. We may think that our lives are good and be mistaken. I shall not labor this difficulty, because it requires justifying objective judgments about lives and much needs to be done before I can attempt that.

But this simple view is mistaken even from a purely subjective perspective. Surely, the goodness of lives cannot depend on satisfying *all* wants, since, while some matter deeply, others are transitory and superficial. So we must amend the simple view and claim that if we succeed in satisfying all of our important wants, then, at least, we shall find our lives good. But even this is not enough, because important wants are routinely incompatible. The satisfaction of one often involves the frustration of others. Often, long-term goals can be achieved only if short-term ones are left unsatisfied, and long-term goals frequently conflict with each other. These difficulties can be avoided by adding the qualification that important wants must be ordered. Thus we obtain yet another amendment of the simple view: if we succeed in satisfying the most important of our hierarchically arranged wants, then we shall find our lives good.

But this will still not do. We aim to satisfy our wants, because we believe that the result will be a good life. However, this belief may be mistaken. The marriage, career, or position we seek may turn out to be disappointing. The satisfaction of even our most important wants is compatible with the subjective estimate that we have failed to achieve good lives. And so an additional requirement of good lives is that the satisfaction of the most important of our hierarchically arranged wants must occur in accordance with ideals we correctly value. My claim, then, is that our lives are subjectively good if we succeed in satisfying our most important wants in accordance with appropriate ideals, and they are objectively good if reasonable observers agree with this appraisal.

This formulation makes evident the significance of the qualification that the achievement of good lives requires that we should do what we want to do, unless there are *good reasons* against it. The good reasons are limitations we must recognize; some of these are external and some internal to the pursuit of good lives.

External limitations derive from the context in which we live. Nature unavoidably restricts the forms our lives can take, and while the limitations society imposes are less ironclad, they must also be observed. For fundamental social constraints are conditions required for the existence of society, and since good lives normally cannot be lived outside of society, these constraints are minimal requirements for the pursuit of good lives. A good reason for not trying to satisfy a want, therefore, is that its satisfaction would violate conditions necessary for good lives.

Internal limitations are imposed by our particular wants and ideals. As we have seen, the wants need to be organized and the ideals need to be justified. This will result in a decision to satisfy some wants and to frustrate others. This complex process is what I mean by self-direction. It involves knowledge of our wants, control of their satisfactions, and commitment to ideals. Self-direction can lead to good lives provided it meets certain conditions. Some of these can be brought under our control; others cannot be. Natural disasters, political upheavals, accidents, or illnesses may prevent us from achieving good lives no matter how hard and well we try. But I am interested in conditions we can control. One of these is the development of character traits that make good lives possible: I shall call them *virtues*. The other is the selection and justification of *ideals*.

These considerations dictate the structure of my argument. I shall begin by discussing good lives in general terms; go on to consider the minimal constraints imposed on pursuing them; continue by giving an account of self-direction; then I shall turn to ideals and their justification; and then to virtues. At the end, I shall discuss the connection between good lives and happiness, as well as the justification of good lives.

The Case of Mill

In his *Autobiography*,[1] John Stuart Mill has left an invaluable record of both having and losing the sense that his life was good.

> I had what might truly be called an object in life: to be a reformer of the world. My conception of my own happiness was entirely identified

with this object. The personal sympathies I wished for were those of my fellow labourers in this enterprise. . . . [A]s a serious and permanent personal satisfaction . . . my whole reliance was placed on this; and I was accustomed to felicitate myself on the certainty of a happy life which I enjoyed, through placing my happiness in something durable and distant, in which some progress might always be making, while it could never be exhausted by complete attainment. This did very well for several years, during which the general improvement going on in the world and the idea of myself engaged with others in struggling to promote it, seemed enough to fill up an interesting and animated existence.

Mill's description of this period in his life needs to be read with an important qualification in mind: being a utilitarian, Mill thought that a good life was a happy life. If by happiness is meant having the life we want, then there is no harm in identifying the two. But if happiness is taken to mean a pleasurable state of mind, then it is a mistake to insist on the identity of good and happy lives. For having an object in life and having an interesting and animated existence need not result in pleasurable states of mind. They may have for Mill; but they have not for many explorers, revolutionaries, artists, statesmen, and athletes.

Mill, then, lived in this manner

until the time came when I was awakened from this as from a dream. . . . [I]t occurred to me to put the question directly to myself: "Suppose that all your objects in life were realized; that all the changes in institutions and opinions which you are looking forward to, could be completely effected at this very instant: would this be a great joy and happiness to you?" And an irrepressible self-consciousness answered, "No!" At this my heart sank within me: the whole foundation on which my life was constructed fell down. . . . The end has ceased to charm, and how could there ever again be any interest in the means? I seemed to having nothing left to live for.

Reflecting on what has gone wrong, Mill offers the following conclusion:

All those to whom I looked up, were of the opinion that the pleasure of sympathy with human beings, and the feelings which made the good of others . . . the object of existence, were the greatest and surest source of happiness. Of the truth of this I was convinced, but to know that a feeling would make me happy if I had it, did not give me the feeling. My education, I thought, had failed to create these feelings in sufficient strength to resist the dissolving influence of analysis, while the whole course of my intellectual cultivation had made . . . analysis the inveterate habit of my mind. I was thus . . . left stranded . . . without any real desire for the ends which I had been so carefully fitted out to work for: no delight in virtue, or the general good, but also just as little in anything else.

Mill's explanation of what deprived him of the sense that his life is good is convincing, but we can go beyond it. He became indifferent to his projects and lost concern for the ideal he previously pursued. He ceased to want what he had been wanting; his self-direction was no longer inspired by the ideal he accepted. The circumstances of Mill's disengagement and the nature of his projects are peculiar to Mill, and so is the extraordinary education that was partly responsible for both his achievement and crisis. But we can abstract from these peculiarities and recognize Mill's case as typical of many lives that have become bad. The precipitating experience is that we awaken, as if from a dream, and realize that what mattered before no longer does. Loss of religious faith, the death of a deeply loved person, the recognition that our commitment was based on self-deception, the realization that the ideal we have devoted our lives to pursuing is hollow, and the discovery that the cause we have made our own in irremediably tainted with evil are such experiences. The result is that we grow indifferent; life becomes a tedious burden. The connection between self-direction and ideals has been broken.

Some Forms of Bad Lives

More specifically, what would make it reasonable for us to regard our lives as bad? One possibility is that we find our activities worthless. We see ourselves as engaged in endless drudgery. We do what we do, not to attain some positive good but to avoid a condition even worse than what prevails. Yet, some intrinsically worthless activities can have a place in good lives, if they have instrumental value. The pursuit of all ideals involves some unpleasant tasks, but such tasks have a point, because of the ideals to which they lead. However, if activities lacking either intrinsic or instrumental value dominate in our lives, then they are bad, because they are pointless. In other cases, the activities dominating may have a point, and yet the lives may still be bad, either because the ideals aimed at are actually harmful, or, because, while not harmful, they are not beneficial either. In the former case, we can say that the lives are bad, because the ideals are destructive or unsuitable. The closer people get to achieving them, the worse off they are; such lives are misdirected. In the latter case, the lives are bad by being trivial. The ideals aimed at cannot provided the benefits sought. Lastly, lives directed at ideals impossible of attainment, ideals that cannot even be approximated, so that not even increments of the hoped for benefits can be obtained, are futile.[2]

We shall understand good lives better if we see that they cannot be identified as those that have worth and point, go in the right direction, and aim at beneficial and possible ideas. Mill reasonably judged his life bad, yet it had worth, for it had the intrinsic merit of being altruistic; it had the important ideal of bettering the condition of mankind, thus it was not pointless, misdirected, or trivial; and it was not futile either, for the amelioration of misery and the increase of general happiness are possible ideals. Mill recognized all these merits in his life, yet he found it bad. There is, therefore, more to good lives than avoiding these pitfalls.

Mill's life would have been made good by his wanting to live it. Before his crisis, he wanted that; after it, he did not. There appeared a break between Mill and the worthwhile, purposeful, well-directed, important, and possible activity of being a reformer of mankind. The connecting link was wanting to engage in it, and that is what Mill had ceased to do.

Mill's case shows that it is a mistake to suppose that goodness is inherent in some lives, so that if we live them, we cannot fail to find them good. Good lives must have the features I have just described, but we must also want to live them. Our contribution is as essential as the intrinsic features.

Another reason often given for regarding our lives as bad is their supposed absurdity. Camus had popularized this view in *The Myth of Sisyphus*, but it needed to be made more precise, and Nagel has done so.[3] He argues that the ordinary occurrence of absurdity is due to "a conspicuous discrepancy between pretension or aspiration and reality: someone gives a complicated speech in support of a motion that has already been passed . . . you declare your love over the telephone to a recorded announcement." However, there is also a philosophical sense of absurdity and "it must arise from the perception of something universal—some respect in which pretension and reality inevitably clash for all of us."[4] What is this clash? "[T]wo inescapable viewpoints collide in us, and that is what makes life absurd." One is that we cannot live lives without energy and attention, nor without making choices which show that we take some things more seriously than others. . . . Think of how an ordinary individual sweats over his appearance, his health, his sex life, his emotional honesty, his social utility, his self-knowledge, the quality of his ties with family, colleagues, and friends, how well he does his job, whether he understands the world and what is going on in it.

The other viewpoint is that

humans have the special capacity to stand back and survey themselves, and the lives to which they are committed, with that detached amazement which comes from watching an ant struggle up a heap of sand. Without developing the illusion that they are able to escape from their highly specific and idiosyncratic position, they can view it *sub specie aeternitatis*. . . . Yet when we take this view . . . it does not disengage us from life, and there lies our absurdity: not in the fact that such an external view can be taken of us, but in the fact that we ourselves take it, without ceasing to be the persons whose ultimate concerns are so coolly regarded.[5]

This is a perceptive analysis of the philosophical sense of absurdity, but it does not help us to understand the loss of self-direction from which Mill and others suffer. Nagel is no doubt right in attributing to us the capacity to view ourselves from an impersonal cosmic perspective, but the fact is that few of us do so. Furthermore, those who do cast this metaphysical look upon humanity are by no means uniformly overcome by a sense of meaninglessness. Plato, Spinoza, and Russell among philosophers; Sophocles and Wordsworth among poets; and Einstein among scientists, come to mind as combining the cosmic view with an intense concern for human welfare. The truths that in the long run we shall all be dead and that from Alpha Centauri we seem like ants for many people enhance rather than diminish the significance of human concerns. Nor do people typically find their lives bad, as Mill did, because of a philosophical sense of absurdity. We know that Mill's trouble was not that from a cosmic perspective his concerns appeared to be insignificant; rather, what bothered him was that he found himself without concerns. He ceased, as Nagel puts it, "to sweat about his appearance, his health, his sex life . . . whether he understands the world and what is going on in it." He carried on in a desultory manner, but he stopped caring. He stopped, not because his caring appeared absurd from a cosmic point of view, but because his ideals no longer inspired his self-direction.

The experience we need to understand is the cleavage that sometimes appears between ourselves and our projects; the projects used to matter, but they no longer do. This may have something to do with the projects, for they may indeed be worthless, pointless, misdirected, trivial, or futile. But it may also have to do with our attitudes to our projects. And it may be that our attitudes are sometimes sapped by a sense of absurdity, but they are typically sapped by an undeveloped or lost sense of self-direction that has nothing to do with absurdity. People often find their lives bad, because they are bad. But certainly, not all lives are. One difference between good and bad lives lies in the activity of self-direction.

Self-Direction and the Simple Will

Self-direction is a much more complicated process than merely putting our will behind our projects. We shall see that this is so if we consider why the simple will is insufficient for making lives good. The simple will is roughly Spinoza's *conatus:* "The endeavour wherewith each thing endeavours to persist in its own being [which] is nothing more than the actual essence of the thing itself,"[6] or that aspect of Schopenhauer's *Wille* that we each find within ourselves. It is a universal instinctive disposition of living things to maintain and perpetuate themselves.

Richard Taylor argues[7] that this conception of the will is the key to the goodness of lives. He takes Camus's gloss on the myth of Sisyphus and asks what would give significance to the utterly desolate life of eternally rolling the rock uphill as it eternally rolls down. Taylor considers two answers. One is that the drudgery would be tolerable if it served some purpose, such as building a temple on the hilltop. But he rightly rejects this as unsatisfactory. The pyramids do not render good the lives of the slaves forced to build them. Nor would it make our lives good to discover that we play a role in the plans of some higher intelligence. Temple building and cosmic purpose may give us a *function,* but that does not make us regard lives spent fulfilling it as good. Only if we *wanted* whatever the activity leads to would the activity seem tolerable to us. And this is Taylor's own answer. We find our lives good if we are engaged in doing what we want to do. The crux is the wanting and not the object of wanting or how we came to want it.

Thus, Taylor says, if the gods wanted to soften their punishment of Sisyphus, they could have implanted a device in his brain that made him *want* to roll rocks uphill. This would not have changed the facts, but it would have changed Sisyphus's attitude toward them. He would still be rolling rocks for all eternity, but he "has been reconciled to it, and indeed more, he has been led to embrace it."[8] In other words, we shall find our lives good if we want to perform many of the activities we do perform. The source of goodness is inside: it is the identification of what we do with what we want to do.

Now I think that this account is essentially right, although as it stands it is not rich enough to account for our experience of living good lives. Two difficulties point to this conclusion. The first is over the distinction between *wanting to live* and *wanting to live well*. An important aspect of the thought of Spinoza, Schopenhauer, and Taylor is the insistence that humanity is essentially continuous with other forms of life. One aspect of this continuity is that we share with living things the basic disposition to maintain and perpetuate ourselves. Let us call this wanting to live. But the satisfaction of this want by the performance of life-maintaining activities cannot by itself give us good lives, for we sometimes rightly find our lives bad, even though the life-maintaining activities are successfully performed. Succeeding in these activities is necessary, but not sufficient for good lives. People suffering from debilitating illness, physical or psychological brutalization, or the loss of all they value may not want to live, because they reasonably think that they cannot live *well*. The insistence on the continuity between human and other forms of life must be supplemented by the recognition that while we seek to make our lives good, and may or may not succeed, plants, animals, birds, and insects do not seek that. What is necessary and sufficient for good lives is the satisfied want to live well. The simple will, striving for survival, is insufficient to bring this satisfaction about.

The second difficulty is that Taylor's account does not allow for the distinction between *self-directed* and *manipulated* wants. According to him, it makes no difference to Sisyphus's finding rock-rolling good whether he spontaneously wants to roll them or whether he wants it because the gods implanted a device in his brain. In his view, the satisfaction of wants is what makes lives good and nothing else matters. But this cannot be right. It seems obvious that there is a difference between finding our lives good as a result of hypnosis, indoctrination, or artificial stimulation of the cortex and finding them so, because, through self-direction, we have discovered and achieved what matters to us. However, it is not easy to say what this obvious difference is.

One consequence of Taylor's view is that the goodness of lives derives from mental states. We seek satisfaction of our wants and we experience their satisfaction by being in a contented mental state. There are two elements in such mental states: the act of wanting and the object wanted. Normally, the satisfaction is produced by their coincidence. Sisyphus wants to roll rocks; he is rolling rocks; thus Sisyphus is satisfied. He can be manipulated about both elements. The gods can implant a device that makes Sisyphus have a want that he normally would not have, or another that can take a genuine want of Sisyphus and make him believe that it is satisfied when it is not. In the first case, he is manipulated so as to want to roll rocks; in the second case, he is manipulated so as to have the false belief that he is rolling rocks. The discovery that either has occurred destroys the satisfaction derived from the activity. If we do not immediately discover it, then we may falsely believe that the activity is satisfying. But, as we shall see, such false beliefs cannot be sustained for long.

Why is the discovery of manipulated wanting destructive of satisfaction? A manipulated want is one that we would not otherwise have. It is possible that we may be manipulated to have a want that we would have even without manipulation. But this is a dubious case of manipulation, so I shall ignore it. A truly manipulated want does not stem from our character and circumstances. There is no internal explanation of why we should have it. It has no place in the causal nexus of our desires, hopes, plans, projects, ambitions, memories, and failures that spur us to action. If we discover that we were manipulated to have a want, we feel violated.

But what if we do not discover it? It would be very hard to avoid making the discovery. For the want prompts us to engage in an activity that is going to look very strange to us. We are bound to ask ourselves: why have we all of a sudden begun to roll rocks? What is it about it that satisfies us? How is this satisfaction related to all the other things we care about? And there will be no answer. So we shall find the activity unreasonable and the satisfaction unimportant. We shall get on with our important projects and ignore this curious incident. Of course, the gods can do more. They can give us a whole new set of wants, make us forget old ones, remove the amazement of our family and friends at our radical change, and persuade our employers not to fire us. The gods could change the world; and they would have to in order to make this logical possibility one that we should take seriously.

Let us, then, turn to the second possibility and ask why is the discovery that we were manipulated so as to believe that our want is satisfied even though it is not destructive of the satisfaction? Wants have objects and they are satisfied when their objects are obtained. We can believe, and can be made to believe, that the object is obtained when it is not. But it is well to recognize how difficult it would be to sustain this false belief. The satisfaction of a want is thickly empirical. Rock-rolling causes fatigue, gives call-uses, and forms muscles. It involves surveying the terrain, chatting with spectators or ignoring them, organizing meals, and so on. Activities overlap, crisscross, depend on each other; as wants stand in an internal causal nexus, so activities stand in an external one. To give us a false belief about the presence of the object of our want requires much more than altering a mental state; it requires simulating the causes that normally produce the mental state. But the original causes are links in other causal chains as well, and will these be simulated too? Once again, great implausibility follows.

But how is this implausibility detrimental to good lives? Good lives depend on satisfactions and a want is satisfied by achieving its object. If we were to discover that we merely believed ourselves to have been successfully engaged in a self-directed activity without actually having done so, it would suddenly seem hollow, because the objects we have congratulated ourselves on having achieved turn out to be nonexistent. And if the belief had been induced, we would discover it, unless the whole world was radically altered.

In our world, however, the distinction between self-directed and manipulated wanting is crucial to finding our lives good. Self-direction involves both making ourselves likely to succeed in our projects and interacting with the world in order to engage in these projects. Satisfaction comes from succeeding at both aspects of self-direction. If we were manipulated to hold the belief, the satisfaction would be lacking, unless the belief in successful self-transformation and engagement with the world were also manipulated. But that, as we have seen, is not a realistic possibility.

What follows is that one deficiency of the simple account is its supposition that satisfaction derives from mental states. I have been arguing that satisfaction is produced by successful activities. Such activities, however, put us in contact with our surroundings.

Consequently, satisfaction is not a purely internal matter, depending on states of mind, but also an external one, depending on
interaction between us and the world. It remains true that what
makes activities satisfying is self-direction. Self-direction, however, is not just simple wanting, but wanting the appropriate
object.[9]

The distinctions between wanting to live and wanting to live
well and between manipulated and self-directed wanting also
make a deeper understanding of Mill's crisis possible. The crisis
was caused by Mill's realization that his wanting to reform mankind was not self-directed. He realized that his education trained
his intellect, but not his feelings and will. He was intellectually
convinced of the truth of utilitarianism, at any rate, of the truth of
its general ideas and programs, and it was supposed by him and
by his father that this was sufficient for making utilitarian practice
his object in life. But it was not, because intellectual assent is not
enough to make a project our own. Mill's project did not spring
from his character and circumstances; it was the result of what his
father taught him. And while we can be taught principles, arguments, and truths, we cannot be taught to have the feelings and
intentions appropriate to these intellectual notions. A project is
our own if intellectual assent to it is combined with feelings of
enthusiasm, approval, interest, urgency, and ambition, and if
these feelings and the intellectual assent spur us to engage in the
appropriate activities. Mill lacked the feelings and the want. His
engagement was induced by his father's authority, not by self-
direction. When Mill discovered that this was so, his crisis ensued.

This, of course, suggests also what would remove such crises
and what would make lives good. In self-directed commitment to
a way of life, we identify with that way of life intellectually and
emotionally, and we are moved to engage in it not merely occasionally, but for the duration of our lives. We want it not as a way
of maintaining our lives, but as a way of making them into what
we regard as good lives. We believe and feel that they are good,
and that is why we want them. The psychological content, then, of
self-directed lives is the coherence of beliefs, feelings, and intentions, and their employment in pursuit of appropriate ideals.[10]

This coherence is necessary, but not sufficient, for good lives,
because the beliefs may be false, the feelings misplaced, and the
intentions unrealizable. If they are flawed, no matter how harmoniously committed we are, we shall not achieve what we regard as
good lives. Self-direction must also have appropriate objects.

Good lives depend on a balance between the subjective psychological aspect and the objective aspect requiring the intellect, feelings, and the will to center on appropriate objects.

"[P]sychological states and their objects [are] equal and reciprocal partners. . . . [I]t can be true both that we desire x because we think x good, and that x is good because we desire x. . . . [T]he quality by which the thing qualifies as good and the desire for the thing are equals and 'made for one another.'"[11] We need not suppose that this has metaphysical implications. Surely, it is not surprising that in the course of evolution there has emerged a fit between what we want and what is good for us. Without it, destruction would have ensued long ago. Yet the fit is very much less than perfect. Objective conditions both shape and constrain our wants, but within the limits imposed by the world on our projects there is much scope and need for self-direction. To understand how appropriate objects can be found for our psychological states, we have to understand how objective conditions limit self-direction.

2
The Limits of Self-Direction: Human Nature

Introduction

Human nature is one of the objective conditions that limit self-direction. It does so by defining our possibilities and by establishing minimum standards to which good lives must conform. Theories of human nature, however, are controversial. The question they must answer is not merely whether there are characteristics shared by all human beings, for there could be such characteristics without significantly affecting our understanding of good lives. We would learn very little if it were discovered, for instance, that the number of pigments in human bodies was unique to humans, or that only humans could serve as hosts to a yet-to-be synthesized parasite. Thus the question is whether there are characteristics possessed by all human beings *and* essential to good lives. I shall call these *important necessary characteristics* and argue that there are such.

Naturalism and Historicism

Let us begin by contrasting two extreme views of human nature: one is a version of naturalism; the other of historicism. (Each has other versions, but I shall ignore them for the present.) According to this version of naturalism, there are important necessary characteristics and they jointly constitute our essential nature. They are historically unchanging, culturally invariant, and uniquely human; they are the same for all human beings, always, everywhere. The contrasting version of historicism denies that there are any important necessary characteristics; human nature is plastic, malleable, and there is no essential human nature.

At first glance, both positions appear quite implausible. Naturalism seems to be contradicted by the undeniable diversity we find among people. But naturalists recognize diversity and explain it in terms of the variable nonnecessary characteristics human beings have in addition to the unchanging important necessary ones. Diversity is superficial; invariability is fundamental. On the other hand, historicism appears to be refuted by the plain fact that we readily identify as human the subjects among whom diversity holds. How could this be done, if there were not some unchanging universal characteristics? The historicist explanation is that the characteristics permitting identification are indeed necessary, but they are not important, for they cannot reasonably be included in the essence of human nature. The constancy of human nature, suggested by the necessary identifying characteristics, is superficial; the diversity of human beings, due to the absence of important necessary characteristics, is profound.

If we reflect on this conflict, it becomes apparent that naturalists and historicists do not disagree about the facts of human nature, but about the interpretation of agreed upon facts. Naturalists can take in their stride anthropological and sociological reports of human diversity and historicists need not be disconcerted by ethological and sociobiological success in tracing facts of social life to our biological makeup. For each will attribute the anomalous facts to superficial aspects of our humanity and continue to hold fast to what they regard as important. The disagreement is over what is important. The first thinks that it is the unchanging component of human nature; the second that it is the changing one. Additional facts will not settle this disagreement, for it is the significance of facts that is in dispute.

If this understanding of the dispute is correct, perhaps we have reached rock bottom. Could it be that these are just two basic and incompatible visions and they are inaccessible to further argument? I do not think so. It will be recalled that we are discussing extreme versions of naturalism and historicism. Reason will get a foothold if we retreat from the extremities. This we are forced to do if we recognize that both sides acknowledge the existence of necessary characteristics; their disagreement is about the existence of *important* necessary characteristics. So there is some common ground, and I shall now explore how far it extends by describing some of the necessary characteristics, which may or may not be important, about whose existence naturalists and historicists do not dispute.

Some, but not all, of these characteristics are physiological.

Upon these depend the structure and function of the human body; they provide the human shape and make possible both voluntary and involuntary human activities. Among these characteristics are the brain and the nervous system. It will be agreed by both sides that the brain is at least an empirically necessary condition of the higher mental processes. So among the physiological characteristics of the human body, I include the basis of the capacity to think, feel, imagine, will, and so forth.

Part of the importance of these necessary physiological characteristics is that their conjunction permits the identification of someone possessing them as human. Of course, the human body can be damaged by the loss of organs or limbs and its functions can be impaired. How much of the body and how many of its functions must be intact to make identification possible, I shall not worry about. No doubt, there are controversial borderline cases, but they have no bearing on what I am discussing.

The second group of necessary characteristics are psychological. Our physiology gives us wants and capacities and our psychology prompts us to satisfy the wants and use the capacities in certain ways. The distinction between physiology and psychology is blurred. But one difference between them is that there is an urgency about responding to the promptings of physiology that is absent from our responses to psychological motivation. This is due to the fact that if basic physiological wants are not satisfied, we die or are seriously damaged, whereas frustrated psychological wants have less serious consequences. So, from the point of view of survival, physiology is primary, psychology is secondary.

One psychological fact is that we want not only to satisfy our physiological wants, but also to do so in a particular manner. What that manner is partly depends on the various social contexts in which we live. The wide variations in social contexts and human psychology are among the strongest reasons for believing in human diversity. But alongside the diversity, there is also similarity. The relevant psychological facts are constituted of similarities among all human beings. They involve such matters as having a view of what we should like our lives to be, a view about our likes and dislikes, and trying to have much of the former and little of the latter; of being able to learn from the past, plan for the future, and make use of these capacities in the course of living our lives; of having some view of our talents and weaknesses; of possessing an attitude, which need not be conscious, toward such inevitable features of life as family, illness, death, having children, maturing, aging, succeeding, failing, coping with adversity, sexual relations, and conformity to convention and going against it. These facts constitute the psychological dimension of our common humanity.

The psychological wants underlying these aspirations, capacities, and attitudes may be frustrated. Human lives may be lived in primitive conditions where all of our energies must be directed at survival. We think of such lives, in subsistence economies, concentration camps, shipwrecks, and other disasters, as dehumanizing. They are so partly because these psychological wants are not satisfied. That this may happen is not evidence against but confirmation of their human necessity.

The third kind of characteristics are social. Human vulnerability, scarce resources, limited strength, intelligence, energy, and skill, force cooperation upon human beings.[1] Social life exists, because only within it can we satisfy our physiological and psychological wants in a manner we find satisfactory. The form social life takes is the establishment of some authority, the emergence of institutions and conventional practices, and the slow development and the deliberate formulation of rules; all these demand conformity from members of a society. This imposes restrictions on what we can do and provides forms for doing what we want and what society allows. Different societies have different authorities, institutions, conventions, and rules. But no society can do without them and none of us can do without some participation in social life, provided we seek the dependable satisfaction of our physiological and psychological wants.

One can retreat from society, but the withdrawal can only be partial. Even lifelong hermits were nourished as children, received some instruction, and were acquainted with the social life they rejected. They relied on tools, clothing, experience, and charity, and these they had only because society provided them. I doubt very much that there can be Mowglis or feral infants, but if there were, they would represent one of those rare borderline cases in which we would not know what to say about their humanity. They would have a human shape, but little else. So I conclude that in addition to physiological and psychological facts, social facts present yet another collection of necessary human characteristics.

Four Types of Human Characteristics

Two distinctions will further clarify what is involved in asserting or denying that there are important necessary human characteristics and how various versions of naturalism and historicism

differ. The first is between universal and variable human characteristics. Both are possessed by all human beings, but the universal
characteristics are the same, while the variable ones are different.
The physiological, psychological, and social facts just enumerated
are universal; eating habits, sexual mores, and attitudes to compe-
tition are variable.

The second distinction is between formal and substantive
characteristics. Formal characteristics are abstract and general;
substantive characteristics are concrete and particular. To say that
we seek to satisfy our wants is to attribute a formal characteristic to
us. If, however, the wants are specified and the manner of their
satisfaction is described, then a substantive characteristic is being
ascribed. Formal characteristics concern the *sorts* of things we can
and may do; substantive characteristics assign *specific* contents to
these capacities and performances. That hunger must be at least
minimally satisfied is a formal characteristic of human beings; that
the satisfaction includes or excludes cannibalism or raw meat is a
substantive characteristic.

Armed with these two distinctions, we can give a general
characterization of naturalism and historicism regarding human
nature. According to naturalists, there are universal and substantive human characteristics and it is their existence that allows us to
speak of human nature. In contrast, historicists maintain that all
substantive characteristics are variable, and if there are universal
characteristics, they are formal; consequently, conceptions of
human nature are bound to be so general, so devoid of content as
to be vacuous. In other words, naturalists assert that there are
concrete and particular characteristics that all human beings have
and historicists deny it.

Both positions permit different versions depending on how
inclusive are the assertions and denials. We began with the most
extreme version of naturalism, namely the view that there are
universal and substantive human characteristics and they jointly
define human nature. Less extreme versions can be formulated by
maintaining that there are universal and substantive characteristics, but denying that they define human nature; they merely
give it some content. Degrees of naturalism may, then, be seen as
depending on how far universal and substantive characteristics go
in specifying the content of human nature.

The most extreme version of historicism would be the view that
there are only substantive and variable human characteristics. I
have ignored this possibility, because it is obviously untenable. A
historicist must explain why human beings count as members of
the same species and how it is that we can all identify each other as

human; the extreme version fails to do so. The explanation given by less extreme historicists is in terms of formal characteristics. So the most extreme tenable version of historicism is that all universal characteristics are formal and all nonformal characteristics are substantive and variable. Thus human nature has no content; it is merely a formal notion, a convenient label allowing us to refer to the general and abstract characteristics on the basis of which we identify our kind as human.[2] Versions of historicism vary according to estimates about how far formal characteristics extend.

Now the test case in the dispute between naturalism and historicism is presented by the physiological, psychological, and social facts just listed. All versions of naturalism and historicism agree that these facts are universal and human characteristics. Naturalists, however, argue that they are substantive, while historicists hold that they are formal. I have previously described this disagreement as turning on the question of whether the characteristics admitted by both sides to be necessary are also important. I can now deepen this description by explaining what leads to these conflicting judgments about their importance. Naturalists think that they are important, because they tell us something substantive about human nature, while historicists regard them as unimportant on the ground that they reveal only formal characteristics and otherwise leave human nature empty.

My view is that in this dispute naturalists are right. But the naturalism I shall defend is of a moderate sort. The relevant facts are universal and substantive human characteristics, yet they give only a minimum content to human nature. This is sufficient to establish their importance, but it is insufficient to define human nature. So I partially agree with historicists: human beings are diverse, and this is an important fact about us. But I also agree with naturalists that there is a core of unchanging constant human nature and that this is another important fact about us. I will now argue that the facts in question are substantive and not merely formal. I shall start with an account of what makes them important. This account is intended to connect facts and values. But instead of adding to the controversy about the possibility of bridging the supposed gap between facts and values, I shall show how the facts of human nature actually provide some values.

From Facts to Values

We may begin with an assumption I take for granted: one aim of morality is to increase human welfare. This includes both the production of good and the amelioration of evil. Good is what benefits human beings and evil is what harms them. Moral good is benefit produced by human agency and moral evil is harm done by people to people. ∕

The importance of my list of physiological, psychological, and social facts is that they are indissoluably connected with moral good and evil. The facts are important, because they constitute the minimum necessary conditions of human well-being. To deprive human beings of these conditions is to harm them, and thus it is evil. To guarantee the conditions is to benefit them, and so it is good.

Just as the facts in question are truisms about human beings, so the associated benefits and harms are truisms about the conditions in which human beings live good or bad lives.[3] To guarantee the conditions in which physiological wants are satisfied, so that people's lives are not in danger, is obviously good; and to jeopardize these conditions is obviously evil. To inflict death, dismemberment, lasting physical pain, and prolonged hunger and thirst are normally evil. (I shall shortly explain the qualification introduced by normality.) Similarly, it is good to make sure that people do not suffer these harms.

The same air of obviousness surrounds the satisfaction of psychological wants. It is obviously good for people to have the opportunity to exercise their faculties, direct their lives, and assess what they regard as important, and equally obviously, it is evil to deprive them of it. The facts of social life provide the social conditions in which physiological and psychological wants can be satisfied and in which people are protected from injury by others. Thus having a stable society, guaranteeing security and some freedom, and providing an authority and known rules for settling disputes and adjudicating conflicts is good, and its opposite is evil.

There can be no stronger argument for the connection between these facts and good and evil than pointing it out. If the connection does not seem obvious, no additional argument will produce conviction. For presupposed by all possible arguments is the common human knowledge that some things are beneficial and others harmful for human beings. There are, of course, deep and serious controversies about good and evil. But they start with far more complicated candidates for good and evil than what I have incorporated into my catalog of truisms.[4]

There are, however, two qualifications implicit in this account, which I must now make explicit. First, to say that guaranteeing the physiological, psychological, and social conditions is good and undermining them is evil, is a general claim. Situations may arise

in which the overall goal of human welfare can be best served by
violating individual conditions. In certain circumstances, the satisfaction of wants may conflict and be incompatible. None of the
goods I have discussed is inviolable. So the qualification I wish to
make is that the general claim holds in the sense that there is a
presumption in favor of guaranteeing the conditions and against
their violation, but the presumption may be overruled. Doing so
requires reasons for depriving people of the benefit or for inflicting harm on them. But these reasons can only be that the situation
is special and what seems to be beneficial or harmful is not, or that
small harm will bring great benefit. Thus we may say that life is
good and death is evil, but helping the incurably ill, suffering
from prolonged and extreme pain, to kill themselves may not be
evil. The amended general claim, then, is that the physiological,
psychological, and social conditions hold normally, and, if they are
supposed not to hold, then reasons must be given for the claimed
exception.

The second qualification is a reminder that the relevant conditions are only necessary and not sufficient for good lives. They are
the minimum conditions required for human beings to live whatever kind of life they choose. For even mystics, devoting themselves to the contemplation of an extramundane world, must at
least minimally satisfy their physiological needs, if they are to go
on contemplating; they must be relatively free to exercise their
faculties in the manner required by their esoteric discipline; and
they must live in a relatively stable and secure environment so that
their contemplation will not be disrupted by such mundane matters as torture, rape, or enslavement. Guaranteeing these conditions is good, because it makes good lives possible. But the
achievement of this good does not assure that the people bene-
fited by it will have good lives. For the lives they go on to live may
be ill-chosen, harmful for themselves or others, unsuited to their
circumstances or personality, or be based on false beliefs about the
world. Hence, the conditions specified provide only the soil in
which good lives can flourish, but they do not, by themselves,
make them flourish. And from this, the obvious corollary follows
that in addition to these universal goods and evils, there are also
many other goods and evils that may vary from context to context,
and from person to person.

Thus my interpretation of the importance and necessity of the
relevant physiological, psychological, and social facts is that they
are important, because we can derive from them conditions required for the benefit and for the avoidance of harm to human

beings, and thus good lives depend on them. Their necessity consists in being universal requirements for human welfare, and in being the foundation upon which other variable goods rest.[5]

Moderate Naturalism

I have discussed what makes some necessary characteristics important in order to support a moderate version of naturalism against the historicist claim that human nature is a vacuous conception, because there are no universal and substantive human characteristics. Such universal characteristics as there are, according to historicists, are formal. It is against this that I have argued that the facts in question are both universal and substantive. What makes them so is that the welfare of each and every human being, at all times, and in all circumstances, depends on the satisfaction of the physiological, psychological, and social conditions these facts prompt. How would historicists respond to this case?

They would concede that the relevant facts must be taken account of in all contexts and for all people, but argue that what count as such facts and what taking account of them come to are determined by the particular context of this or that society. In other words, historicists would hold out for the claim that the necessary characteristics are formal and not substantive.[6] Historicists would charge naturalists with having reversed the right order of priority. It is not that human nature determines the conceptions prevalent in society; rather the society determines the conception of human nature that prevails in it. And, since societies differ, so do conceptions of human nature. Thus human nature is not the sort of primary datum naturalists take it to be, but a derivative socially variable one. Historicists may grant that there has to be some conception of human nature, at least implicitly, in every society, but what that conception is varies among societies. This is why conceptions of human nature are formal and variable, rather than universal and substantive.

The reason for rejecting this historicist position is that it overlooks plain and uncontestable facts. Societies are composed of human beings and of the traditions they establish. Of course, the traditions that spring up in a society deeply influence the people living in it. But it cannot be that what human beings are, their essential nature, depends on any society, for people come first and societies second.

A historicist may reply that what depends on societies is the prevailing theory of human nature and not human nature itself. But this will not do. A society needs an adequate theory of human nature to know what benefit and harm are for its members. But an adequate theory is not made of whole cloth; it must be based on something solid. And what it is based on, at least its minimum content, must be those necessary characteristics I have included in my list of physiological, psychological, and social facts. Social variations, of course, exist among theories of human nature, but the variations cannot involve these necessary characteristics, for without them no one could be human.

The historicist position is an invitation to think that theories of human nature could ignore or deny that human beings have a body with its basic physiological wants and capacities, that human beings wish to do and have what they like and avoid what they dislike, and that human beings are unavoidably connected with a social context. No adequate theory of human nature can deny or ignore these facts.

Human beings may be regarded as the children of God, as Promethean heroes, as absurd, as insignificant episodes in an indifferent cosmos, as the playthings of competing gods, or as the crowning glory of evolution. But whatever theory a society favors, it cannot fail to incorporate into it those simple, basic, necessary characteristics I have described. They give content to theories of human nature, thus rendering them substantive and not merely formal. Furthermore, the content they give is important, because it is indissoluably connected with the possibility of living good lives. Historicism is mistaken, because it overlooks these facts. It is so impressed by human diversity that it fails to notice the underlying invariability.

Some Implications of Moderate Naturalism

My argument for the existence of important necessary characteristics that partly compose human nature is now complete. It remains to explore the implications of moderate naturalism for theories of good lives. Such a theory must provide a systematic and reasoned account of the nature of good and evil and of how to go about pursuing the first and avoiding the second. Moderate naturalism influences theories of good lives by setting for them a minimum standard of adequacy; any adequate theory must do justice to the relevant physiological, psychological, and social facts. The reason for this is that since theories of good lives are concerned with human welfare, and since these facts establish the minimum requirements for the welfare of any human being, theories of good lives either take these facts into account or they cannot be adequate.

Moreover, adequate theories of good lives must take these facts into account both positively and negatively. They can do so positively by recognizing that whatever account they give of good and evil it must incorporate the facts in question. Failure to do so renders such a theory indefensible. And they must also take account of these facts negatively by excluding from their account any practical imperative that leads to the violation of these minimal conditions. If they fail to do so, they cannot possibly achieve their goal of pursuing good and avoiding evil. The positive guidance sets a minimum standard of explanation by providing a set of facts any adequate theory of good lives must recognize. The negative guidance is to establish a minimum standard of practice by providing a set of conditions no adequate theory can violate. The force of necessity in both cases is that since theories of good lives aim at the achievement of good and the avoidance of evil, they must abide by the minimum requirements necessary for both the achievement and the avoidance.

If it is borne in mind that by good and evil I mean benefit and harm for human beings produced by human agency, and that the facts I have cited concern the minimum satisfaction of physiological needs, some opportunity to pursue what one likes and avoid what one dislikes, and the maintenance of social conditions in which both can be done, then the general claim I am defending may appear platitudinous. To show that moderate naturalism goes beyond banality, I shall indicate how some theories of good lives are excluded by the minimum standard.

The positive guidance is violated by certain interpretations of relativistic theories. If by relativism we understand the claim that theories of good lives prevailing in different societies may have no common ground at all, then it is mistaken. For such relativistic theories suppose that conceptions of good and evil are completely dependent on the context in which they arise.[7] And since contexts radically differ, so also do conceptions of good and evil. But this cannot be so, since adequate conceptions of good and evil must do justice to human nature. Diversity there can be and there is, but only within the limits set by the relevant facts. There cannot be an adequate theory of good lives that would prescribe the nonfulfillment of basic physiological wants, the loss of all opportunity to do as we like, and the destruction of social conditions conducive to good lives. Of course, theories of good lives have much to say about how physiological wants are to be satisfied, how people should choose to live, and how society should be organized. And of course what they say about these matters varies with their social context. But these variations must have in common the facts I have identified, if they are to embody an adequate theory of good lives.

The negative guidance is violated by all theories that recommend practice inconsistent with the pursuit of goods and avoidance of evils that moderate naturalism recognizes as implicit in human nature. If matters were simple, this would mean that no theory advocating slavery, racism, or chauvinism, for instance, could be adequate. But matters are not simple. There is a difficulty I must now consider.

There are theories of good lives advocating radical discrimination among human beings. Plato and Aristotle supported slavery, John Stuart Mill regarded most races as insufficiently developed to enjoy freedom from paternalism, and Marxists have no doubt about the moral superiority of communistic societies over capitalistic ones. What can we say about these theories?

It would be wrong to claim that they fail to qualify as theories of good lives, because their authors disregard human welfare. For, quite obviously, defenders of such theories do have regard for human welfare. The issue is that they do not have equal regard for everyone's welfare. According to them, slaves, savages, and those living with false consciousness are, morally speaking, inferior; they are not be be treated badly, but like children. They are human, but they have not realized their humanity as fully as some others. I shall call such theories elitist, in contrast with egalitarian ones. Elitists deny and egalitarians assert that all human beings deserve equal regard for their welfare.

The dispute between elitists and egalitarians is a substantive moral dispute. They agree that morality is about human welfare, but they disagree over the question of whether there can be adequate moral grounds for discriminating in favor of or against some human beings. And, although we may be revolted by slavery, racism, and the excesses of communism, elitism should not be dismissed out of hand. It is by no means obvious, for instance, that in a just war putting higher value on the lives of our soldiers than on the enemy's is morally indefensible. Nor is it a foregone conclusion that we should not favor the welfare of our family over the welfare of strangers.

I do not propose to enter into this moral dispute; I merely want to indicate that it is open. Its existence has a bearing on the negative guidance the mimimum standard provides. Elitists and egalitarians can both accept the universality and necessity of my list of facts, and they can both agree that because of them there is a presumption in favor of having equal concern for the welfare of all human beings. Elitists think, however, that this presumption can be overruled, because there are morally relevant differences among human beings and these justify treating them unequally. Egalitarians deny this. The negative guidance of the minimum standard, therefore, is that no theory of good lives advocating discrimination can be adequate, unless the presumption in favor of equal treatment has been justifiably overruled. Whether or not this condition has been met by a theory of good lives depends on the theory, the context, and the justifications offered. So the positive guidance of the minimum standard excludes as inadequate radically relativistic theories on the ground that they fail to take into account human nature. And the negative guidance excludes theories that advocate unjustified discriminatory practices.

There is yet a further theory of good lives excluded by the minimum standard.[8] The inadequate theories discussed up to this point have been excluded, because they have not made enough of human nature. Another source of inadequacy is to try to make too much of it. This is the fault of naturalistic theories that go far beyond the moderate version I am defending. The supposition underlying them is that the content of human nature is sufficiently rich and invariable to allow the formulation of one particular theory of good lives. This theory, then, would be superior to all others, because it would give a better account of good and evil and of how to go about obtaining one and avoiding the other than any other competing theory. Its account would be better, because, given its understanding of human nature, it is more conducive to human welfare than other theories with less adequate conceptions of human nature. The traditional aim of such theories is to describe the summum bonum.

The minimum standard excludes these versions of extreme naturalism, because the universal physiological, psychological, and social facts do not give a rich enough content to human nature to provide a means of choosing one among the many theories consistent with these facts. Moderate naturalism influences theories of good lives by eliminating those that fail to do justice to the facts. But there is a plurality of theories that do do justice to them, and human nature cannot be cited as evidence against any of them. Extreme naturalism is faulty, because it is committed to supposing otherwise.

Moderate naturalists, therefore, agree with extreme naturalists about human nature limiting theories of good lives. They part company over the extent of this limitation. Moderate naturalists also agree with historicists about the diversity of theories of good lives, because contexts change and what serves human welfare changes with the context. But historicists suppose that there is no limit to these changes, while moderate naturalists think that human nature sets a limit beyond which the changes cannot go.

In conclusion, I offer the general observation that theories of human nature are evaluative through and through. In them, facts and values are inextricably mixed. This is so, because we, human beings, form these conceptions and we care about ourselves. Good lives would not be possible without this care. But this does not mean that there is something metaphysically special about human beings. It means that we think, and cannot help thinking, about good and evil in human terms. The basis of good lives, therefore, is not metaphysical; rather, it is the possession of a point of view, a perspective from which the world is judged. And that perspective is *sub specie humanitatis*.[9]

3
The Context of Self-Direction: Moral Tradition

Introduction

Through self-direction we aim to satisfy our most important wants in accordance with appropriate ideals. I have tried to show how this process is necessarily influenced by human nature. I shall argue here that it is also influenced by the conventions of the moral tradition in which self-directed agents live.

The extent to which nature and convention influence human conduct is one of the old questions of moral philosophy. One traditional answer is to attempt to draw a sharp distinction between their respective influences. According to it, nature is the part of reality not made by human beings, while conventions are human constructions. Thus we may say that we have innate or instinctive natural wants, independently of the social context in which we live; among them are those created by the physiological, psychological, and social facts of human nature. We also have conventional wants, and these we have been conditioned or taught to have by being brought up in a society. These are shaped by education, custom, fashion, style, and the like.

But the attempt to maintain this sharp distinction fails when we come to apply it to actual human conduct, for natural and conventional elements seem to be altogether mixed in us. To begin with, it is natural for us to have conventional wants, for it is part of our nature to live by conventions. As bees build hives, so we construct conventions. Furthermore, we are conscious of many of our instinctive and acquired wants, and through consciousness we can, at least to some extent, control them, assign priorities to them, and, in normal circumstances, choose the manner in which we satisfy them. The first consideration renders many conventions natural; the second makes much of our nature inseparable from the conventions we have created.

The third consideration derives from the impossibility of separating the manner and the substance of our attempts to satisfy wants. I have argued that many of our wants stem from our nature and not from the conventions we have created. However, these wants must be satisfied in some manner or another, and the manner is determined by the conventions of the society into which we are born and in which we are educated. Wanting food, for instance, is natural, but what counts as food and how it is prepared and consumed differs from context to context. Thus, even the most natural of our wants have conventional satisfactions, and while our nature demands that they be satisfied, our society supplies the manner of their satisfactions. Consequently, in such necessary human practices as consumption and elimination, work and leisure, sex and marriage, the treatment of illness and injury, birth and death, and maturing and aging, natural and conventional elements are inseparably mixed.

Nature, Required Conventions, and Variable Conventions

For these reasons, the interpretation postulating a sharp distinction between nature and convention should be replaced by a threefold distinction between *nature, required conventions,* and *variable conventions.* Nature is the nonconventional part of reality. In human beings, the basic physiological, psychological, and social facts are natural, and so are the wants created by these facts. I have nothing to add to the understanding of nature, presupposed by the sharp distinction I reject. But the existence of two kinds of convention and the fact that one of them is required have considerable importance.[1]

Required and variable conventions are similar in some respects. They are both formulatable as rules prescribing appropriate conduct. Yet neither needs to be actually formulated for its prescriptive force to be felt. They are not so much conscious guides as customary ways of doing things. When the conventions are observed, there is no need for articulation, for bringing them into consciousness. Those who abide by them, normally do so routinely, matter-of-factly, habitually. Conducting themselves in conventional ways has become their second nature. Explicitness may be called for in difficult cases, when the routine is interrupted, or in the course of explaining to outsiders or novices the significance of the conduct guided by conventions.

Another similarity between required and variable conventions is that they concern the manner in which wants should be satisfied. This connects both kinds of convention to human welfare, and thus to morality. Their function is to guide members of a society in obtaining various supposedly beneficial satisfactions, in avoiding those regarded as harmful, and in harmonizing the conduct of individuals, so as to create optimal conditions for the satisfaction of wants.

And lastly, the two kinds of convention are alike in that they differ from society to society. The source of their diversity is that the manner in which wants are satisfied varies. It is crucial to my case, however, that the inference from the diversity of conventions to the diversity of wants whose satisfactions they guide is illegitimate. Conventions may be diverse either because their objects are different, or, because, while their objects are identical, the ways in which they prescribe attaining them are different. The first is true of variable conventions, the second of required ones.

There is a useful analogy here with language. As language, so required and variable conventions are necessary elements in our characteristically human lives; without either, we would not be the species we are. But what is necessary is that there be a language or a system of required and variable conventions, and not that it should be of a particular kind. As there are many different languages, so there are many different systems of required and variable conventions. And as the diversity of languages does not warrant the conclusion that the human potential realized through them varies with language-groups, so the diversity of systems of required and variable conventions does not warrant the inference to the diversity of human wants.

The fact is, as I have argued, that some wants all human beings share, while others are peculiar to individuals and societies. This is what calls for going beyond the similarities between required and variable conventions and noticing their differences. The fundamental difference is that required conventions guide the satisfaction of wants all human beings have, while variable conventions prescribe appropriate satisfactions for wants that differ from person to person, and from context to context.

Some conventions are required, because they are prescriptions guiding the satisfaction of wants created by the physiological, psychological, and social facts of human nature. These conventions are universal and necessary, because the specific satisfactions obtained through them are required for the welfare of all human beings. They are also natural, because their universality and necessity are due to the facts of human nature. Calling conventions natural seems like an oxymoron, because the error involved in the sharp distinction between nature and convention is reflected in the language. But it is an error nevertheless. The human situation, created by our nature and the world, requires the existence of some conventions, and, although it is true that we have created them, it is also true that we could not have failed to create them. For had we not done so, we would have perished long ago.

Yet the universality, necessity, and naturalness of required conventions do not consist in the specific rules embodied in these conventions, but in the existence of some specific rules or others. Societies must have specific rules about the division of labor, the protection of life, security, property, sexual relations, child rearing, treatment of the old, and so on. But what specifically these rules are, will depend on the traditions and circumstances of various societies. That these sorts of conventions are required means that all societies must have them. Thus their requiredness is compatible with their diversity.

By contrast, variable conventions are particular, social, and optional. They are particular in that they guide conduct or practices that may not exist in other societies at all. Conventions regulating public confession, cohabiting extended families, the religious dimension of healing, prophesying the future, the arrangement of marriages, and undertaking pilgrimages are examples of practices important in some societies and unknown in others. The explanation of the particularity of these conventions is that their origin is social. Their roots are in the contingent customs and ceremonies of the society, rather than in the facts of human nature. Nothing in human nature would be damaged or frustrated if a society treated healing as a secular craft or if marriages were not arranged by others, but depended on the inclinations of the partners. And this means that the observance of these conventions is, in one sense, optional. These are the respects in which a society is most open to change or reform; the arena in which the inevitable battles of conservatives and liberals will be waged.

There is, however, another sense in which variable conventions are not optional at all. Human welfare will not be jeopardized if a society favors one variable convention over another or if it does not have one that another society has. But human welfare requires that there be some set of variable conventions. Thus the *existence* of a system of variable conventions is not optional; what is optional is the *identity* of the particular variable conventions that comprise the system. The reason for this is that the satisfaction of universal human wants through conformity to required conventions is not sufficient for good lives. Required conventions merely secure the ground upon which good lives can be built. But they are built out of the variable conventions that prevail in a society. This may be expressed by saying that it is a required convention that there be variable conventions in general, but not that there be any particular variable convention.

The conclusion that follows from my discussion of required and variable conventions is that just as human nature sets limits within which self-direction must operate, so also do required and variable conventions set limits. The assumption implicit in the sharp distinction between nature and convention is that conventions are in some sense arbitrary, and so self-direction may well take the form of pitting ourselves against the conventions into which we are born. I have argued against this assumption that conformity to required conventions is just as necessary as observing our natural limits is, that the existence of variable conventions is equally necessary, and that the domain of self-direction is the particular variable conventions in accordance with which we aim to live good lives. I shall now proceed to clarify and provide additional support for this view.

Conventions and Principles

By a moral tradition I mean a society's required and variable conventions. In a sound moral tradition, conduct conforming to required and variable conventions is largely unreflective and spontaneous. People do their jobs, live their lives, and act appropriately, without thinking much about it. True, complications inevitably arise; conflicts and temptations disturb the even surface of moral life. But these ripples are exceptional; smoothness is the rule. Extreme situations and people devoid of conscience are remote and rarely demand attention. The prevalent moral failings are not monstrous, and moral education, guilt, shame, fear, goodwill, self-respect, and lucky circumstances unite to keep them that way.

What guides moral conduct in this desirable way? "Custom," I say with Hume, "is the great guide of human life."[2] This is not a widely shared view in contemporary moral thinking. The received opinion is that moral conduct is guided primarily by principles. The main principle is said by Kantians to be some version of the

categorical imperative; some utilitarians think that the principle is
the greatest happiness; the recent contractarian proposal of Rawls
combines two of them: the equal liberty and the difference principles; and there are many other candidates as well. The content of
these principles does not affect the objection to regarding them as
fundamental moral guides, nor does it matter whether they are
said to be one or many. What does matter is the explanation of
how they guide moral conduct. They are said to do so both
consciously and unconsciously.

The principles are taught unconsciously in moral education.
Underlying the many "dos" and "don'ts" of a moral tradition,
there is assumed to be the pervasive influence of basic principles.
Derivative moral rules reflect the basic ones. And morally well-
trained people, having acquired derivative rules, naturally, without thinking or deliberation, follow the basic ones. This is all that
most people most of the time need to do to behave in a morally
praiseworthy way. The basic principles can also be, and occasionally need to be, conscious guides. For the derivative principles may
conflict; they may be challenged internally by people wishing to
know why they should follow a principle that obliges them to
frustrate some of their wants; and they may also be challenged
externally by coming into contact with another moral tradition.
When this happens, basic principles are appealed to as justifications of derivative ones, and this, of course, requires the conscious
recognition of their guiding force.

It is true that principles guide conduct. By they cannot be the
basic guides they are supposed to be for three reasons. First, how
do principles come to be formulated and accepted? The reasonable answer is that they are extracted from conventional conduct
prevailing in the society. Thus formulated, the principles find
general acceptance, because they exemplify what people have
been doing anyway. The principles grow out of the practice they
aim to guide. If the moral tradition of a society does not already
embody, say, the Golden Rule, then it is useless to try to graft on to
it this alien principle. The graft will take only if the host is
receptive. Thus practice is primary and principles are secondary.
And the practice from which moral principles are extracted is
conventional conduct in a moral tradition.

Secondly, potential principles for a moral tradition may be
rejected, accepted, or revised. How could this be if the principles
were basic? The answer, of course, is that they are not basic,
conventional conduct is, and the fate of newly proposed princi-

ples depends on how well they reflect prevailing practice. Lastly, the application of a principle presupposes approval of the practice the principle is supposed to legitimate. For cases must be recognized as coming under the jurisdiction of a principle before they can be evaluated in its terms. I can follow the principle of paying debts only if I recognize that what I received from you constitutes indebtedness. If I do not recognize it, the principle will not help; and if I do recognize it, I do not need the principle. Principles, therefore, cannot be the basic guides of conduct. They are useful only as formulas that can be taught in the early stages of moral education and as efficient ways in which participants in a moral tradition can communicate to each other the grounds of their approval and disapproval.

Moral Tradition

Moral principles grow out of and receive their sustenance from conventional conduct. If conduct ceases to be conventional, the principles lose their force. The result is chaos, for people do not then know what to expect of each other. Suspicion replaces trust; friendliness turns into hostility; and sympathy, politeness, and altruism become unaffordable luxuries. The great importance of moral tradition is that it helps to protect society from this kind of dissolution.

We need to distinguish between two kinds of tradition.[3] The first is an association of people guided by a specific and common ideal. This specialized tradition provides the framework in which participants aim to achieve whatever their ideals happen to be: profit; world domination; the composition, performance, and appreciation of music; historical research; athletic achievement; helping the poor; and so on. There will be many such specialized traditions in a society. The other comprises general traditions designed to maintain the necessary conditions for the continued existence of specialized traditions. This sort of tradition does not aim to achieve specific ideals; it aims to create a context in which specific ideals can be achieved. Legal, political, managerial, and law enforcement traditions are examples of it. And it is to this class that moral traditions also belong. Moral traditions, then, are gound-clearing rather than architectural; enabling rather than productive; protective rather than venturesome. A moral tradition has achieved its purpose if no one in a society needs to be aware of its existence. For the society, then, shows itself to be morally untroubled and people are living their lives in the framework thus established.

It is a great and rare achievement for a society to reach this state of moral harmony. Our society and the vast majority of societies in recorded history fall more or less short. Approximating this desirable state depends, in the first instance, on moral education, which hands down the moral tradition from generation to generation in a society. This is the context in which principles acquire their importance. For moral education begins with imitation, but that cannot go very far. If we are morally well-trained, we do not merely know how to do what others have done in our situation; we also know how to recognize situations that call for specific types of moral response. Principles help to advance our moral training from mere imitation to intelligent performance. But such performance is more than knowing how to follow principles; it also involves knowing how to conduct ourselves in new situations. This kind of knowledge cannot be based on generalizations from the past; it requires creative participation in the tradition. It is based on experience, and requires good judgment and a deep appreciation of the spirit of a tradition. It calls for judging which of several conflicting principles should guide us in a particular situation; when to adhere steadfastly to a moral guide and when consistency has turned into soulless ritual; when the letter of the moral tradition is at odds with its spirit; when an individual's interests should take precedence over the common good; when the good to be achieved is great enough to risk the evil that failure may produce; or what specific actions do kindness, justice, or charity actually call for in the case confronting us. These are difficult matters to judge and moral knowledge is hard to acquire.

One reason for making the required effort is that a sound moral tradition is inspiring. A moral education provides us with a vision of the possibilities of good lives; it trains us in the development of a sensibility in terms of which we perceive good and evil for ourselves and others. And it is also the teaching of shared ideals that guide our conduct. Thus allegiance to a moral tradition is not merely to conform habitually to conventional conduct, but, in addition, to be motivated by a moral vision to do so, and the sharing of that vision by fellow members of the tradition.

Vision is perhaps too chiliastic a term to describe what I have in mind. People in a moral tradition are rarely visionaries; in fact, moral traditions usually exercise a restraining influence on the millenial flights of fancy of their members. Yet we receive more from a moral tradition than an outlook. An outlook need not guide action, it need not inspire, it need not provide a framework for interpretation and evaluation, and it can leave our emotions unengaged. But a moral tradition provides all this.

The evaluative dimension of a sound tradition is deep. It goes beyond knowing how to use such terms as good and evil, or right and wrong. Its depth comes from familiarity with the discriminations, nuances, judgments of importance and priority, and from sensitivity to sources of conflict and tension, all of which form the texture of the moral conduct guided by the tradition. What we know is not merely that this person is good and that evil, but also what makes them so, and why one is better or worse, more or less culpable or admirable, weaker or stronger, more capable of improvement or hopelessly corrupt than another person in similar circumstances. It is to know what is courageous, shocking, or offensive, rather than a sophomoric attempt to provoke, an assertion of independence, or a cry for help. Full-fledged participants in a moral tradition know these and thousands of similar things in a particular manner. They do not know them as a judge knows the law; they do not reflect and then carefully select the appropriate rule or precedent that best fits the case at hand. Moral knowledge of the sort I have in mind has become their second nature. Making the discriminations; noticing the nuances; and being alive to the conflicts, priorities, and temptations no longer requires reflection. Just as an accomplished violinist knows how to play adagio and a rock climber knows how to manage an overhang, so moral agents know about moral matters. Of course, on occasion they may have to stop and think. But that happens only in difficult cases. The daily flow of moral life can be handled spontaneously by participants in a sound moral tradition.

Nor is moral knowledge like that of anthropologists observing a society. Anthropologists stand outside of what they observe. They may approve or disapprove of the tradition; they may feel sympathy, revulsion, or be indifferent; or they may compare it favorably or unfavorably to other traditions. Participants in a moral tradition are necessarily inside it. They can observe it perhaps as accurately as any anthropologist, but they cannot be indifferent. It is not that they are bound to judge their own tradition as being superior to others; rather, whatever moral judgments they make are made in terms that tradition provides. Their belonging to it means that they see the moral aspect of the world in that way.

Allegiance to a moral tradition, then, will shape how we think and feel about our lives and how we judge the disclosures of our experiences. But by being so shaped, we become part of a moral community and we share with our fellow members the vision and sensibility of our common tradition. Thus a moral tradition provides an evaluative dimension to the lives of its members and it unites them into a community.[4]

Conventions and Satisfactions

One way moral traditions guide us is by fostering conventional conduct that leads to a favorable balance of benefit over harm for its members. As we have seen, conduct may conform to required or to variable conventions. If a moral tradition is in order, conformity will produce benefits in the form of satisfying the appropriate wants of its members. But just as we must distinguish between required conventions, aiming to satisfy wants everybody has, and variable conventions, guiding the satisfaction of wants that differ from context to context, so also we must distinguish between the corresponding required and variable satisfactions. Both kinds of satisfactions are obtainable through participation in a moral tradition, but there are significant differences between them.

Required satisfactions are related to tradition as a foundation is to the structure erected on it. The many types of conduct guided by required conventions are those necessary for obtaining the satisfactions of the wants created by the facts of human nature. These satisfactions are required for good lives whatever forms they may take. Consequently, any sound moral tradition will aim to provide them. Periclean Athens, Confucian China, early medieval Christendom, Puritan New England, and Victorian England all had required conventions conformity to which provided required satisfactions for their members. Of course, these moral traditions were vastly different. Their differences, however, were not due to differences in required satisfactions, but to the existence of different conventions aiming to achieve the same required satisfactions and also to the differing variable satisfactions they had made possible.

Variable conventions perform two main functions. One is to guide conduct so as to provide variable satisfactions, The other is to establish and reinforce the cohesion of the members of a moral tradition. I shall discuss these in turn. Variable satisfactions are related to moral traditions as some parts are to a whole: they partially constitute it. Thus the identity of a moral tradition is logically connected with the identity of the variable satisfactions obtainable through it. But obtaining variable satisfactions is not like winning a prize, enjoying a musical performance, or solving a difficult problem to one's satisfaction. Variable satisfactions are enjoyed as the forms good lives may take. These forms are manners of living, acting, and being connected with others, prescribed by variable conventions. They are the forms of conventional conduct that partially compose a tradition. Participants more or less consciously inherit conceptions of good lives from their tradition—conceptions that are their special individual amalgams of such opportunities, defined and made possible by their tradition, as they find attractive and applicable to their own cases.

We can tell, in general terms, that satisfactory conceptions of good lives must include, first, the main theme of this book, self-direction: some view of what we want to make of ourselves and what character traits we need to have and cultivate to achieve it. We must ask and answer such questions as whether we want to live a retiring private or a gregarious public life; whether we have the talents and personality required by our chosen form of life; whether that form will be scholarly, artistic, commercial, or athletic; whether we prize achievement, contemplation, service, risk-taking, casting our net wide, or specializing in a distinct endeavor; whether we aim at exercising power; remaining quiet, private, and reflective; enjoying the luxuries wealth can provide; receiving the recognition status and prestige bestow; basking in the reciprocated love of a few intimates, or devoting ourselves to a cause.

Secondly, conceptions of good lives must leave room for intimate personal relationships based on love and friendship; without them, a life can not be good. But whether the satisfaction will be derived chiefly from marriage, parenthood, solidarity with comrades in a joint cause, shared admiration of some ideal, love affairs, discipleship to a great person, or from the affection and loyalty of one's students will vary from life to life.

Thirdly, we cannot have good lives unless we have settled on an acceptable way of relating to the vast majority of people in our society whom we do not know and yet continually encounter in the routine conduct of our affairs. The desired attitude here is decency, that is, appropriate conduct as judged by the conventions of our society. Its marks are casual friendliness, spontaneous goodwill, politeness, giving others the benefit of the doubt; or negatively, the absence of hostility, distrust, suspicion, and of the litigious disposition bent on exacting its pound of flesh.

The variable satisfactions of a moral tradition, then, are derived from the forms of self-direction, intimacy, and decency that the variable conventions of a society provide for its members. Conceptions of good lives in a moral tradition will be combinations of the forms we consciously or otherwise aim to follow in our lives. In a sound moral tradition, the available forms are much more numerous and various than what we can reasonably aspire to follow. In a society enjoying such a rich tradition, conventions do not appear as rigid codes, rules that bind, or principles demanding obedience; customary conduct according to variable conventions will provide many different ways, and an option to follow them, in which people can make good lives for themselves. Such a society will be pluralistic, by virtue of the multiplicity of available forms of conduct, and it will be free, because its members can choose between the forms their lives could take. A moral tradition, therefore, is a necessary condition for the development of self-direction.

I come now to the second function of variable conventions. At other times, when societies were smaller and more homogeneous, participants in a moral tradition were likely to know each other personally or by reputation, and if they did not, their clothing, demeanor, and language identified their membership. This has been changing, because societies have grown larger and more impersonal, so that fewer and fewer outward manifestations remain reliable indicators of inner processes. Yet moral traditions need visible marks of belongingness and these, in our times, are the variable conventions regarding cues, rituals, and ceremonies.

The cues are the gestures, frowns, smiles, nods, scowls, laughter and tears, sniffings and cluckings, winkings, head scratchings, yawns, clearings of throat, stares, gazes, looks and taking care not to look, gaze, or stare, the speed and emphasis with which something is said, the occasion and direction in which it is said, flushes, blushes, blanches, and the multitude of other ways in which people emphasize, embellish, soften, and indicate the seriousness or levity of what they say and do. But the cues are appropriate only if they communicate what was intended or meant by them, and this, of course, requires that the actor and the spectator, and the agent and the recipient, share an interpretation of the significance of what has passed between them. This, once again, is rarely a conscious reflective process. The cues are frequently given and understood without either party being aware of their passage. To a very considerable extent, people in a moral tradition are united, and feel comfortable and familiar with each other, precisely because they depend on thus being understood.

This sense of belongingness is enhanced by the rituals that permeate everyday life: handskakes; openings of doors; taking off of hats, coats, or jackets; sharing of meals, coffee, or drinks; kissing and embracing; telling secrets; sharing confidences; exchanging gossip; use of formulas for expressing respect, condolence, enmity, or sympathy; and occasions and manners of congratulations for success and commiseration for failure or misfortune. And the ceremonies marking significant occasions like birth, marrriage, death, graduation, birthdays, anniversaries, arrivals and departures, promotion and retirement, and holidays and festivities, are similarly unifying forces. Fellow members of a moral tradition recognize their connectedness, because they share the knowledge of what is appropriate to the events of their lives and they share also the knowledge of the ways in which these events are to be marked. And this remains true even of those rebels, eccentrics, nonconformists, and iconoclasts who refuse to do what is appropriate. For the moral tradition against which they protest determines the occasions on which they can express their disdain. Only genuine indifference, uninvolvement, and ignorance of what is appropriate place one outside of a moral tradition.[5]

Thus the source that sustains a tradition is not that its members know, love, or even like each other, nor is there a fundamental commitment to a principle to which they have sworn allegiance. There is largely spontaneous, unreflective, conventional conduct, the unarticulated feeling of ease in each other's company, because the rules are generally understood and participants are secure in the knowledge that there is much that need not to be said, and that when something needs to be done, they know how to do it. The signs of their connectedness are the cues, rituals, and ceremonies, and the consequences are that people recognized as fellow members are given the benefit of the doubt, and they are treated in a friendly polite way. Principles derive what force they may have from the concrete goodwill that participants in a moral tradition spontaneously have toward each other. Without this goodwill, the principles would be unavailing. And because goodwill is founded on conventional conduct, Hume is right in regarding custom as the great guide of life.

The justification of conventions, therefore, is that they supply an indispensable condition for living good lives. They do this by guiding our conduct in the satisfaction of our wants. But there are different wants, satisfactions, and conventions. In this chapter, I have been trying to sort out some of their differences. Human nature, whose minimum content is defined by basic physiological, psychological, and social facts, creates wants whose satisfaction is a universal requirement for all good lives we may try to achieve. The explanation and justification of required conventions is that they prescribe conduct that will produce required satisfactions.

Required conventions and satisfactions, however, merely supply the necessary foundation upon which good lives can be built. Variable conventions and variable satisfactions are also needed. Variable conventions contribute to good lives by giving form to the satisfactions required by our nature; by establishing customs regarding self-direction, intimacy, and decency; and by assuring the cohesion of a society through the rituals and ceremonies of everyday life.

My concern is with self-direction, with the attempt to create good lives for ourselves. Participation in a moral tradition and observance of the required and variable conventions that constitute it provide the context in which self-direction can take place. Just as human nature creates the basic requirements of good lives, so our moral tradition creates the forms of good lives. I have said nothing so far about self-direction leading us to view critically and creatively the moral tradition into which we are born. That we may do so is crucial to my thesis. But my present purpose is to emphasize that moral traditions provide the context in which self-direction must begin. This could not be otherwise. For we are given by our tradition conceptions of good lives; what it is to be morally good; what personal characteristics are virtuous and admirable; how people should treat each other; what the acceptable forms of personal relationships are; how to cope with misfortune, adversity, and the prospect of failure; and what the duties and privileges are of the various stations in life our society affords. These constitute the substance of good lives and form the sensibility by which we interpret and evaluate whatever happens.

The Justification of Moral Traditions

It will be recalled that I have already dissociated my account from moral relativism, the view that, since moral judgments can be justified only within the tradition in which they are made, independent moral judgments of traditions are impossible. I have argued that any sound moral tradition must guarantee the satisfaction of the wants created by the facts of human nature. A moral tradition guaranteeing these satisfactions can reasonably be said to be superior to one that does not. And one that guarantees more of them is superior to one that guarantees fewer. Moral relativism is mistaken, because moral traditions can be compared and evaluated on the independent ground of whether and how far they satisfy the universal wants created by the facts of human nature.

But this will not take us very far, because moral traditions provide much more than the minimum conditions; variable conventions strongly influence the conceptions of good lives participants will have. Different traditions provide different conceptions, and it is proper to ask whether these conceptions can be rationally judged. I think that they can be, but only negatively. Moral traditions can be criticized. But if one's moral tradition passes critical scrutiny, it is reasonable to live according to it. This view supports the supposition that there is a plurality of rational moral traditions prevailing in different societies. Yet, the relativistic conclusion that we cannot resonably compare and criticize traditions does not follow from it.

Moral traditions can be criticized by showing them to be self-defeating. An unsatisfactory moral tradition cannot achieve its own purposes, because features internal to it stand in the way. The form of particular criticisms will depend on what features of a moral tradition handicap it. And since many features may do so, possible criticisms of moral traditions are not specifiable in advance. Nevertheless, there are some fairly standard defects, and I shall discuss some of them by way of illustration.

The simplest defect is that the beliefs inherent in a moral tradition about good and evil are false. It will be recalled that moral good and evil are understood as benefit and harm to human beings produced by human agency. If it turns out that what members of a tradition think benefits or harms themselves or others does not, then their tradition cannot achieve its purpose of providing good lives for its members. Examples of this are not hard to find: slavery, foot binding, female circumcision, torture, human sacrifice, and enticing the young to drug addiction are harmful, and thus evil. A moral tradition fostering them, therefore, undermines rather than guarantees the minimum conditions of its members living good lives.

Let us now consider less clear-cut cases in which the minimum conditions for good lives are guaranteed, but the tradition incorporates defective forms such lives may take. The most obvious case in point is a tradition that has only a very limited number of forms. In such a context, self-direction is severely curtailed and so, therefore, are people's chances of making good lives for themselves. Such traditions are rigid; they have an impoverished conception of human possibilities. The rigidity may be due to adverse physical conditions forcing members of a society to adhere to activities directly related to maintaining subsistence. Or the rigidity may be imposed by some orthodoxy that has achieved unquestioned authority. Turnbull's description of the Ik in *The Mountain People* and the horrendous vision of Orwell in *1984* are examples of these aberrations. But however they come about, the fault lies in a reduction of human options, a curtailment of the directions in which members can develop themselves. Since part of the purpose of a tradition is to provide such opportunities, a rigid moral tradition is faulty in its own terms.

Another source of weakness is if a moral tradition fails to inspire its members. Recall the realization that preceded Mill's crisis; he asked himself:

> Suppose that all your objects in life were realized; that all the changes in institutions and opinions which you are looking forward to, could be completely effected at this instant: would this be a great joy and happiness to you?' And an irrespressible self-consciousness distinctly answered, 'No!' At this heart sank within me: the whole foundation on which my life was constructed fell down. . . . I seemed to have nothing left to live for.[6]

This passage describes a personal experience. Imagine, however, that the experience is not due to psychological factors peculiar to a person, but to a realistic appraisal of a moral tradition. The signs of this happening are widespread boredom, ennui, anomie, decadence, and the feverish pursuit of thrills. When this happens, and its cause is internal to a tradition rather than the fault of some of its members, the tradition is played out. It is supposed to move its members to action by appealing to their imagination, exciting them to admiration, by inspiring their feelings by giving a cast to their emotional lives in which feeling and doing, and imagining options and being moved to realize them are closely bound. A tradition that fails to inspire, fails to be action-guiding. Its more conscientious members may continue to carry on in a desultory way, but its soul is gone. This, I think, is what happened to the Roman tradition, due largely to the impact of Christianity, and to the ancien régime before the blood of the Revolution washed it away.

These are some of the ways in which traditions can come to grief. Other ways can be added, because there are as many potential criticisms of traditions as there are contexts and aspirations. They can fail by allowing custom to turn into a ritual whose point is forgotten, by the breakdown of institutions for adjudicating conflicts, by cataclysmic changes to which they cannot respond, by the appearance of another tradition that does better justice to the experience and aspirations of its members, and so on. The upshot is that since a tradition can be successfully criticized, it can be rational. But if a preponderance of available criticisms do not convict a tradition, then it is reasonable to adhere to it. A sound moral tradition provides rich opportunities for self-direction and intimate personal relationships. Thus its members have goodwill toward each other, and decency prevails. A society, therefore, is justified in jealously guarding its moral tradition, if it is sound, and improving it, where it is defective.

4

Self-Direction

What Is Self-Direction?

The aspiration at the core of self-direction is well captured by Isaiah Berlin. "I wish my life and decisions to depend on myself, not on external forces of whatever kind. I wish to be an instrument of my own, not of other men's, acts of will. I wish to be . . . moved by reasons, by conscious purposes, which are my own, not by causes which affect me, as it were, from outside. I wish to be a doer . . . deciding, not being decided for, self-directed and not acted upon by external nature."[1]

It is a fact of life, however, that self-direction is limited by conditions set by human nature and by our moral tradition. I have been arguing that we should not see these conditions as forces of oppression, but rather as minimum requirements of our welfare. We cannot live good lives unless our basic physiological, psychological, and social wants are met. But meeting them is not a burden imposed on us from the outside; rather, it is a source of pleasure and security. Furthermore, self-direction takes place in various traditional contexts regulated by conventions to which we must conform, if we are to satisfy our wants in a manner we find acceptable. However, these conventions are not arbitrary restrictions, but civilizing channels for the energy that gives self-direction its impetus. The aim of this chapter is to begin developing a conception of self-direction that goes beyond the limiting conditions, and thus beyond the minimum requirements of human welfare.

By its nature, self-direction is the direction of a particular self by itself. It is a process of self-transformation involving the gradual change of our present self into a future self that approximates more closely the ideals we aim at. I shall discuss self-direction by reflecting on the life of Montaigne. His life exemplifies a case of extremely successful self-direction. He was conscious of being engaged in it and articulate about what it involved, as shown by his

Essays,[2] one of the classic works on the subject, and he discovered at the end that the significance of the lessons he has learned about himself extended beyond his life. So by concentrating on Montaigne's life, we can come to a better understanding of self-directed lives in general.

The salient facts of Montaigne's life are easily told.[3] He was born in 1533, into a Gascon Catholic family of lesser nobility, residing not far from the city of Bordeaux. He was educated first at home, where he learned Latin before French, and later at one of the best schools of France. He was trained in law, and, at the age of twenty-four, he became a councillor in the Parliament of Bordeaux, where his duties required him to participate in legislation and to act as something like a magistrate. During this period he married, had six children, all but one of whom died in infancy, and formed the most significant relationship of his life: a friendship with La Boetia, who died from a painful illness four years later. After thirteen years of service, Montaigne retired to his estate "long weary of the servitude of the court and of public employments . . . where in . . . freedom, tranquillity, and leisure" (ix–x) he intended to reflect and write. In 1570, he began work on the *Essays*. But two years later he was interrupted by being called out of retirement to act as a mediator between the warring Catholics and Protestants of France; as a moderate Catholic and an experienced man of affairs, he was acceptable to both parties. He was intermittently engaged in this four years. In 1580, when he was forty-seven, the first edition of the *Essays*, containing Books I and II, appeared. It was well received. Montaigne, then, traveled for almost two years in Switzerland and Germany, but mainly concentrated on Italy. In his absence, he was elected mayor of Bordeaux, a prestigious office he did not seek and was reluctant to accept. But the was prevailed upon, and, when his two-year term came to an end, he was given the rare honor of reelection for a second term. After this, he once again took up residence on his estate, finished Book III of the *Essays*, and kept revising the first two books. The three books were first published together in 1588, when he was fifty-five years old. He continued revising them until the end. He died in 1592, a few months before his sixtieth birthday. He was generally regarded as a wise and learned man, an eminent scholar, and a distinguished public servant.

From the point of view of self-direction, one of the most interesting aspects of Montaigne's life is its relation to the *Essays*. The *Essays* were consciously intended by Montaigne as the instruments of his own self-transformation. They were meant as replacements of conversations with his dead friend; vehicles for articulating and reflecting on Montaigne's attitudes; records of changes in his thought and sensibility; ventures in trying out arguments, thinking through various complicated matters, and expressing scorn and admiration; they formed "a book consubstantial with its author" (504). As Montaigne says: "I have no more made my book than my book has made me . . . . [It is] concerned with my own self, an integral part of my life." (504). The *Essays* shaped Montaigne's life, not merely because they reflected it, but also because Montaigne reflected in them on his reflection and changed himself accordingly. "In modeling this figure upon myself, I have had to fashion and compose myself so often to bring myself out, that the model itself has to some extent grown firm and taken shape" (504). Thus the *Essays* were both causes and effects, and symptoms and diagnoses, efforts to take stock of how things were with Montaigne, to firm up the resolve to change them, and planning how to change them. I propose to approach self-direction by examining how Montaigne coped in his own life with some of the tensions typical of human lives.

Public Service and Private Life

In one of the first essays composed after his retirement began, Montaigne wrote: "the wise man . . . if he has the choice . . . will choose solitude. . . . [T]he aim of all solitude, I take it, is the same: to live more at leisure and at one's ease. . . . [But] by getting rid of the court and the market place we do not get rid of the principal worries of our life. . . . Ambition, avarice, irresolution, fear, and lust . . . often follow us even into the cloisters and the schools of philosophy" (175–76). The answer is to concentrate on the improvement of our soul, make it

> withdraw into itself: that is real solitude, which may be enjoyed in the midst of cities and the courts of kings; but it is enjoyed more handily alone. (176). We must reserve a back shop all our own, entirely free . . . our principal retreat and solitude. Here our ordinary conversation must be between us and ourselves. . . . We have a soul that can be turned upon itself; it can keep itself company; it has the means of attack and the means to defend, the means to receive and the means to give: let us not fear this solitude (177).

But this is only one strand in Montaigne's thinking. About fifteen years later, he adds the following comment to these passages: "Solitude seems to me more appropriate and reasonable for those who have given the world their most active and flourishing years (178).

The other strand is represented by what Montaigne did during his "most active and flourishing years." Public service was a traditional and expected part of the life of nobility, and, as we have seen, Montaigne played his part with distinction as a councillor, a mediator, and as mayor of Bordeaux, even though these activities interrupted his solitude. His view was that "I do not want a man to refuse, to the charges he takes on, attention, steps, words, and sweat and blood if need be" (770). And Montaigne, we know, acted according to this view. But why did he do it? Because he saw himself living in the "sick age" of sixteenth-century France. "I perceive . . . the strife that is tearing France to pieces and dividing us into factions" (760), and he felt that it was his duty to do what he could. But he found the laws he was administering unjust, the system corrupt, and the religious wars, with their massacres and cruelty, disgusting (759). "Consider the form of this justice that governs us: it is a true testimony of human imbecility, so full it is of contradiction and error" (819). "How many condemnations I have seen more criminal than the crime" (820)! "There is no hostility that excels Christian hostility. . . . Our religion is made to extirpate vices; it covers them, fosters them, incites them" (324). But how could Montaigne lend himself to what he knew was corruption? Not for gain. "I sometimes feel rising in my soul the fumes of certain temptations toward ambition; but I stiffen and hold firm against them" (759). He did it because, although "[t]he justest party is still a member of worm-eaten and maggoty body. But in such a body the least diseased member is called healthy; and quite rightly, since our qualities have no titles except by comparison. Civic innocence is measured according to the places and the times" (760).

Throughout his life, Montaigne felt the tension between public service and private life. His sense of duty, nurtured by the obligations of his social position; the admired examples of his father and his friend, La Boetia; the expectations of the court and his fellow noblemen, all impelled him toward public service. The attractions of personal happiness and tranquillity, the development of his thought and sensibility, and his fondness of reflection and rural life, impelled him toward private life. His conception of a good life was connected with both. In some fortunate lives, spent in times less turbulent than those of sixteenth-century France, this tension calls for a judicious balance, and it may be achieved by experience and judgment. But Montaigne was not so fortunate; for him, public service conflicted with living a good life, because, due to the corruption of his age, public service routinely required him to perform immoral acts. Montaigne saw this clearly, but he also saw the need for it. "In every government there are necessary offices which are . . . vicious. Vices find their place in it and are employed for sewing our society together. . . . The public welfare requires that a man betray and lie" (600). Montaigne's conflict is known to us as the problem of dirty hands, from Sartre's eponymous play.

Now the obvious temptation is not to dirty our hands. But Montaigne did not give in to it. To do so would have meant abandoning his conception of a good life and leaving public service to those who would corrupt it even further. It would have meant betraying his responsibility both to himself and to others. Instead, Montaigne struggled with the conflict and articulated a *modus vivendi* of enduring significance.

Reflecting on his conflict, he wrote: "The mayor and Montaigne have always been two, with a very clear separation" (774). What was the separation? On the one hand, "[a]n honest man is not accountable for the vice and stupidity of his trade, and should not therefore refuse to practice it: it is the custom of his country and there is profit in it. We must live in the world and make the most of it as we find it" (774). And again,

> I once tried to employ in the service of public dealings ideas and rules . . . which I use . . . in private matters. . . . I found them inept and dangerous. . . . He who walks in the crowd must step aside, keep his elbows in, step back or advance, even leave the straight way, according to others, not according to what he proposes to himself but according to what others propose to him, according to the time, according to the men, according to the business (758).

On the other hand, "I have been able to take part in public office without departing one nail's head from myself, and give myself to others without taking myself from myself" (770).

But how is this possible? How can we both remain ourselves and engage in vicious and stupid practices? Montaigne's answer was: by offering only "limited and conditional services. There is no remedy. I frankly tell them my limits" (603). He will soil himself up to a point, but not beyond it. "I do not . . . involve myself so deeply and so entirely" (774). The limits beyond which Montaigne will not go separate the depth he will not allow his involvement to penetrate and the malleable surface of his life that he is prepared to adjust according to the time, the men, and the business. In his self, there is a hard core and a soft periphery. He is willing to perform public service, and thus both do his duty and participate in corrupt arrangements, so long as they affect only the periphery and do not compromise the hard core of his self. But he does not depart one nail's head from himself, because there is an area reserved for his private life, his "back shop," his "principal retreat," the object of his reflection when he withdraws into himself, into "real solitude."

The general significance of the answer Montaigne found for himself is that since we live in a world that has not become appreciably purer since the sixteenth century, and since reason and morality require only our conditional services, we must learn to distinguish between the core of our selves, where our deepest commitments lie, and the outer layers, which we can afford to compromise, if we need be.

One central tasks of self-direction is to draw and maintain this distinction. But we can do so only if we know what our commitments are and if we have decided upon their respective importance in our conception of a good life. And these, in turn, require that we possess the capacity and willingness to work for that knowledge and to make the appropriate decisions. Commitments are connected with ideals, and the capacity and willingness depend on the development of some specific virtues. Thus a full account of self-direction, and a deeper appreciation of Montaigne's answer, requires an account of ideals and virtues, as they bear on the possibility of self-direction. In subsequent chapters, I shall propose such an account.

Tradition and Individuality

Montaigne's resolution of the tension between public service and private life depends on the possession of a strong and clear sense of self. As we know from his life and the *Essays,* Montaigne had such a sense. However, my primary interest here is in self-direction, not in Montaigne. What I want to get clear about is how *we* can go about developing the sort of self that would enable us, as it enabled Montaigne, to live in tranquillity in the midst of turmoil and to perform public service in a corruption-ridden context without compromising our deepest commitments. As we think about this, we encounter the second of the tensions characteristic of human lives in general and of Montaigne's in particular. And, as before, we can learn from Montaigne by understanding how he coped with it.

It is tempting to think that having a strong and clear sense of the self depends on maintaining a sharp distinction between the tradition, which influences us, and our individuality, which gives content to our selves. If we think this way, self-direction becomes something like the moral analogue of economic protectionism. It keeps out foreign products, the corrupting traditional influences, and it invests into the development of native resources, by nurturing innate potentialities. As a result, we see the development of our individuality in opposition to our tradition. The more tradition influences us, the less self-directed we are supposed to be; and the stronger our self-direction is, the more we are said to succeed in developing our individuality by freeing ourselves from traditional influences.

This way of thinking about self-direction has become widespread, but, in my view, it is seriously mistaken. Tradition influences us not only by undermining our moral commitments, but also by strengthening them; it provides not only limitations to the development of our individuality, but also possibilities for growth; it is a respository not only of temptations we should resist, but also of ideals we should pursue. If we were to succeed in excluding traditional influences, as this view of self-direction recommends, we would all have to begin anew. We would not know which of our many potentialities we should develop; we would not know their respective importance; we would not have ideals to guide us; we would deprive ourselves of the experiences and examples of those who lived before us. In effect, this view of self-direction obliges us to reject the possibility of developing ourselves in the light of history, literature, morality, and politics. It is a recipe for primitivism.

Nevertheless, it is not an accident that this way of thinking strikes a responsive chord in us. For alongside the promise tradition holds out, there is also the danger with which it threatens. If we concentrate on the promise, we risk becoming mindless conformists, apologists for the status quo, reactionary obstacles to reform. But the remedy is not to concentrate on the other extreme, the danger, and reject tradition altogether. The remedy is to strike a balance: to take what is good and say no to what is bad.

This suggests another way of thinking about self-direction. According to it, self-direction consists in maintaining a balance between tradition and individuality; its role is not to exclude traditional influences, but to control the influences tradition has on the development of our individuality. Since one of the dominant aspirations of Montaigne's life was to strike this balance, and since he was eminently successful at it, I turn to him once again to illustrate the general point.

Montaigne was a conservative; not a reactionary, not a sentimentalist about the tradition, not blind to how bad things were. "Our morals are extremely corrupt, and lean with a remarkable inclination toward the worse; of our laws and customs, many are barbarous and monstrous; however, because of the difficulty of improving our condition and the danger of everything crumbling into bits, if I could put a spoke in our wheel and stop it at this point, I would do so with all my heart" (497). There was a real danger in sixteenth-century France that, as Yeats wrote, reflecting on another time, "Things fall apart; the center cannot hold; mere anarchy is loosed upon the world."[4] Order, even corrupt order, is better than anarchy. There must be laws and customs, otherwise we can do nothing about what is barbarous and monstrous. "The worst thing I find in our state is instability. . . . It is very easy to accuse a government of imperfection, for all mortal things are full of it. It is very easy to engender in people contempt for their ancient observances. . . . But as for establishing a better state in place of the one they have ruined, many of those who have attempted it achieved nothing for their pains" (498). So what should we do? Should we acquiesce in evil?

Of course not. To begin with, "it is the rule of rules, and the universal law of laws, that each man should observe those of the place he is in" (86). For obviously, one source of evil is the failure to conform to the tradition. But what if the tradition is defective and conformity to it will merely perpetuate evil? The answer, then, is to understand that "[t]o compose our character is our duty . . . to win, not battles and provinces, but order and tranquillity in our conduct. Our great and glorious masterpiece is to live appropriately" (850–51). If everyone aimed to do that, and if we but knew what living appropriately meant, then we would know how to accept what is good and reject what is evil in our tradition.

Yet there is an obstacle to following the advice. For "[t]he laws of conscience, which we say are born of nature, are born of custom" (83). If the tradition is corrupt, it will corrupt the conscience from which we derive our understanding of what it means to live appropriately. And Montaigne saw that too, "the principal effect of the power of custom is to seize and ensnare us in such a way that it is hardly within our power to get ourselves back out of its

grip and return ourselves to reflect and reason about its ordi-
nances" (83). Notice, however, that crucial qualification: "hardly."
It is not beyond our power to step back and reflect, only it is very
difficult to do so. But nobody said, and it is naive to suppose, that
living appropriately was easy. So we return to the question: how
can we do *that,* if the very judgment of appropriateness is in
danger of being poisoned by the corruption of the tradition?

The key to the answer is to recognize that "[t]hings in themselves may have their weights and measures and qualities; but
once inside us, she [the soul] allots them their qualities as she sees
fit. . . . Health, conscience, authority, knowledge, riches, beauty,
and their opposites—all are stripped on entry and receive from
the soul new clothing . . . which each individual soul chooses. . . .
Wherefore let us no longer make the external qualities of things
our excuse; it is up to us to reckon them as we will" (220). There
are two centrally important points to note here.

First, living appropriately begins with taking into ourselves
traditional influences, rather than in pitting ourselves against
them. Among these influences are the various ideals, some of
which Montaigne lists, out of which we construct our conceptions
of good lives. Thus traditional influences are part of the raw
material with which self-direction begins. Consequently, tradition
influences the development of our individuality in two crucial
ways: by providing a stable and secure social context in which we
can concentrate on making good lives for ourselves through self-
direction and by providing a repertoire of possibilities from which
self-directed agents can choose some appropriate ideals of good
lives.

So we must not think that when Montaigne says that "I turn my
gaze inward, I fix it there and keep it busy" (499), then he is
retreating from his tradition in order to nurture the homegrown
products of his private, individual, inner life. What his gaze fixes
on are the traditional ideals by which he has been influenced.
These ideals are a rich mixture of those he derived from Catholicism; stoicism; pyrrhonism; the remembered extremely influen-
tial conversations with his friend, La Boetia; from the prevailing
life-style of a country squire; from his extensive reading of Plu-
tarch, Plato, and Herodotus; from his own travels and conversations with other travelers; from his experience as a public
official; and so on. And when he says that "I have a soul all its own,
accustomed to conducting itself in its own way" (487), then what
he has in mind is that he is accustomed to finding his way among
the manifold influences on him. "[T]he liberty of judgment" of
which he is so jealous (500) means the liberty to weigh, to assess

the appropriateness of various traditional ideals to his character and circumstances.

The second point of note in the passage just quoted is that when we exercise our "liberty of judgment" to appraise the appropriateness of traditional ideals, when we "reckon them as we will," then we are engaged in what I mean by self-direction. So self-direction essentially involves judgment, reckoning, and returning into ourselves to reflect and reason, but the objects upon which we concentrate are traditional ideals. And what self-direction consists in, inter alia, is adapting some of these traditional ideals to our own cases.

A distinction between the formulation and the acceptance of ideals will help to sharpen this point. We usually do not formulate the ideals we accept. Normally, ideals receive their authoritative formulation in a traditional text, like *The Republic, Nicomachean Ethics,* or the *Bible;* or they are exemplified in the life of a person, such as Socrates, Alexander, or Jesus; or they come attached to the traditional expectations of a public office, like the justice of a magistrate, the courage of a soldier, the wisdom of a statesman, and so on. One of the benefits of belonging to a tradition is that we can find in it clearly formulated, well-tested ideals that command general admiration and that represent accepted standards of excellence. Self-direction assumes its importance in the context of our acceptance of traditional ideals, not in their formulation. It involves deciding whether we, ourselves, would wish to conduct some important aspect of our lives in accordance with a particular traditional ideal, and, assuming that we do, what the acceptance of the ideal comes to in our individual lives shaped by our characters and circumstances.

Take, for instance, the ideal of public service. It consists in contributing to the tradition from which we derive many of the benefits that make good lives possible. Assume that reasonable people accept this traditional ideal and are prepared to act according to it. This is not the end, but the beginning of self-direction. For we need to decide what form our public service should take, how important it is in comparison to our other ideals, whether it should concentrate on criticizing the shortcomings of the tradition, contributing to its smooth functioning, defending it against detractors, or trying, creatively, to enrich it. Unless we answer these and similar questions, our acceptance of a traditional ideal may amount to nothing more than mindless conformity. The development of our individuality requires that we choose and adapt traditional ideals, and this is one function of self-direction.

The importance of self-direction, however, does not mean that we are, each of us, the final judges of the reasons for or against particular ideals. It means, rather, that we are the final judges of the reasons, and of how heavily they weigh, for or against *our acceptance* of a particular ideal. These two sets of reasons overlap for rational people, but not even for them do they coincide. For our reasons for accepting an ideal take into account *our* characters and circumstances, while the reasons *per se* for an ideal are independent of such personal considerations. Traditions carry a great deal of authority about reason per se, but self-direction ought to be authoritative about our own reasons. Of course, neither authority is infallible. It is just that they are more likely to be correct in their own context than other candidates.

However, if we go a little deeper, we find that not even the traditional authority responsible for the formulation of ideals is unconnected with self-direction. For traditional authority rests on the accumulated experiences of many individuals. And these individuals had also to make the sorts of judgments that we have to make. Their judgments became subsumed into traditional authority, because they proved reliable. So there is nothing mysterious about traditional authority: it is a repository of good judgments tested by long experience, from which we can benefit, if we are reasonable. Thus tradition is not an enemy of self-direction, but a testimony to its importance, for both the formulation and the acceptance of ideals essentially involve it. This, I think, is the significance of the closing words of Montaigne's *Essays*. "There is no use our mounting on stilts, for on stilts we must still walk on our own legs. And on the loftiest throne in the world we are still sitting on our own rump" (857).

But knowing the importance of self-direction and understanding that it involves balancing the traditional influences upon us and the requirements of our individuality are insufficient for good lives. We also need to know how we should weigh the acceptance of ideals and how we can achieve the desired balance. Thus, just as the resolution of the tension between public service and private life requires us to look more deeply into ideals and virtues, so also does the aspiration to maintain a balance between tradition and individuality.

Self-Direction and Good Lives

Self-direction is important, because it is a means to good lives. However, not even the most assiduously self-directed people have good lives guaranteed to them. For the goodness of lives also depends on circumstances over which we have no control; illness, social upheavals, the death of people we love, accidental injury, being unjustly victimized, lack of merited appreciation, and similar misfortunates can present obstacles that no amount of self-direction may be able to overcome. But internal obstacles may also prevent self-direction from leading to good lives. For self-direction can be done badly. The ideals it aims to realize may be flawed or inappropriate to our characters and circumstances and we may fail to develop to a sufficient extent the virtues it requires. In the rest of the book, I shall discuss how to avoid these pitfalls.

However, we can already specify some conditions that successful self-direction must meet. I argued in chapter 1 that good lives depend on the coherence of our beliefs, feelings, and intentions; on these psychological states having appropriate objects; and on these objects including the reasonable satisfaction of our important wants. But, as we have seen in chapters 2 and 3, this pattern, aiming at coherence, appropriate objects, and reasonable satisfactions, is limited by objective conditions set by human nature and by our moral tradition. Successful self-direction must involve at least the minimal satisfaction of universal physiological, psychological, and social needs, as well as conformity to all the required and some of the variable conventions of our moral tradition, so that the general framework for good lives is protected. The present chapter has added to these requirements two others. First, self-directed lives should involve participation in the world, but it should only be a conditional participation, without compromising our deep commitments. And second, there should be a balance between our tradition and individuality, achieved by being open to the possibilities of good lives our tradition provides, while, simultaneously, assessing those possibilities, opting for some among them, and adapting them to our own cases.

Successful self-direction should meet these requirements, but it should also go beyond them. It will aid our inquiry if we have an initial sketch of at least one good life, so that it would be clearer what sort of thing we aim at in our search for additional conditions. Here, once again, we can appeal to Montaigne, for he had succeeded, through a lifetime of self-direction, in making a good life for himself.

Montaigne's ideal was clear. "It is an absolute perfection and virtually divine to know how to enjoy our being rightfully" (857). Thus the ideal is enjoyment, the enjoyment is of a way of life, but it must be a rightful enjoyment. If we achieve this, "tranquillity and gladness shine from within. . . . The surest sign . . . is constant cheerfulness" (119). This is the state of "virtue—this supreme, beautiful, triumphant, loving virtue, as delightful as she is courageous, a professed and implacable enemy of sourness, displeasure, fear, and constraint, having nature for its guide, fortune and pleasure for companions" (119). Its "tool is moderation. . . . She is the nursing mother of human pleasures. By making them just, she make them sure and pure. . . . If she lacks the fortune of ordinary men, she rises above it or does without it, and makes herself a different sort of fortune that is all her own. . . . She loves life, she loves beauty and glory and health. But her own particular task is to know how to enjoy these blessings with temperance, and to lose them with fortitude" (120). This is the ideal, and the good life, for Montaigne, required learning how to achieve it. This life is not one "of scholastic probity . . . a slave to precept, held down beneath fear and hope. . . . What I like is the virtue that laws and religions do not make . . . that feels in itself enough to sustain itself without help, born in us from its own roots, from the seed of universal reason that is implanted in every man who is not denatured" (811).

The first step toward achieving such a life is to understand ourselves. "We seek other conditions because we do not understand the use of our own, and go outside of ourselves because we do to know what it is like inside" (857). In trying to come to understand ourselves, then, what do we find? First we find the requirements of nature, but "what Nature flatly and originally demands of us for the preservation of our being is too little" (772). We need to go beyond it. "Let us grant ourselves something further: let us also call the habits and condition of each of us *nature*. . . . Habit is a second nature, and no less powerful" (772). And the function of habit is "to give form to our life . . . it is all-powerful in that" (827). As a result, we "have a pattern established within us by which to test our actions, and, according to this pattern, now pat ourselves on the back, now punish ourselves. I have my own laws and court to judge me, and I address myself to them more than anywhere else" (613). In possession of this pattern, Montaigne can truthfully say of himself, "My actions are in order and conformity with what I am and with my condition. I can do no better" (617). And when he surveys what he in fact had done, "I find that in my past deliberations, according to my rule, I have proceeded wisely, considering the state of the matter proposed to me, and I should do the same a thousand years from now in similar situations" (618). Thus he can apply the ultimate test to his life and have perhaps the greatest satisfaction of all: being able to say, "If I had to live over again, I would live as I have lived. I have neither tears for the past nor fears for the future" (620).

None of this means that the road was always smooth from the ideal of enjoying his life rightfully to the retrospective judgment that he had done so. In fact, Montaigne encountered and coped with much adversity. He was kidnapped by brigands and imprisoned by religious extremists; he survived the plague raging around him; his castle was invaded by enemy soldiers and he and his family were at their mercy; he suffered for many years severe pain caused by kidney stones; five of his children died; he witnessed the agonized death of his beloved father and of his closest friend and mentor, La Boetia; he lived in the midst of a brutal civil war and risked much as a go-between. And the turmoil was not only external. His education and early studies gave an unsuitable cast to his mind, and it took him many years to modulate and adjust his thought and sensibility so as to fit harmoniously with what he was coming to understand about himself. Dogmatic Catholicism and unquestioning acceptance of the Church's authority were mixed with stoical and pyrrhonic influences. As he had gone on to reflect, his Catholicism became moderate, his recognition of the Church's authority was confined to theological matters, the resignation advised by stoics turned into an exuberant humanism, the sceptical doubt he learned gradually changed from a fideistic anti-intellectualism to a suspicion of dogmatism and an emphasis on the importance of common sense and good judgment. In all this, he grew, he became more reflective, and his self-direction improved. He understood that this was the process he was going through, and he guided himself through it by the method he invented: he wrote the *Essays* and used them as devices for understanding himself and for changing himself from what he was to what he thought he ought to be. Thus the epigraph to the final edition of the *Essays* he lived to see through the press. "*Viresque acquirit eundo*—He gains strength as he goes."[5]

In closing, I want to take stock of the requirements of self-direction we can derive from Montaigne's example. First, we must take from our moral tradition ideals, adapt them to our characters and circumstances, and forge out of them our individual conceptions of a good life. This requires us to assess the importance of various ideals and commit ourselves to their realization. Some of these commitments will be deep, others superficial. Deep commitments constitute part of our individuality, give us our identity, and define a private sphere that we should protect from the intrusion of the world. Second, we must make ourselves into the kind of agents who are capable of living according to their ideals. This requires the development of four virtues that jointly make self-direction possible. We need self-control to change ourselves from what we are to what our ideals prescribe we ought to be. We need self-knowledge to develop a realistic view of ourselves. We need moral sensitivity to appraise the suitability of ideals to our lives. And we need wisdom to understand our limitations and possibilities and to conduct ourselves accordingly. These requirements, ideals, and commitments to them, and the four virtues of self-direction, constitute the topics for the next five chapters.

5
Ideals and Commitments

Introduction

Aristotle's advice about achieving a good life is that "every one that has the power to live according to his own choice [should] . . . set up for himself some object for the good life to aim at . . . with reference to which he will then do all his acts, since not to have one's life organized in view of some end is the mark of great folly."[1] The objects Aristotle has in mind are roughly what I mean by ideals, and the purpose of this chapter is to consider what ideals are and what it is like to be committed to them.

Plato's story of Gyges's ring suggests an initial answer.[2] By the turn of the ring on one's finger, one is rendered invisible. Glaucon asks: what would be the difference in the conduct of just and unjust people if they had Gyges's ring? And the answer he gives, as a challenge to Socrates, is that there would be no difference. If people could steal, kill, and take their pleasure with impunity, they would do so. The difference betwen just and unjust people is that the former behave according to the laws of their society, while the latter do not. But if we ask why the just ones obey the laws, we find that they do so because they care about their reputation and fear punishment. Gyges's ring removes these constraints and so the laws would have no hold on someone possessing it. To be committed to an ideal is to be the sort of person whose conduct would *not* be changed by the possession of Gyges's ring. Such people would not act differently, because what motivates them is what *they* regard as good, and that has not been changed by Gyges's ring.

The story of Gyges's ring allows us to envisage people freed from the normal constraints of society. They do exactly what they want; only self-direction guides them. However, self-direction, in turn, is guided by ideals. Of course, ideals still come from outside, from the moral tradition of their society. Self-directed people have them, however, because reflection, not social conditioning, has prompted their acceptance.

A Description of Ideals

Ideals are goals that guide conduct. One way of understanding why people do something is by understanding the goals they aim at. Knowing these goals also makes it possible to judge success and failure. The first consists in approximating or achieving the goals, the second in having attempted, but not having gotten closer.

Conduct may be guided by many goals, but only some of these are what I understand by ideals. For goals to qualify as ideals, they must be valued. People may act to achieve goals they do not value, because they are forced, or act out of revenge, rage, indifference, or boredom. They may pursue goals they dislike in order to avoid something even worse, and they may be ignorant or unconscious of the goals they in fact pursue.

Ideals, then, are valued goals: to accept an ideal is tantamount to recognizing it as something we want, because we think that it is good. That we act so as to achieve what we regard as an ideal is natural and expected. What needs explanation is when we are conscious of having an ideal, have the opportunity to act according to it, and yet refrain from doing so. Self-sacrifice, stupidity, love, a sense of duty, laziness, or scruples may account for it.

In accepting an ideal, we accept a particular view about what is a good life. Our ideals represent our judgment about what, in the long run, in our lives overall, would make them good. And this, of course, is the reason why we commit ourselves to ideals, why we value the goals implicit in them, and why we think that their pursuit will make our lives better.

To this two qualifications need to be added. First, the judgments that lead us to accept ideals are fallible. We may think that an ideal will make our lives good, and we may be mistaken. How to form reliable judgments of this sort is a question to which I shall keep returning. The second is that while ideals are accepted, because we think that they will give *us* good lives, their acceptance may be deeply influenced by love and justice. Good lives, as we have seen, are not selfish

Much has been written about the lofty status of ideals. It has been supposed that they are metaphysical entities existing in an extramundane world. I do not share this Platonic view of them; I think that ideals are concrete open to inspection. They are to be found in the lives of actual people, in the factual or fictional representations of such lives, or in the imaginative portrayal of lives nobody has ever lived. Ideals exist embodied in people, books, and works of art; in drama, novels, biographies, paintings, sculptures, films, religious tracts, and philosophical treatises. Ideals, therefore, are in the public domain, accessible to all who seek them. They are part of the riches of our moral tradition, a repertoire of possibilities it affords us.

Ideals are complex. They are composed of many elements and each makes a contribution to the ideal being what it is. Some of these elements are contingent; others are essential. What makes an element essential is that without it the ideal would become unrecognizable as that ideal.

Consider, for instance, the ideal represented by the life of Spinoza. He was a foreigner in Holland; a Jew in a Protestant country; a heretic among Jews; a philosopher without a school, patron, or students; a scholar who earned his living as an artisan; a man with profound religious sentiments who rejected the God of the Bible, of his country, and of his family. He was a quintessential outsider. But unlike many outsiders, he sought his own exile, because he had a deep purpose. His life was of a piece with his philosophy. As his philosophy taught that freedom comes from understanding the essential structure of the world and recognizing the irrelevance of the particular manifestations that happen to surround one, so in his life he tried to free himself from the encumbrances of religion, society, and family to make it possible for him to concentrate on the essential questions by penetrating below the surface on which most people live. His life was outwardly placid, inwardly a passionate quest. He was alone, because you do not take company to Mount Sinai. This quest, of course, is not an ideal for everybody. But if Wittgenstein, Nietzsche, Simone Weil, Montaigne, and St. Theresa had known about Spinoza, they would have recognized him as a kindred soul.

Reflecting on his life, we can identify some elements of it as essential. Without intellectual passion, rationality, solitude, self-control, independence, and introspectiveness, he would not be the Spinoza that matters to us. Being a Jew, earning his living as an artisan, having been influenced by Maimonides and Descartes, and modeling his major work on Euclid are far less important to his being the ideal for a certain kind of life. These elements, therefore, are contingent.

The complexity of ideals helps to explain both the nature of arguments about them and their capacity to inspire us in different circumstances. Arguments about ideals may concern the acceptance or rejection of a particular ideal, or, given that the ideal is accepted, its interpretation. I shall call the first kind of argument *external,* the second *internal,* and ignore external arguments for the moment.

Internal arguments about ideals occur among adherents who accept the same ideal and disagree about its interpretation. This disagreement occurs, because, while in accepting an ideal they accept its essential elements, they have not thereby accepted any judgment about the respective importance of the essential elements. Thus two people may be equally inspired by Spinoza's life, and try to model themselves accordingly; one may regard rationality and self-control as dominating among the essential elements, while the other may think that of all the essential elements intellectual passion and solitude matter most. These people have a genuine disagreement about one particular form of good life, even though they agree both about the guiding ideal and about its essential elements.

Can such disagreements be settled? The answer depends on bearing firmly in mind the point of the argument. If the dispute concerns the canonical ranking of the essential components of the ideal, it is pointless. To argue, in abstract terms about which element is more important is like arguing which organ of the body is more important, or which piece in chess should be given pride of place. But such arguments need not be silly. If people argue about the respective importance of the elements in an ideal, then, given their lives, the context in which they live, and their characters, talents, and weaknesses, the argument is capable of settlement. For it hinges on whether a person has succeeded in living a good life following that ideal and its interpretation. But I must still postpone detailed discussion of how such arguments can be settled.

The other important consequence of the complexity of ideals is their endurance. For better or worse, many ideals continue to exercise powerful attraction, even though the lives embodying them were lived in contexts drastically different from the contexts of those who are attracted by them. Their endurance is made possible, because the complex mixture of essential and contingent elements permits openness, and thus the adaptability of ideals to different contexts. As an illustration, consider the lives of Socrates, Alexander, and Gandhi. One essential component of each was courage. But what courage came to in their vastly different personalities and situations was, of course, quite different. Superficially, we may say that they all risked their lives. We shall not really understand them, however, if we fail to see why they took the risks. Socrates wanted to remain true to himself, Alexander wanted to conquer the world, and Gandhi wanted to free his people. Thinking about their cases, we soon realize that integrity, military ambition, and nationalism are incidental to courage; they are merely the forms their notable courageous conduct took. If we go deeper, we see, however, that what was common among them was the willingness to take risks to protect the ideal to which they had committed themselves. The openness of ideals is due to the presence of these contingent features. And their endurance and continued attraction is made possible by coming to see that the essential feature of their courage is applicable in many varied contexts. So the complexity of ideals permits the interplay between the essential enduring elements and the contingent variable ones. And this, in turn, guarantees that the ideals will be modifiable to fit changing circumstances.

Ideals, then, are goals valued by their adherents, because they take them to be constituents of good lives. They are publicly available, readily observable, rather than metaphysical entities. They are complex, composed of essential and contingent elements, and because of them, ideals are open to interpretation and modification. As a result, they can continue to attract their adherents in radically different circumstances.[3]

Ideals and Attitudes Toward Them

If an ideal attracts us, our attitude toward it will be a mixture of cognitive, emotive, and imaginative appreciation. To know how things would be evaluated if we had accepted an ideal is one thing; actually evaluating them that way is another. The difference is partly that in the latter case we feel that some things are shocking, surprising, reassuring, delightful, obscene, or threatening. Another part of the difference is imagining how we would respond in different situations, if we were guided by that ideal. Imagining possible feelings is no less important than having present ones, for, to a considerable extent, that is what guides self-direction. It strongly influences what we want to bring about or avoid; how hard we should work for or against particular ideals; how happy, miserable, offended, honored, outraged, or proud we would be if we approximated them.[4]

Consider trying to understand the lives of a Christian and an atheist. Observation of their behavior may not make it possible to identify them, because behavior is not usually explicit about these deeper convictions. Indeed, apart from a direct statement of their beliefs, it may not be possible to judge their religious leanings. The difference between them may not come from what they do, but from how they think and feel about what they do: their internal lives differ. The Christian regards life as a preamble to eternity, and hopes to spend it in the proximity of God. His moral convictions receive their ultimate sanction from transcendental authority. He fears, trusts, and loves God and recognizes his universal jurisdiction. The feelings of the atheist are not invested in any transcendental authority; he believes that this present life is the only one. His moral convictions are determined by his judgment about what is likely to benefit humanity, assuming that he is one kind of atheist. The Christian regards humanity, good and evil, the past, present, and future as the observable, sometimes mysterious unfolding of a divine plan. For the atheist, there is no plan; there is only choice and chance, and there is no design behind the obstacle race humanity is running.

Part of the difference between them is in their emotional and imaginative responses to their lot. These constitute a species of moral attitudes that are essential components of such responses as pessimism or optimism, resignation or pleasure-seeking, anxiety or trust, awe or irony, and the like. However, in the present case, these are not directed toward particular objects, but toward reality; it is the scheme of things that makes us anxious, pessimistic, or awed. And when the attitudes are expressed with reference to particular objects, the objects are being perceived as instances of something quite general. These kinds of moral attitudes frequently prompt and color our responses to reality and our perception of our relation to it. Such attitudes are partly in terms of which we answer what Kant regarded as one of the main questions of philosophy: for what may I hope?

This question has two closely connected aspects. One is the consideration of what we may hope for in terms of an ideal. In asking this, we have not accepted the ideal; we are simply trying to understand it. Feeling and imagination help us to do so. However, they may lead us to become attached to unjustifiable ideals. So the second aspect of the question of what we may hope for is whether it is reasonable to repose our hopes in a particular ideal. This can be answered through a sensitive appreciation of the ideal.

The ideals of Christians and positivists, Spinoza and Jeremy Bentham, and Marxists and Plato, to offer some obvious contrasts, differ partly because to accept one rather than the other is to have one rather than another moral attitude toward reality and our place in it. This is the reason why understanding an ideal is not merely an intellectual matter, but also an emotive and imaginative issue. And this explains why we can appreciate, say, the austerity and nobility of Spinoza's ideal, while recognizing that it does not survive objections. It explains also why Christians may refuse to abandon their beliefs, even though they accept the inadequacy of the arguments supporting their position. And it is why we may say that the arguments for determinism are strong, but we would not like determinism to be true. The simple fact is that we hope for the justification of some ideals and recoil from the implications of others.

Many people, including philosophers, however, are not disposed to recognize this commonplace. These moral attitudes are rarely mentioned in discussions about ideals. What underlies this widespread avoidance is the suspicion that such moral attitudes are prejudices writ large. Intellectual integrity and self-interest require us to be on guard against what we wish to be true. However, in striving to avoid wishful thinking, we have come to underplay the role of feeling and imagination as important aspects of good lives.

It might be said that these moral attitudes should be ignored. Ideals, after all, are supposed to be capable of justification; they rest on assumptions that could be true or false, but the moral attitudes I am discussing are neither. This is indeed true. But, although moral attitudes have no truth-value, they may still be more or less appropriate, or altogether inappropriate. Furthermore, we may be concerned with rationally appraising their appropriateness, and we may be prepared to revise them, if we judge them to be inappropriate.

Consider, for example, an atheist who is also a positivist. Suppose that over a period of time he meets one misfortune after another through no fault of his own. People he loves die, he is seriously injured in an accident he was not responsible for, lightning destroys his house, he is falsely and unjustly accused of a crime, and so on. He may become resentful of the scheme of things. His previous attitude toward nature's supposed neutrality is replaced by anger mixed with fear, and he is indignant about the unfairness of it all.

Of course, these attitudes are inappropriate, given that he is a positivist. Nature cannot be both impersonal and unfair, nonsentient and yet a proper object of anger and resentment. We can understand how he has come to have these attitudes, nevertheless, it is unreasonable to have them and simultaneously to accept positivism. Recognition of the inappropriateness of his attitudes may not make them disappear, but it may be the first step toward controlling them.

Ideals and Presuppositions

The appropriateness of moral attitudes depends on the justification of the ideals toward which the attitudes are directed. And the justification of ideals depends on the justification of their presuppositions. Presuppositions are essential components of ideals; they are the fundamental assumptions upon which ideals rest. To abandon a presupposition is tantamount to abandoning the ideal that rests on it. For example, rationality if fundamental to the ideal embodied by Spinoza, but that it should take axiomatic form is not; a calm sceptical frame of mind is fundamental to the Humean ideal, but that it should center on religious or epistemological beliefs is not. The fundamentality of presuppositions makes them intrinsic to ideals. They are like the structural elements of a building and unlike its decoration, or like the organs of a body and unlike hair or eye color. Presuppositions are not means to achieving ideals, but parts of the ideal to be achieved, so if a presupposition fails, being intrinsic to an ideal, the ideal thereby also fails. In contrast with fundamental assumptions, there are also contingent assumptions implicit in ideals, but ideals can survive their failure.

Consider Spinoza once more. The fundamental assumptions of the ideal he came to represent include the necessity of rationality, independence of life and mind, devotion to truth, and the desire to understand so as to live a good life. If he had been motivated by resentment against his elders rather than by intellectual passion, if his solitary life was due to chronic shyness and not to the need to concentrate on very difficult intellectual matters, or if he had interpreted his excommunication as a sign of personal animosity and not as a conflict of basic principles, then the ideal his life represents would be flawed and its inspirational force would be weakened. The contingent assumptions of the ideal were that the conflict happened to concern Jewish dogma, that in the Holland of his days there was sympathy for principled opposition to religious authority, that he supported himself as an artisan, and that he was attracted by the model of Euclidean demonstration. Part of understanding Spinoza's splendid life is to see that we do not need even to consider the contingent assumptions to be inspired by the ideal; and that to be inspired by it involves taking the fundamental assumptions for granted. If we believe that they are mistaken, we have lost the ideal.

To say that presuppositions are fundamental is to say something about their form; but what about their content? What sort of things are fundamentally assumed by ideals? Such assumptions, of course, vary with ideals; so the content of particular ideals cannot be specified in general terms. But we can go beyond purely formal characterization and make some general observations about content.

The presuppositions involve factual assumptions, assumptions about the possibility and suitability of the ideal, and assumptions about the consequences of the realization of the ideal. Now all these can be true or false, and it is a plain question of fact which they are. It may be that in some cases it is hard to discover the truth of the matter, but such difficulties do not occur more frequently in this domain than in historiography, literary criticism, jurisprudence, or ethnography. So the justification of ideals through their presuppositions is not an especially daunting task.

One kind of presupposition involved in ideals, then, is factual. Ideals rest on some facts, and if these turn out to be otherwise, the ideal cannot be rationally held. Consider, for instance, Christianity. Its factual assumptions include the existence of God, the Resurrection, the Immaculate Conception, and the miracles attributed to Jesus. If these assumptions turn out to be mistaken, then the Christian ideal fails. Of course, it can still be held irrationally, or it can be reformulated so as to exclude supernatural elements. These strategies, however, violate the original ideal. The existence of a supernatural realm is essential to Christianity and it is also essential that it is reasonable to think so. And whether it is reasonable to think so can be decided by looking at the evidence.

Other ideals, of course, rest on other factual assumptions. Spinoza believed that reality has a rational scheme, or in Einstein's version, God does not play dice; Plato's Socrates thought that we have a faculty, reason, that establishes a qualitative difference between animals and mankind; Lenin, Trotsky, and perhaps Stalin, moved by the Marxist ideal, believed that there are historical laws whose agents they were; the liberal ideal of Locke rests on the assumption that humanity can be improved by education; and my ideal of self-direction presupposes that we can transform ourselves through our own efforts.

A second kind of presupposition is about the possibility of

ideals. This may be either logical possibility, concerning the coherence of ideals, their freedom from internal contradictions, or
it may be the assumption that ideals are not inconsistent with
human nature and required conventions, so that they do not
violate limitations to which all of us, regardless of our circumstances, are subject. Ideals are pursued on the assumption that it is
possible to satisfy our important wants in accordance with them. If
ideals are logically or humanly impossible, this satisfaction cannot
be obtained, and thus the ideals are defective.

Consider, for instance, the persistent human aspiration to develop a view of reality *sub specie aeternitatis.* This would involve
coming to understand the scheme of things, in itself, as it is
independently of human beings. Theologians, metaphysicians,
mystics, scientists, poets, and especially Utopians frequently suppose themselves to have hit upon a device, be it revelation, deductive demonstration proceeding from indubitable premises, arcane
exercises and meditation, the hypothetico-deductive model, or the
discovery of the laws of psychology, sociology, or history, and this
device enables them to rise above human limitations and see
things as they are, with God's eye. Having made this discovery,
they can, then, instruct others how they should live, so as to
conform to the general scheme of things.

All such ideals are impossible. For all of us must start with the
information our senses provide and stay within the limits our
physiology imposes. Technology can push these limits further
back, but even technology can only extend what is already there.
The dimensions of human comprehension of the world are set by
human nature. There is no reason to suppose that the world is
exhausted by the parts that we can comprehend, and so we cannot
see the world in its totality, as it really is. The attempt to go beyond
human limitations is the impossible aspiration of being and not
being human at the same time.

Not only is the aspiration epistemologically doomed, it is also
morally and politically dangerous. For time and time again, these
perfervid prophets have used their certainties to increase immea-
surably human misery in the world. Excommunications, holy
wars, final solutions, revolutions, swords of God, defenders of
faith, and agents of history, those with the future in their bones,
have killed, maimed, tortured, and persecuted in the name of
their certainties. They knew the truth, they thought, and those
who resisted it were either stupid or wicked. The stupid had to be
forced to learn, for their own good, and the wicked had to be

punished, for the common good. If our time has a moral achievement, it is the realization of this danger.[5]

A third kind of presupposition concerns the suitability of ideals to us and to our circumstances. Ideals may have only true factual presuppositions and they may conform to the limitations of logic, human nature, and conventions, and yet fail to satisfy our wants. This can happen if our character and talents make it extremely unlikely that we could successfully pursue the ideal, or if the historical or social context is incompatible with it.

Obvious instances of the first kind of unsuitability are restless and impatient people trying to be artisans; those lacking manual dexterity wanting to succeed as surgeons; people revolted by the physical functions of the body aspiring to be nurses; private, reflective people, needing time and peace for contemplation, aiming to become politicians; and blustery, tactless, forthright characters wishing to be negotiators. In each of these cases, there is a perfectly acceptable ideal and yet the people pursuing it are doomed to have unsatisfactory lives, because their ideals are unsuitable.

Another source of unsuitability is bad planning. Ideals may be unobjectionable and suitable. Yet we may be guided by more than one ideal and they may conflict with each other in different ways. One may simply exclude the other. A promiscuous sexual athlete, for instance, cannot have the comfort and security of a close marriage. Ideals may also conflict by calling for greater psychological resources than a person can have. Perhaps it is possible to be a first-rate painter and to earn one's living as a stuntman, but to add being a serious historian to these is to surpass human capacity. Failure in these cases comes from trying to do too much, not, as in the previous case, from trying to do the wrong thing.

Even an otherwise unobjectionable ideal may become unsuitable, because of changes in the world. Philosopher-kings cannot flourish in a democracy; civility is impossible in revolution; a life of quiet contemplation is immoral in a society gone mad, as Nazi Germany had; chivalry has its home in feudal societies and it is quixotic under capitalism; nor can one be far from the madding crowd in a highly industrialized small country.

The last kind of presupposition concerns the consequences of the adoption of an ideal. Living according to an ideal is a project in self-transformation. For, when we are guided by an ideal, we not only satisfy wants, but also strengthen or weaken our dispositions, and thereby shape our characters. We are endeavoring to become the kind of persons our ideals represent. We are engaged in this, because we are attracted and inspired by the ideal, and because we believe that transforming ourselves will be worth the effort. This rests on understanding what life according to the ideal is like. And this understanding may be deficient: we may believe that the consequences will be different from what they turn out to be.

This may occur because we have simply overlooked some consequences. A life of scholarship may seem attractive, because it appears to leave room for leisurely contemplation, and time for reading and pondering deep questions. But, then, we may discover that the leisurely contemplation is in fact the terribly hard work of imposing an interpretation on a domain and simultaneously remaining open to fundamental challenges; that the reading required is indeed much, but not wide, and it is a constant struggle to keep abreast of the best that has been thought and written on the field; and the pondering of deep questions soon turns into the need to analyze minutiae. The discovery of overlooked consequences may result in the realization that we do not like the life that initially seemed good. But the discovery may come too late, for having opted for one life, we have rejected others. Frequently, there is no scope for a new beginning, because in forming ourselves we cannot discard the material and start anew.

And even if we have taken into account the important consequences, we may still be wrong in our assessment of just how largely they figure in the future. In this case, our sense of proportion is at fault. In deciding to be a politician we may know that compromise and negotiation are essential to the political process, so that we cannot be dogmatic and righteous about our beliefs. And yet we may not be prepared to accept that no ground is firm, that everything is negotiable, that even the finest principles die by the piecemeal process of a thousand qualifications, exceptions, and complications. Of course, we can always resign. But in politics that is an admission of failure. So we may discover that what we supposed ourselves realistically to see as one of the inherent but manageable difficulties of political life, actually looms as an unavoidable obstacle in the way of realizing the aspirations that led us to politics in the first place.

We can say, then, that the essential components of ideals are presuppositions. The justification of ideals may be external or internal. External justification depends on the truth of presuppositions; internal justification involves the ranking of essential elements. Ideals guide the satisfaction of wants and faulty ideals will result in frustrated wants and in consequent dissatisfaction with our lives. The process of justification, therefore, is not an externally imposed rigmarole to which those with rational pretensions must pay lip service, but a prudent effort to increase the chances of good lives for ourselves.[6]

The justification of presuppositions, however, is difficult. It involves predicting the future on the basis of inadequate knowledge. We have to extrapolate from our imperfectly understood present selves to make judgments about our projected future selves. We have to ask and answer the question of how our future selves will think and feel when they come into existence. We can ease this difficulty by coming to as good an understanding as possible of the ideal we want to achieve. The great aids here are feeling and imagination, enabling us to form appropriate moral attitudes toward ideals.

Ideals and Commitments

We commit ourselves to ideals, because they represent desirable ways of satisfying our wants. By such commitments, we aim to transform our present selves into future ones that approximate more closely our ideals. As an illustration of this process, I shall consider Thomas More as portrayed by Robert Bolt.[7]

Bolt writes of More that he was

> a man with an adamantine sense of his own self. He knew where he began and left off, what area of himself he could yield to the encroachments of his enemies, and what to the encroachments of those he loved. It was a substantial area in both cases, for he had a proper sense of fear and was a busy lover. Since he was a clever man and a great lawyer he was able to retire from these areas in wonderfully good order, but at length he was asked to retreat from the final area where he located his self. And there this supple, humorous, unassuming and sophisticated man set like metal, was overtaken by an absolutely primitive rigor, and could no more be budged than a cliff.[8]

The key to understanding More's "adamantine sense of self" is to understand his commitments. As Bolt tells it, More was prepared and eventually did go to his death, because he would not take an oath falsely. The details are irrelevant, but I mention in passing that the issue was whether Henry VIII was legally and morally entitled to marry Anne Boleyn. What matters is that More had committed himself to certain moral views, and he was unwilling to take an oath, not even to save his life, which would involve violating his commitment. More had many other commitments as well, and from these he retreated when pressed in "wonderfully good order." Thus some commitments matter more than others. We may order them by distinguishing between primary and secondary commitments.[9]

Primary commitments can be dishonored only at the cost of inflicting grave psychological damage on ourselves. More was a hero and a saint, and he died rather than violate his primary commitment. Most of us are made of softer stuff, but the violation of such a commitment is no less damaging to weaker people. There is a crisis, we do something, and we realize that we cannot come to terms with it. If we had been what we conceived ourselves as being, we would not have done that, so we are not what we took ourselves to be. The result is that an abyss opens up at the center of our being. We disintegrate, go mad, or carry on in a desultory way looking in vain for a chance to undo the dreadful thing we have done.

One example of what happens when primary commitments are violated is Conrad's Lord Jim who spent a lifetime expiating for his one cowardly act. Another is the guilt felt by many survivors of concentration camps who suspect that they survived at the expense of others who did not, because they accommodated themselves to unspeakable evils that the dead, their betters, rejected. Further cases in point are the people who find themselves guilty of what they regard as sacrilege, as Oedipus was of incest and parricide; or Othello and King Lear whose character flaws caused them to injure those who loved them most.

Primary commitments need not be universal, for many of them vary from person to person. Nor are they categorical, for we may decide to violate them. They are primary, because they are fundamental conditions of being ourselves. Their violation causes crippling psychic injury. If people make no such commitments, they have no clear sense of themselves; they resemble Diderot's description of Rameau's nephew or of Camus's stranger.

Primary commitments may be thought of as the secular analogues of the sacred. They are at the core of our moral outlook, the deepest, the most serious convictions we have. Among them are our commitments to the required conventions of our moral tradition. Primary commitments can be discovered by finding out what it is that we would not do; what we regard as outrageous, deeply offensive, or horrible. And if through fear, weakness, or necessity we do do it, profoundly damaging consequences follow for us. Thus primary commitments involve great risks, for we are vulnerable to their violation and so risk disintegration. If we take nothing deeply seriously, we are less likely to suffer lasting psychological damage than people who have thus committed themselves. And so, it is natural to ask: why should we make primary commitments?

Because without them good lives are impossible. Living good lives requires self-direction, and that, in turn, is possible only if we have a clear view about the satisfaction of our wants in accordance with our ideals. Primary commitments are to the satisfaction of the most important wants. Not to make primary commitments, therefore, is either to be ignorant of what really matters to us, or to be indifferent to its realization. This is an option we can take, but only at the cost of frustrated and dissatisfied lives.

Secondary commitments are less serious. They are normally honored, but doing so may be overruled by countervailing reasons. The difference between primary and secondary commitments is that in the case of the former we shall accept no reason that could override them, while the latter may be overridden. The explanation of this difference is that our judgments about what reasons are weightiest are dictated by our primary commitments.

As Bolt describes him, More was deeply in love with his wife and he loved his children no less. However, his commitment to them was secondary, because he decided, upon due reflection, that his commitment to God was deeper. And so he went to his death, and left his family to fend for themselves. When it came to the point, someone in More's position could have taken the oath falsely, because his family came first. But that could only have been done by a person More could perhaps have been, but was not. More was what he was, because his God took precedence over his family.

Many secondary commitments are dictated by our station and its duties. We can be upright and live a life of common decency just by living up to our secondary commitments. The appeal to primary commitments needs to be made only in crises when the guidance of conventional morality is found wanting, as it may be in conflicts between mercy and justice, love and duty, or charity and responsibility. Or they may occur when we find the conventional morality of another moral tradition preferable to our own. Moving from one class to another, undergoing religious or political conversion, being an exile or a refugee, understanding the ethos of our enemies through being occupying victors or defeated subjects are cases in point.

Primary commitments are at the core of our morality. Secondary commitments range between the core and the outer fringes of morality. Many secondary commitments are to the forms taken by our primary commitments. These forms are the particular variable conventions of a moral tradition. More was a patriotic man, but his commitment to England was secondary. The form it took was fealty to his king. But obedience to his monarch was for More secondary, for the author of *Utopia* understood that the demands of patriotism are historically and socially conditioned.

Some secondary commitments are comparable to aesthetic style. Artists must have a style, but if it is to be more than decoration, it should be a vehicle for the expression of substance. Similarly for moral agents: their primary commitments must be expressed on appropriate occasions, but the particular ways in which this is done is of secondary importance.

Secondary commitments are teachable. Children can be instructed to observe the conventions relevant to them in specifiable contexts. As Aristotle saw, morality begins with such habits. But if it ends there, it is no more than the moral equivalent of decoration: etiquette. To be sure, a habit of polite consideration of others is better than nothing. But unless we understand the substance behind the forms, we are shallow and incapable of self-direction, because we have failed to be influenced and inspired by the ideals that animate the moral tradition presupposed by secondary commitments.

Hume called secondary commitments "a kind of lesser morality."[10] Clearly, adherence to the forms of morality is not a particularly praiseworthy achievement. Nevertheless, the connection between the forms of morality, embraced by secondary commitments, and the substance of morality, to which primary commitments lead moral agents, need not be superficial. Ours is not a ceremonious age, and so we tend to suspect that attention to form is prompted by hypocritical attempts to disguise lack of content. But in cultures and historical periods more homogeneous than ours, there is a seamless continuity from primary to secondary commitments. In such context, forms have a natural affinity with content. It is true that the occasional hypocrites may, then, take advantage of the reasonable presumption of having deeper commitments indicated by their observance of the forms, but most people do genuinely have them. There is not much point in regretting that our society is not like that. But even the most tough-minded scourge of hypocrisy must recognize that it is easier to be moral when there are ready-made and generally recognized forms reflecting primary commitments.

Be that as it may, the passage from secondary to primary commitments is toward greater self-direction. In some context, it is easier to achieve it than in others. But in all context, two different components must be distinguished: one is seeing the situation as falling under the guidance of a particular ideal and the other is being impelled by this perception to action. This process essentially involves becoming clear about the hierarchical structure of our commitments. And clarity, in turn, requires articulation. If we have no suitable vocabulary, we cannot make distinctions, and so we cannot be conscious of our ideals and commitments. We have inchoate feelings of importance about some things. These may surface only when we are provoked by their violation. Deep disquiet, horror, or an unfocused sense of evil, of things being really wrong without being able to point at any particular event responsible for it are its symptoms. Moral progress is impossible without articulating these feelings. For only by doing so can we discover our primary commitments, the things most important to us. This is why consciousness and articulation play a crucial role in self-direction.

Normally, we achieve articulateness in terms provided by our moral tradition. This is the deeper sense in which one aspect of morality is conventional. Morality is partly an individual struggle to express an inchoate sense of values in a conventional vocabulary. This makes critical reflection and action possible, and it is in terms of that vocabulary that we can clarify to ourselves what we are about. The available moral vocabulary, embodying the accumulated lessons of the moral struggles of people engaged in the same enterprises as we are, enables us to do it. The shared conventional aspect of morality, giving us the same vocabulary, enable us to recognize in each other fellow travelers along the same road. Thus we can understand, encourage, criticize, be inspired by, and learn from each other.

As members of a tradition, we share some ideals and a vocabulary; this unites us. But we do not share the sense of importance we attach to different ideals, and consequently to the selection of terms describing particular situations, and this sets us apart. What guides our choice of moral terms is the project of creating our better selves.

More's life once again illustrates this. The facts were that unless he swore an oath he knew to be false, he was going to beheaded. He did not, and he was. More was a deeply reflective man; thus he knew where he stood. He was aware of many different ways of characterizing his situation—inarticulateness not being one of his problems—but he did not hesitate between them. What made his decision the only one possible for him was the hierarchy of his commitments. He saw the good life in terms of a primary commitment to God. Ultimately, he interpreted his predicament as a matter of faithfulness. There were other options and, of course, temptations. If he had perceived his situation primarily in terms of patriotism, he may have interpreted it as a choice between allegiance to his country and allegiance to Rome. Or, he may have characterized it primarily in terms of love, and then it would have seemed to him that the happiness of his wife and children dictated taking the oath falsely. Alternatively, he may have suspected himself of pride, of putting too high a value on his own word, and then humility would have required him to deceive. But he rejected all these interpretations and the perceptions they suggested. He was aware of them, but they did not express his primary commitment. Robust, happy and hungry for life though More was, he gave it all up, because he knew that being what he was was more important than boons.

More of the drama is a moral hero. Heroes are important to morality, for they inspire us and they embody in a clear form the qualities we may aim to cultivate in ourselves. They are the stuff of which ideals are made. More's dramatized life illustrates what it is to have a clear sense of ourselves, how that involves a distinction between primary and secondary commitments, and how actions flow naturally from what we are and in what terms we see moral situations. This leads us to the question of what qualities we should cultivate in ourselves, so that we can increase our chances of living good lives. The required qualities are the four virtues of self-direction, to be discussed in the next four chapters.

6
Self-Control

Introduction

It is customary to distinguish between self-regarding and other-regarding virtues. The first contribute to our own welfare, the second to the welfare of others. Thus temperance and courage are thought of as self-regarding virtues, while justice and benevolence are classified as other-regarding. This is an important distinction, but it is misleading. It correctly identifies some virtues whose exercise primarily affects ourselves, in contrast with some others whose primary effect is on others. Yet it is misleading, because it suggests that self-regarding virtues benefit us, while other-regarding virtues are altruistic. But temperance and courage often benefit others, because by possessing them people often contribute to the welfare of others, as mothers or fire fighters may. And justice and benevolence may benefit ourselves, if our ideals of good lives require them; those wishing to be good judges or teachers, for instance, require these virtues to make good lives for themselves.

Self-regarding and other-regarding virtues should be distinguished, but not on the basis of who benefits from their exercise. The distinction should be based on who is primarily affected by their exercise. Since my interest is in virtues required for self-direction, I shall concentrate on self-regarding virtues. But to get rid of the misleading contrast between selfishness and altruism, I shall rename them as virtues of self-direction. They are self-control, self-knowledge, moral sensitivity, and wisdom. They will be discussed in separate chapters.

These four virtues are requirements, but not guarantees, of good lives. They are requirements, because unless we have them at least to some extent, we cannot be self-directed. But they are not sufficient, for, first, good lives require other virtues in addition to those of self-direction; for instance, justice and benevolence. Of these, I shall say nothing in this book. Second, even if we have all the virtues required for good lives, we may put them to evil or misguided uses, because our ideals may be faulty. Third, virtuous people, guided by justified ideals, may fail to attain good lives, because circumstances beyond their control may prevent it.

Self-control is the first virtue of self-direction I shall consider. It is the process whereby we strengthen dispositions in ourselves we judge to accord with our ideals and weaken those we think violate them. In Hume's words; "By our continual and earnest pursuit of character . . . we bring our own department and conduct frequently in review. . . . This constant habit of surveying ourselves, as it were in reflection, keeps alive all the sentiments of right and wrong, and begets, in noble creatures, a certain reverence for themselves as well as others, which is the surest guardian of every virtue."[1]

The four virtues of self-direction are intimately connected. From a psychological point of view, however, self-control comes first, concerning as it does the beginning of self-direction; and only after this can the rest follow. Unless we develop the "habit of surveying ourselves . . . in reflection," we cannot begin to shape our lives in directions we want them to go. Self-control prepares the ground so that the attempt to achieve good lives can go forth.

Quite apart from its desirability, self-control is essential to responsibility. We can be held responsible only for what is in our control. Consequently, only people with at least some self-control can be moral or legal agents. Ethics, the law, and our social arrangements all assume that normal human beings have at least some control over their activities, and, therefore, that they are responsible agents.

Self-control, however, is not innate. No doubt, we are born with the capacity to develop it, but that capacity must be nurtured. Different people develop it to different degrees; consequently they are responsible to different degrees. On what does the development of self-control depend? Can we decide to acquire a habit of surveying ourselves reflectively or is it a matter of fortuitous circumstances involving a combination of our genetic makeup and the social setting into which we happen to be born? If we can do nothing about developing self-control, then what is the point of praising us for having it and blaming us for its lack?

It appears that the more we learn about ourselves through biochemistry, biology, and the other sciences, the less justification there is for thinking of self-control as something in our power. For what these sciences seem to tell us is that we are governed by natural necessity. Human actions and decisions are governed by laws of nature in the same way as all other natural events are. If this is so, then nature controls us, and we have no more control over that part of nature that falls within our skin than we do over parts exterior to us. Natural necessity, therefore, seems to conflict with self-control, the source of responsibility.

This conflict raises the question of the possibility of human freedom. Can we act freely or are our actions subject to natural necessity rather than to our own control? I shall argue for three connected propositions: the conflict between natural necessity and free actions is apparent, not real; natural necessity and free actions both exist and they are compatible; and free actions are self-controlled actions. Since freedom and self-control come to the same thing, as we understand free actions, so we shall understand the nature of self-control.

In a remarkably suggestive passage, Iris Murdoch has written, "Freedom is, I think, a mixed concept. The true half of it is simply a name of an aspect of virtue concerned especially with the clarification of vision."[2] Self-control is the virtue whose aspect freedom is. The vision with which they are both connected is of good lives. And the clarification of that vision occurs through the kind of reflection Hume has mentioned. A full account of this reflection will emerge only gradually. Here, I shall concentrate on freedom and self-control, and merely note that reflection is essential to them.

I shall begin by considering two existing attempts to show the compatibility of free actions and natural necessity: the *Humean* and *Spinozistic* strategies.[3] I think they both fail, but not totally. For each contains an important component of the right answer.

My topic is large and I must impose some restrictions. I shall state these without supporting arguments. First, the claim that human actions are subject to natural necessity is narrower than the claim of determinism that everything is subject to natural necessity. I shall not discuss determinism. Second, by an action I mean a conscious, deliberate, overt or psychological, human performance or abstention from performance. This general description is meant to provide a sufficiently large sample about which the question of self-control can be raised. It is not a definition. There are many difficulties about defining actions, but I shall ignore them here. Third, by a cause I mean sufficient condition. Thus an event is the cause of another if, in normal circumstances, its occurrence assures the occurrence of the other.

The Failure of the Humean Strategy

The fundamental Humean idea is that free action is unconstrained. Thus natural necessity can be overcome by the performance of unconstrained actions. The ideal state of affairs is the performance of completely unconstrained actions. I shall call this idealized version, the *romantic* conception of freedom, because it pictures a person who would be free as a hero grappling with immense forces against incalculable odds. Prometheus who pitted himself against the gods and Camus's Caligula who sought freedom in going against all law, custom, reason, his own feelings and well-being are illustrations of attempts to achieve the romantic ideal of freedom.

All such attempts are doomed before they start, because they try to achieve the impossible. For, the romantic search for total lack of constraint pictures human beings as heroes trying to free themselves from their own intellect, will, feelings, and body. This is impossible, because no action can escape from having causal antecedents in the body and the circumstances of the agent, and so from having at least some constraints.

A more realistic approach along the same lines is the *Humean* attempt to reconcile natural necessity with the possibility of free actions. It consists of a two-part solution of the problem. One part is to weaken the link between cause and effect. The other is to distinguish between internal and external causation, and to identify free actions with internally caused actions and constraints with external causation.

The first part involves the denial that we have any reason for supposing that the necessity holding between causes and effects exists in nature. The alternative is to suppose it to be projected onto nature by our minds. Thus the apparently binding force of necessity is due to the way the human mind works. Consequently, there is no reason for supposing that so-called natural necessity can act as an external constraint on human actions.

There are two objections to this view. The first is that even if we grant everything it asserts, all that follows is that we do not know whether natural necessity exists. So the Humean analysis of causation may be true and natural necessity could still constrain human actions. The second is that the Humean argument rests on untenable psychological beliefs to which classical empiricists committed themselves. They had suppposed that the mind is a passive recipient of discrete impressions and that its active role is to organize these discrete impressions in accordance with the laws of association. It is clear, however, that the mind is actively inquiring. Furthermore, it does not receive discrete impressions that it then proceeds to organize; it receives already organized stimuli. So natural necessity is denied on faulty psychological grounds.

The second part of the Humean solution, however, is stronger. This is the idea that causality is involved in free action, but it is internal causality, generated by the agent, and not external causality, produced by natural necessity. Internal causality is not a constraint on free actions, but the propelling force behind them. The internal causal agent that brings about human actions is the will. Unconstrained people do what they will to do. We have power over our actions; we can deliberate about them, and thus strengthen or weaken our will; and we can put our will behind one or another of several possible actions. In this way, the Humean approach accepts that causality is involved in free action and denies that this amounts to constraint. The free action is the last link in the causal chain, but it is preceded in the chain by the will of the agent.

The trouble with the idea of internal causation is that there is no reason for supposing that the causal chain that ends in the action starts with the will. What we will is itself the effect of causes and many of these causes exist independently of our will. The will may not constrain the actions that follow from it, but the causes of acts of will do constrain what is willed, and so, indirectly, they constrain willed actions. The fundamental difficulty with the second part of the Humean attack is that it fails to provide a reason for thinking that internal causation is anything more than an insignificant episode in a long chain of external causation. There is no Humean answer to the question of what it is about internal causation that makes it markedly different from external causation. As we shall see, however, this question has an answer.

The Failure of the Spinozistic Strategy

The key idea of the Spinozistic strategy is that we are subject to natural necessity and freedom consists in willing to do what we have understood to be dictated by necessity.[4] This is an ancient conception of freedom, and, perhaps for this reason, appears paradoxical to contemporary minds. How could the recognition of necessity be freedom? Resignation, perhaps. But is not doing what we must the very opposite of free action? We feel the force of these questions, because we have largely accepted the idea of freedom as lack of constraint. Its hold on us ought to weaken, however, as we see its great difficulties.

According to the Spinozistic view, natural necessity should not be thought of as the rule of an omnipotent despot. Natural necessity is rather the scheme of things; it is just there, informing everything that exists, including human lives. There is no question of escaping it. The Promethean revolt is not heroic, but silly.

Whether we conform to the scheme of things is not an open question. But whether we do so with understanding is open. We have the capacity to understand and exercise our will. Of course, the result of understanding and willing cannot be an escape from necessity. There is only wise or stupid conformity. Wisdom is to arrange our lives in accordance with the scheme of things. However, the arrangement can only be to curtail our temptation to engage in ineffectual resistance and resentment. Only unhappiness can come from a stupid protest against the impersonal, inevitable, irreversible flow of events. Wisdom is to understand the scheme of things; and since we are part of it, to understand ourselves. To be free is to act in accordance with our nature.

But it is unclear what our nature is according to this view. It includes the intellect, the will, feelings and emotion, the body, imagination, talents and handicaps, genetic and acquired dispositions, and much more. How are we to take the injunction to act in accordance with our nature? All of it? Some of it? How should we act when different parts of our nature impel us in different directions?

Again, there is a limiting case: the *tragic* conception of freedom. According to it, acting in accordance with our nature should be taken to mean the totality of our nature. Parts of our nature may conflict, but one part will prevail eventually and result in action. An action is free when the necessity that governs it is implicit in ourselves. When we act in accordance with it, we are responsible for what we do, for the action stems from our nature. Praise and blame attach to us for being the way we are. Our actions are symptoms of our nature.

The tragedy of Oedipus exemplifies this. Oedipus killed a man, who turned out to be his father, and he married a woman, who turned out to be his mother. He did not mean to kill his father; but he did mean to kill the man who angered him. Nor did he intend to commit incest; yet he wanted to marry the queen to satisfy his desire and ambition. He acted in accordance with his nature and he paid for it. This conception is tragic, because there are flaws in the nature of all of us. If we are held responsible for all actions that stem from our nature, regardless of whether we intend them or not, then freedom is a terrible burden.

One difficulty with the tragic conception of freedom is that it treats all parts of our nature as if they were on an equal footing.

One part will prevail and it will issue in action. But we, who are the battlefield on which this war for domination is fought, are supposed to be passive onlookers. We know from introspection that this is not so. We can take sides and support or discourage tendencies in our nature. This is indeed part of the point of Plato's myth of the soul in *Phaedrus*. His answer is clear: the rational part of our nature should dominate over the others. This is the ground of disagreement between the tragic and the *Spinozistic* conceptions of freedom.

The Spinozistic view accepts the existence of natural necessity, and so the Humean analysis of causality is rejected. Also rejected is the empiricist view that the mind is a passive receptacle on which nature makes its imprint. The mind is an active agent, capable of reflection and understanding, quite independently of whatever empirical information it may have. Freedom must be understood as the combination of a nonempirical discernment of natural necessity and the employment of the will for accepting what has thus been discerned.

Natural necessity and free action are not in conflict, because freedom does not mean opposing or overcoming natural necessity, but accepting it. The negative side of the understanding and the will that makes freedom possible requires us to control our emotions and our animal nature, and so to prevent uselessly pitting ourselves against natural necessity. The positive side requires us to employ our understanding and will to live in harmony with the scheme of things.

The spirit of the Spinozistic view is illustrated by the Stoic metaphor for the relation between human beings and nature. They speak of a dog who is tied to a horse-drawn cart. Its position is unenviable, but it can still make it better or worse. To make it better, it must fall in with the movements of the cart: run with it, if it moves fast; amble, if it moves slowly; rest, if it stops. To resist is to make its bad lot worse, for the cart will drag it, and then the going will be even rougher.

The central difficulty in the Spinozistic view is that the mind, which does the understanding and willing, is also part of the scheme of things. It too is subject to the prevailing laws. This being the case, what could be the point of the recommendation that we ought to understand and will the inevitable course of events? For whether we do so is also dictated by natural necessity. Furthermore, the Spinozistic reconciliation of natural necessity and free action comes to accepting the inexorability of natural necessity and giving up the ordinary notion of freedom being both passive and active. It can involve doing things and refraining from doing them. The Spinozistic view allows only for passive compliance or useless resistance. The idea of freedom conflicts with common experience and shrinks out of all possibility of recognition if it amounts to no more than this.

Nevertheless, the Spinozistic view contains an extremely promising idea and it takes a step further the Humean notion that freedom has to do with internal causation. The idea is that freedom consists in our modification of ourselves. So that internal causation is not externally, but internally directed. The Spinozistic view commits itself to this modification being entirely negative, amounting to not trying to do certain things. I shall now explore the possibility of reconciling natural necessity with free action without this handicap.

Freedom as Self-Control

There are two parts to my attempt to show that there is no conflict between natural necessity and free action. The first is to combine the salvageable portions of the Humean and Spinozistic views with an uncontroversial description of standard features of common human experience. This description will be a reminder of facts whose denial is absurd. The second is to spell out the implications of the descriptions. The view I shall defend is that free actions are all and only actions within the control of the agent.[5]

Let us begin with the Humean idea of internal causation. A paradigmatic instance of it is wanting something. Causation is internal, if it goes on inside or on the surface of the body. The boundary of internal causation is the skin. Pain, desire, fatigue, thought, belief, stupidity, and love may be internal causes. A gun being pointed, the sun shining, or the request of a friend may act as causes, but not as internal ones. Of course, if we act because we are afraid of the gun, or we feel hot because of the sun, or we believe ourselves to be indebted to a friend, then the causation is internal.

Internal causation, then, is not without external causes. Everything we do has causes, the causes also have causes, and some are internal, some external. The distinction between them is not ontological. I am not claiming that the skin marks a break in nature. The distinction is epistemological: causal explanations can be reasonably terminated at certain points. If we ask: Why did she open the window? the answer: She felt hot, is a satisfactory internal causal explanation. Of course, she felt hot, because the temperature was ninety degrees, and because human beings have a certain physiology. But we do not need to talk about all that in order to explain her action.

Internal causal connections may be conscious or nonconscious. We may or may not know what prompts us to act in a certain way. My interest here is exclusively in conscious internal causes. Such causes may produce external or internal effects. Thus the object of a want may be to win the approval of the world, or it may be to cease caring about the approval of the world. Internal causes may lead to altering the world outside of the skin or to changing some aspect of ourselves. The kind of internal causation that I want to concentrate on results in altering our own psychological states. I take it as noncontroversial that there are occasions on which we consciously try and succeed in changing some particular want, feeling, or belief we have. For instance, we may stop wanting to smoke, if we come to believe that it is harmful.

By self-control I mean the kind of causation that is internal, conscious, and whose effect is the modification of some psychological state of ourselves. Self-control, thus, leads to self-modification. So far, this is in the Spinozistic tradition. However, I depart from it, because in that tradition self-modification can only be one of resignation: Internal causation can only result in not wanting to do what we, in any case, could not do. I think that self-modification can have both positive and negative effects. Changing beliefs may squelch desires, but they may also produce them. Reflection may lead to giving up mistaken beliefs, or to adopting new ones.

Let us now take a case of self-control and see what is involved in it. Suppose that a man wants to travel from New York to Washington. In normal circumstances, he would fly. But as he is making his plans to do so, he hears about a collision of two airplanes in which many died. He interrupts his normal procedure and reflects on it. This may lead him to depart from his normal procedure or to adhere to it. Let us suppose that his actual decision is to overcome his fear and fly. We need to discuss several points about this case of self-control.

First, the decision is made against a vast background. It includes the sort of person he is, his character, motivation, beliefs, habits, and the like. So part of the background is made up of the *internal conditions* of his decision. The other part consists of the facts external to him, such as the availabiltiy of alternative means of transport, his financial resources, and the timetable of his projected visit. These are the *external conditions* in which his decision must be made.

What has happened in my hypothetical case is that the man became aware of a consideration possibly relevant to the external condition: the collision. His decision requires that he should evaluate the importance of the new piece of information. He has beliefs about it, such as accepting the truth of the news reports and remembering accident statistics about various forms of travel; and he also has feelings, such as fear, fatalism, or trust in his luck. The external conditions may change the internal conditions, and in this instance they have.

Now the case I am describing is a case of self-control, because part of what has gone into the decision was that the man changed his internal conditions that partly determine his decision. The traveler convinced himself that his fear, caused by the report of the collision, is misplaced, since statistical evidence indicates that air travel is actually safer than other forms of travel. Self-control resulted in self-modification; the self-modification changed the internal conditions of the background; and the changed background altered the connection between the cause, wanting to fly to Washington, and the effect, flying. The decision could have gone the other way. For the man could have found that his fear, unreasonable as it is, is so strong that he cannot get rid of it, and then he would have taken the train. In that case, changed internal conditions would have resulted in another decision.

This decision is an episode in the life of a man. In normal human lives, there are countless such episodes. One episode rarely causes significant changes in a life. But episodes accumulate and they make or break dispositions. And developing or changing dispositions does significantly alter us. Character depends to a great extent on dispositions, and dispositions, in turn, are similarly fostered or thwarted by episodes. So the significance of the decision leading to an episode is not merely that it changes the internal conditions in a particular case. It also tends to change us through the patterns formed of accumulated episodes. If we are reasonable, we realize that this is so. We shall, then, reflect not only on what we want to do then and there, but also on the effects of doing something on the shaping and forming of our characters. We shall ask ourselves What shall I do? Do I want to become the sort of person who does that sort of thing? Thus self-control has a short-term significance and also a long-term character-building one.

In the context of our discussion of freedom, the significance of self-control is that it modifies the internal conditions of the causal process, and thereby modifies the causal process. I do not, of course, mean that the modification is not itself causally explicable. The important thing that the possibility of self-control shows is that it is too simple to think of a causal chain linearly, proceeding in a more or less straight line from the past to the future. Cases of self-control are, as it were, loops in causal processes, where the progression involves the process turning back and altering itself. The possibility that self-control establishes is not the suspension of the causal process, but its alteration. What makes the alteration possible is that normal people can change their own psychological states and thereby change the internal conditions upon which the direction of the causal process depends. This is the sense in which we can be said to have control over what we do.

Self-control is a matter of degree. Different people have it to a different extent and the same people have it to a different extent at different periods in their lives. The explanation of this is that we differ in respect to the external and internal conditions of our lives. The more reflection there is, up to a self-stultifying neurotic level, the greater may be our self-control. But how much reflection is possible for particular people in particular situations depends both on how urgently the external conditions demand response and on their personality, abilities, and wants. It is clear, however, that the more self-control we have, the better it is for us, for it increases the chances of satisfying what we want.

Self-Control and Choice

This description of self-controlled actions shows that we routinely perform actions prompted by our beliefs, feelings, wants, and other psychological states. Frequently, these states are modified by reflection. Without further ado, I shall identify self-controlled action with free actions and claim that since self-controlled actions are clearly possible, so are free actions.

Free actions, in this sense, are obviously compatible with natural necessity. For free actions are the effects of causes. The causes are psychological states modified by us in the light of our reflection. There is no a priori reason why the connection between psychological states, functioning as causes, and free actions, regarded as effects, could not be expressed in terms of law-governed regularity.

The obvious objection I must now consider is that it is a mistake to identify self-controlled actions with free actions. Self-controlled actions may frequently occur, but, it might be said, there is more to free actions than that. Well, what more is there supposed to be?

The answer that comes readily to mind is that the missing element is choice. A self-controlled action is free only if we have a choice about it. But if there is a law-governed connection between self-controlled actions and their causes, then how could we have a choice? This is a seemingly plausible objection, but as we inquire about what choice is supposed to mean here, so its plausibility diminishes.

If we can be said to have a choice only if we can perform uncaused actions, then absurdity follows. For if we, or some parts of us, are not the causes of our action, then there is no reason to suppose that the action is ours, nor that we performed it. The supposition that we can perform an uncaused action is, in fact, incoherent.

A more tenable interpretation of choice is that it depends on the possibility that we could act in a number of different ways. So if an action is chosen, we could have acted otherwise. This way of putting the matter allows that each alternative has its causes, thus escaping the incoherence just noted. The objection now becomes a demand for explaining how a self-controlled action, subject to natural necessity, need not have been performed, and can be replaced by the performance of another action.

My answer is twofold. First, it is a mistake to identify free actions with actions in whose case the possibility of acting otherwise *must* exist. For that possibility is neither necessary nor sufficient for an action being free. Second, there is a perfectly good sense in which we could be said to have done otherwise than to perform very many of the self-controlled actions we in fact perform.

Let us consider again my traveler. Assume that there are only four efficient means of transport from New York to Washington: airplane, train, bus, and car. According to this mistaken suggestion, the traveler is acting freely only if he chooses to go in one of these ways. He goes by plane, but he could have taken the train.

That the possibility of doing otherwise is not *necessary* for free action is shown by the following. Imagine that the traveler has decided to overcome his fear, trust his luck, take whatever small risk he supposes there is, and fly. However, unknown to him, there is a civil defense exercise in Washington and all ground transportation is halted. Regardless of his decision, he could not have gone to Washington except by flying. So he could not have done otherwise than to fly, yet his act of flying was free.

Nor is the possibility of doing otherwise *sufficient* for free action. Assume that the four ways of going are available to our traveler. Yet, in the course of a busy day in New York, he forgets about the whole thing until the last moment, and instructs his travel agent: Get me to Washington! He finds himself on the plane, he could have gone otherwise, but, all the same, his act of flying was not free.

The point is that what is necessary and sufficient for free action is that the action should be caused, in part, by psychological processes modified by reflection. Whether or not the external conditions or the nonconscious internal conditions allow other courses of action is irrelevant to the question of whether an act is free. So the possibility of choice is not a requirement of free action.

My second answer to the objection that if a self-controlled action conforms to natural necessity, then we could not have done otherwise, and so a self-controlled action cannot be free, is to show that this conditional statement is false. If an action is self-controlled, and if it accords with natural necessity, it is still possible for us to have acted otherwise.

A self-controlled action is caused. Given knowledge of the relevant laws and of the external and internal conditions determining our conduct, what we shall do is predictable and explainable. It may be said that this possibility establishes that we could not have done anything else but what we in fact did do. And if so, self-controlled actions cannot be free.

But this is not true. Even though self-controlled actions have causes, we are capable of acting in different ways, because we can often alter the conditions in which the predictable and explainable causal process occurs. The significance of self-control is just the possibility that we can change the internal conditions of the causal process by reflecting on what to do. To say that we could have done otherwise is to say that we could have altered the internal conditions of our action. This does not exempt us from natural necessity, but it changes the aspect of natural necessity under which we act.

The possibility of self-control does not characterize all situations of all people: it does not always obtain, and even when it does, it does so to varying degrees. As we go further back in the lives of people, so the balance between the external and internal determinants of their conduct tilts in favor of external ones. Correspondingly, self-control diminishes. The reason for this is that reflection is learned slowly in the course of physiological and psychological maturation.

Furthermore, there are fully mature people who have a diminished capacity for self-control. Mental defectives and the insane lack the required degree of cognitive, emotive, or conative powers. And even people who have the powers may not be able to exercise them, because their external situation leaves no room for deliberation. In wars, serious illness, and disasters people may find themselves unable to exercise self-control, even if they can normally do so. Life *in extremis* is dehumanizing, precisely because we are deprived of self-control.

It may be objected that this account is superficial, that if we go deeper, we find that we have no control over the degree of self-control we have. Our initial capacities and situation are given; our scope for self-control is initially determined by causal conditions we cannot alter. This is true, but I do not accept the charge of superficiality. Natural endowments are never, and external circumstances are rarely within, our control. But what we make of natural endowments and how we respond to external circumstances often can be controlled. The degree of control depends only partially on natural endowments and external circumstances, because to the extent to which we can alter the internal conditions determining our conduct, we can develop our natural endowments and be guided by reflection in responding to external circumstances.[6] These are my reasons for claiming that the possibility of acting otherwise is compatible with self-controlled actions that conform to natural necessity. So if by choice we mean the possibility of acting otherwise, then very many self-controlled actions allow for choice.

Self-Control and Responsibility

Suppose that self-controlled actions conform to natural necessity and allow for choice. They are free actions, then. However, it remains to be shown that we can be held responsible for them. But is this really difficult? The simple answer is that if we have control over what we do, then we are responsible for what we do.

However, there is an objection to this simple answer. Responsibility depends on self-control, and self-control is a matter of degree. Its extent depends on the balance of the external and internal conditions causing the action. And, the objection runs, the further back we go in human lives, the more the balance shifts in favor of external conditions. Correspondingly, the degree of self-control diminishes, and responsibility diminishes with it. The difficulty is that while we can be held responsible for self-controlled actions, self-control is not itself self-controlled, and so we cannot be held responsible for it. Also, being responsible depends on natural endowments over which we have no control. Whether we are capable of reflecting on our psychological states and modifying them depends on having a certain degree of intelligence, a suitable temperament, and a disciplined will. Since we are not responsible for our natural endowments, and since natural endowments determine the amount of self-control we have, we are not responsible for self-controlled actions either.

My reply is that this objection rests on two mistaken assumptions. One is that we are responsible primarily for our actions, and the other is that we have no control over our natural endowments. The truth is that we are responsible primarily for what we are, and only derivatively for what we do; and we do have control over our natural endowments, because we can aid and hinder their development.

The following considerations show that we are responsible primarily for being in a certain way rather than for doing a certain action. First, the question of responsibility for an action cannot be answered unless the psychological states and natural endowments of the agent are taken into consideration. If we did not intend our action, or if we intended it but, due to mental illness or low intelligence, did not really understand it, or if we acted in a fit of passion, our responsibility for the action is diminished. Second, if an action we perform is in character, we are held responsible for it. Others would say that is just the sort of thing we would have done. And if our characteristic action is good, we are praised, and if it is bad, we are blamed. But if we act out of character, then judgment about our responsibility is suspended until it is understood why we have acted in this uncharacteristic way. Something unusual must have happened, and it must be known before responsibility can be assigned. These two considerations do not alter the fact that actions *occasion* the assignment of responsibility. We are responsible for what we do. But what we do, and this is the third consideration, depends on what we are, so that primary responsibility attaches not to the surface manifestations, but to the deeper structures to which the manifestations are due.[7]

These considerations notwithstanding, there is reluctance to ascribe responsibility for the way we are, rather than for what we do. The source of this reluctance is that moral worth is closely connected with responsibility, and responsibility depends on natural endowments. Intelligence, even temperament, unencumbered, will give some people advantages they have done nothing to deserve. Many find it repugnant to make moral worth dependent on unearned advantages. This repugnance leads to the second mistaken assumption involved in the objection to my assignment of responsibility for self-controlled action. The assumption is that we are not responsible for our natural endowments.

Now it goes without saying that we are not responsible for having been born with or without some natural endowments. My claim is, however, that what we do with the endowments we happen to possess is, in varying degrees, within our control, and so we are correspondingly responsible for it.

Let us recall part of the description of what is involved in a self-controlled action. I noted that each self-controlled action has a dual significance. One is the short-term answer that the performance gives to the question: What shall I do? The other is a long-term character-building significance, and that is what concerns us here. Self-controlled actions are episodes in our lives. Our dispositions are strengthened or weakened by such episodes. If we are reasonable, we realize this, and we ask whether an action strengthens or weakens a disposition we should have. We shall ask whether we want to be the sort of person who has this disposition. And the answer adds its causal force to the modification of psychological states that eventually cause the action. In this way, we can control our natural endowments.

This is borne out by the common human experience. We cannot perhaps change our temperament in the sense of acquiring feelings we do not have or rid ourselves of ones we do have. But we can learn to minimize some and enhance others: shyness can be overcome; ambition can be curbed; gregariousness can be encouraged or discouraged. I do not know whether it is possible to change our intelligence. But we can compensate for its shortcomings by improving our concentration and memory, and by working harder; and we can abuse it by tackling only easy tasks, by being flippant, and by refusing to think hard. The will can also be trained. We can put ourselves in situations where effort is required; we can indulge ourselves by never attempting anything difficult; we can delude ourselves by saying that if I really wanted to, I could do it.

It will be objected that while we can strengthen or weaken our dispositions, and so have some control over our characters, whether we shall do so is not within our control. For that too depends on our natural endowments. This, of course, is true. People with greatly diminished intelligence are mental defectives; with seriously impaired emotions, they are often mentally ill; with an incapacitated will, they are neurotics. These are generally recognized examples of just the kind of diminished self-control and responsibility I have in mind. What follows, however, is not at all damaging to my case. We do have different native capacities for self-control, and so we are responsible in varying degrees. But this presupposes rather than undermines my thesis that self-control is possible and that responsibility is coextensive with it.

To sum up; free actions require us to reflect on and modify our psychological states; doing so is what I mean by self-control. We are responsible for our free and self-controlled actions. Freedom or self-control are matters of degree, depending on our characters, endowments, and circumstances. But since we normally have a degree of control over our characters and the use of our endowments, we are responsible for the degree of self-control.

A corollary point is that free or self-controlled actions are not determined by the state of the world outside of our skin. It may influence what we do, but it is neither necessary nor sufficient for free or self-controlled actions that the world around us should be in any particular way. Freedom and self-control depend on what goes on in the consciousness of human beings.

In this rather deep sense, therefore, Spinoza has succeeded in identifying one essential component of freedom, namely, that it is an individual matter, having to do with what goes on in our minds. But he was led astray, perhaps by Stoic influences, and came to suppose that this implies resignation to the scheme of things. Hume's robust common sense is a welcome antidote to Spinoza's pessimism about the difference we can make. Hume did not doubt that we are capable of overcoming some external constraints and making a difference through free actions. But he failed to explain how this capacity is possible. My view of free action is a combination of Spinoza's and Hume's. The idea that free action is self-controlled action, and that self-control involves the modification of our psychological states joins together the Spinozistic attention to what happens within our consciousness and the Humean optimism that this can affect the world outside us. I have gone beyond this combination only by offering an explanation of how the capacity for free action is possible and by defending the combination against some objections.

Self-Control and Good Lives

The successful pursuit of good lives depends on many things; some are in our control, others not. If we wish our lives to be good, we shall want to control as many factors contributing to them as possible. Self-direction is the process whereby we enlarge the sphere of our control to try to achieve good lives. Self-control is the first requirement of self-direction, for through it we can achieve control over ourselves. So all of us wanting to have good lives, however we conceive them to be, should want to cultivate self-control in ourselves.

Self-control is exercised in a multitude of forms, because we have different selves to control and we must do so in different circumstances. But there is an underlying principle that unifies these many episodes and renders them instances of self-control. It is that we act or refrain from acting, because we want to strengthen or weaken in ourselves dispositions of which actions are instantiations. In this way, we shape our characters and try to become the sort of persons our ideals guide us to be.

Self-control is a matter of degree, for various reasons. One is that the majority of people cannot afford the luxury of thinking about the long-term consequences of their actions, because their immediate survival is at stake. This sad fact shows that billions lack the opportunity to pursue good lives: they have to struggle for life itself. Self-control is a requirement of good lives. From the fact that people living in inhuman conditions do not have or care about having self-control, it does not follow, of course, that self-control is not a virtue.

But what about people who have the opportunity to develop self-control, because they live in a civilized society, and yet do not do so? One possibility is that there may be some people who do not need it, because all their dispositions accord with their ideals and they live in totally harmonious circumstances. Such people are exceedingly rare and lucky. I do not deny that their existence is a possibility, but it is so remote as to be irrelevant to the vast majority living in civilized circumstances.

A far more frequent situation is that people realize that self-control is required for good lives; they try to develop it, but fail, because the attractions of short-term satisfactions outweigh those of their long-term projects. Such people are self-indulgent, and we all are that to some extent. Self-indulgence is a weakness, and if it is excessive, it seriously damages our attempts to achieve good lives. Reasonable people will, or can be brought to, understand this and then they will do what they may to replace indulgence with control. Not to do so damages them, a price they may choose to pay.

Another possibility is that there are people who deliberately refuse to develop self-control, because they reject the possibility that their lives could be good. They may think that no life can be good, because all ideals are illusory and we are by nature irremediably corrupt. Or, they may think that good lives may be possible for others, but not for themselves. My response to the first alternative is that it is mistaken. We know that some lives can be good, because some lives have been good. Socrates, Montaigne, Bach, and Hume establish that possibility.

The second alternative is that there may be people incapable of good lives, because they totally lack self-control. This is different from even a thoroughgoing self-indulgence, because self-indulgent people realize, or can be made to realize, that this disposition of theirs is a weakness and that it stands in the way of good lives. But the people I am here considering reject the possibility of good lives, and so they do not regard their own attempt to satisfy all their wants as a weakness at all; they do not accept the sort of reason that is accepted, even if not heeded, by self-indulgent people.

It is as difficult to find examples of such people as it is to find ones with complete self-control. Literature, however, helps. The main characters portrayed by Sade in *The 120 Days of Sodom* and Caligula in Camus's play illustrate what I mean. People of this sort are ruled by caprice. They need not be consistently evil, for caprice may lead to acts of kindness. They can act with great discipline, but also with great abandon. Whim, not principle, guides them.

What we need to say of such people is that they are corrupt. Furthermore, they are corrupt in the most fundamental way possible. For it is not that they aim at a good life and mistake its nature; they repudiate the possibility of good lives, by repudiating self-control, one essential part of them. Self-hatred, rage occasioned by real or imaginary wrongs, cynicism, believing themselves to be the scourge of God or the instruments of history may be some of the motives that drive them. They are the terrible examples of what happens to us without the virtue of self-control.

7
Self-Knowledge

A Description of Self-Knowledge

The injunction that we should know ourselves is at least as old as the famous inscription, "Know Thyself!" on the Temple of Apollo at Delphi. It enjoins us to know our possibilities and limitations. The possession of this knowledge liberates us by removing one impediment in the way of good lives: ignorance of what we want and are capable of achieving. This is how self-knowledge is connected with self-control. As we have seen, we are self-directed to the extent we control what we do. But to control it, we must know it, and so we must have self-knowledge.

The emphasis on self-knowledge, thus understood, is a distinctive mark of contemporary sensibility. The influence of psychoanalysis; the popularity of autobiographical writing; the widespread attention to false consciousness, bad faith, and self-deception; and the frequent use of interior monologues in literature are some of the signs of our celebration of self-knowledge.

Self-knowledge is a requirement of good lives, because unless we know what we want, how to decide the respective importance of our various wants, and which ideals are to guide us, we cannot satisfy our wants reasonably, and so we cannot have good lives. We have seen that each episode of satisfying or frustrating a want has a dual significance in our lives. Part of it is the immediate effect and the other part is the long-term influence on our characters. The accumulated episodes form dispositions, and the patterns of dispositions we develop constitute our characters. If we are reasonable, we realize this, and so we reflect on the long-term effects our actions have on the sort of person we are and are becoming. Self-knowledge is essentially involved in this reflection.

Self-knowledge has a descriptive and a practical aspect. In its descriptive aspect, we know facts about ourselves. If we know ourselves well, we can draw up an accurate psychological self-portrait. We know our talents and weaknesses, hopes and fears, and desires and aversions. We can make reliable predictions about what we would or would not do in certain situations. This kind of knowledge is objective. It is connected with truth, verification, and falsification. Knowing ourselves in this manner is the same kind of knowledge as we have of others. Of course, in self-knowledge the knower and the known are the same, while in knowledge of others they are different. As a result, we normally have a far better chance of coming to know ourselves than of coming to know others. But this is not due to the nature of the kind of knowledge involved: it is because we are more interested and better informed about ourselves than about others. Self-knowledge *is* different from knowledge of others, but their differences lie elsewhere.

One of their differences emerges in considering the practical aspect of self-knowledge. Self-knowledge is internally connected with action; knowledge of others is not. By internal connection, I mean that being action-guiding is not an accidental but a constitutive feature of self-knowledge. To know something about ourselves creates a presumption in favor of employing the knowledge. The presumption can be defeated, but if it is not, this kind of knowledge leads to action. If I know that I need privacy, I tend to seek it. But if I know something about another person, there is no analogous presumption in favor of my doing anything at all. I may lack the opportunity, or I may merely observe it passively, or I may not want to meddle. But I cannot meddle in my own case, passive observation is extraordinary, and the opportunity to act normally exists. Thus, self-knowledge guides action in a way knowledge of others does not.

Both descriptive and practical aspects are necessary for self-knowledge. To see why this is so, consider what would happen if we lacked either. Suppose that we know ourselves descriptively, but not practically. We have constructed an accurate psychological portrait of ourselves; however, we are not moved by it to action. Take people who know that they are impulsive, without this having any effect on their conduct. We must regard this as evidence that their self-knowledge is not deep enough, that it is lacking in something. Why must we so regard it? Because our characterization of ourselves is not neutral. We are not indifferent to the facts we know about our own psychological makeup: we approve or disapprove, regret or cherish, and are proud or ashamed of being in various ways. If I know that I am impulsive, I must have an attitude toward it. I may think that it is part of creativity, spontaneity, and adventurousness of spirit, and so I value it. Or, I may think that it is dangerous, encourages irresponsibility, and lacks tact, and so it is not a good way of being. In either case, my knowledge inclines me to view my impulsiveness under the aspect of action: giving it scope or curbing it.

But what if we genuinely have no attitude to some important psychological feature we have? Surely, this is possible? Yes, it is possible and it produces defective human beings. The outstanding example is Camus's Meursault in *The Stranger*. He was dead to himself. Of course, this kind of depersonalization need not be as complete as his was. But the extent to which we have it is the extent to which we are incapable of forming ourselves. And that, in turn, is a measure of our incapacity to live good lives. So when I say that descriptive self-knowledge *must* be supplemented by practical self-knowledge, the necessity is conditional on wishing to have a good life.

Is this true the other way as well? What if we have quite adequate practical self-knowledge, but lack the descriptive aspect? Consider an instinctive salesman. He knows how to use himself very well indeed. He knows how to charm, placate, efface himself, be forceful, and so on. He can play himself like a musical instrument. He knows not just *when* he should be one way or another, for that has to do with his knowledge of customers, but also how to draw on his own resources. Let us further suppose that he does this without reflection. He could not explain to others what he is doing; nor could he teach it. If it were pointed out to him that his conduct forms this pattern, he would be mildly surprised and largely indifferent. He has no theoretical interest in the matter; it is selling that concerns him. Just so as not to muddy waters, assume that this man is honest and the product he sells is useful.

Why does he need to supplement his practical self-knowledge with descriptive self-knowledge? Because if something goes wrong for him, he will not be able to correct it unless he does. He may be in perfect control of the instrument into which he has made himself. But instruments break, malfunction, and need to be tuned from time to time. Knowing how to play it is enough only if it is working properly. However, repairing it takes knowing something about how it is put together. Furthermore, human lives are not simple instruments with only one use. This man is not only a salesman; he is also a husband, a father, a brother, a competitor, and a neighbor. Even if things go so smoothly in selling, there are unavoidable problems in other areas of his life. These require reflection. And the demands of the many roles he plays encroach on each other. He must monitor them, establish priorities, resolve conflicts, think about the future, try to learn from the past, and compare himself to others in similar positions. Descriptive self-knowledge is needed, because practical self-knowledge is insufficient to cope with changing circumstances and inevitable conflicts.

Thus, descriptive and practical self-knowledge are both required for good lives. Descriptive self-knowledge enables us to be objective about ourselves. It makes it possible to hold up a mirror and see ourselves as others see us. It is a means whereby the usual indulgence with which we view ourselves is overcome. And it is a means also of predicting how we would respond to yet unencountered situations. To lack it is to be incapable of self-correction and planning for the future. Practical self-knowledge enables us to make decisions about how we should act. Through it we translate what we have understood about ourselves into an influence on our conduct. It is indispensable for self-improvement, for preparing ourselves for good lives.[1]

Self-Knowledge as Interpretive

Through descriptive self-knowledge we know facts about ourselves. But there are facts and facts. Some are simple episodes, like being surprised at the tiger cub as a birthday present. Others are complex patterns, involving, say, the realization that we have a passionate nature. From simple events to complex patterns, there lies a continuum. Descriptive knowledge of simple items at one end is different from the knowledge of complex items at the other end. But in the middle these two kinds of self-knowledge shade into each other. I shall refer to knowledge of complex items as interpretive self-knowledge.[2]

Descriptive self-knowledge of simple episodes is objective, truth-directed, and empirically testable. What we know of ourselves in this way, others can also know. But they know it only inferentially, while we, ourselves, may know it directly. Others infer from our conduct and from what we say or fail to say what psychological events are happening to us. Some of these inferences are quite certain; but not all are. You can confidently conclude what I think of rock music by observing the pained expression on my face whenever I am exposed to it. However, my refusal to attend a funeral may be attributed to my dislike of ritual, to unwillingness to honor the person being buried, or to fear of sentimentalism. But we, ourselves, need not bother with these inferences, because we can directly experience the psychological processes of which others can see only signs and symptoms.

I am not suggesting that descriptive self-knowledge cannot be inferential; for instance, we can infer from our own conduct that we cannot laugh at our own expense. The point is that others can know our psychological states inferentially, if at all; while we may know them both inferentially and directly. By experiencing them, we can have an access that others lack.

If we had only descriptive self-knowledge, we would deprive ourselves of great benefits. For knowledge of simple episodes in our lives does not provide any information about how important the known items are. Facts, including facts about ourselves, acquire their significance from the interpretations placed upon them. It is interpretive self-knowledge that enables us to distinguish between momentous and trivial events in our lives, between formative and banal experiences, and between the everyday occurrences and the exciting, unexpected, dangerous, or shameful signs that we are not what we supposed ourselves to be. Furthermore, the possibility of predicting what we would do in a new situation also depends on interpretive self-knowledge. And this prediction is crucial to change and development, for only through it can we imaginatively explore and form an attitude toward possibilities open to us.

Interpretive self-knowledge imposes a pattern on what is descriptively known about ourselves. It is unclear where the description ends and the interpretation starts. But both are essential to self-knowledge, for description without interpretation is devoid of significance, and interpretation requires description to give it content. Descriptive self-knowledge may or may not be action-guiding. Interpretive self-knowledge, however, cuts across the distinction between descriptive and practical self-knowledge. For through interpretive self-knowledge we not only know the significance of our wants, and the pattern of dispositions they form, but we are also impelled to action. If we know what we want, if ideals lead us to recognize some wants as important, then we shall act to satisfy them in appropriate situations.

Interpretive self-knowledge, therefore, incorporates both the descriptive and practical aspects of self-knowledge. From now on, I shall concentrate on interpretive self-knowledge (and refer to it simply as self-knowledge). It is both truth-directed and action-guiding; it makes possible predictions about our future conduct and decisions about acting or not acting to satisfy particular wants.

Everyone has wants and everyone's wants form patterns. But the extent to which we know the patterns of our wants varies greatly from person to person and from time to time within each person. Self-knowledge is difficult. We are not born with it, since what is known is largely what we become after birth. It cannot be taught, since its content is different for each of us. It is possible to explain what we must do to acquire it and why we should have it, but we must achieve it ourselves. Nobody else can construct for us the partly descriptive and partly practical pattern formed of what we want and do not want, of how important various wants are for us, of what ideals guide us, and of how to interpret the pattern formed of various more or less important wants. Furthermore, self-knowledge is a lifelong process. For so long as we live, we are driven by our wants and must reflect on whether their satisfaction fits in with the ideals we seek our characters to reflect.

Given that self-knowledge is difficult, we may justifiably wonder why we should pursue it. Additional point is given to this doubt by understanding that self-knowledge requires standing back from ourselves and adopting a reflective stance to survey our active struggling selves. This aloofness may seem impractical and possibly harmful. It is impractical to reflect on the long-range significance of what we are about to do when the situation calls for prompt action. And it is possibly harmful, because it removes us from a wholehearted involvement in the business of living. It poisons spontaneity, exuberance, innocence, and makes us divided in ourselves.

My answer is that self-knowledge *is* difficult, but it is neither impractical nor harmful. Its difficulty is worth enduring, because the alternative is to be left without guidance about how to choose between various courses of action. Of course, we may act on the strongest want making itself felt at the time of action. But strong wants may be harmful, and self-interest, if nothing else, calls for the kind of reflection that self-knowledge involves. That self-knowledge is the opposite of being harmful follows from this. If our wants were equally beneficial and none of them were harmful, and if we did not constantly have to choose between wants we could satisfy, and if some wants were not more important than others, then spontaneity, innocence, and exuberance would not need to be curtailed. But since the facts are otherwise, self-knowledge is needed.

What about impracticality? Let us remember that living a good life is possible only in civilized conditions. Therefore, the kinds of emergency that makes reflection and thus self-knowledge impractical cannot be constant. Conditions are civilized if emergencies are the exceptions, not the rule. Yet, it is undeniable that even in civilized conditions prompt action is frequently called for, and reflection would hamper it. But this truism is not incompatible with putting a high value on self-knowledge. Self-knowledge is a disposition; it should be exercised in appropriate situations, and emergencies are not such. There is a time to reflect, and there is a time to act, and the two need not always coincide. My claim is that they should frequently coincide if we wish our lives to be good.

Self-Knowledge as Evaluative

I have subsumed all forms of self-knowledge under its interpretive aspect, and claimed that it is truth-directed and action-guiding. It is possible to go further by noticing that interpretation may or may not be evaluative, but in the case of self-knowledge it always is. If the nature of this evaluation is understood, it becomes clearer why it is reasonable to care about the accuracy of our self-knowledge and why we should want it to guide our actions.

Interpretations play a central role in history, literary criticism, biography, and jurisprudence, to mention some examples. Offering an interpretation in these contexts involves no commitment about the evaluation of the pattern imposed on the facts. A historian may believe that the worldliness of the clergy was an important factor in the rise of the Reformation. But this belief carries no necessary judgment about the priesthood. Accuracy, not partisanship, is what matters to the historian.

Contrast this with John Stuart Mill's claim that Harriet Taylor exercised a profound influence on his philosophical development. This is an interpretation essentially connected with Mill's self-knowledge, and as such, unavoidably evaluative. Now, opinion on Taylor is divided. Some thought of her as a ghastly woman, infused with great fervor about half-baked ideas, fueled by unrealistic ambition and petty resentments. Others regarded her as a fine human being whose sterling intellectual and moral qualities made her prevail over Victorian stupidity about women. I shall prudently avoid taking sides on this, but Mill could not have done the same. He could not have said that Taylor had a profound influence on my thoughts and feelings, but I am indifferent to whether she was a virago or a moral hero. Why could Mill not be neutral? Because his view of Taylor was essentially connected with his view of what makes life good, and the connection was established through his hard-earned self-knowledge. It is this complicated connection that we need to understand.

As a first approximation, it may be said that our accurate judgment about what is important to us, a judgment that can be made only on the basis of self-knowledge, derives from our ideals of good lives. Interpretations of importance about influences in our lives are thus always evaluative, because they are justifiable or criticizable in the light of our ideals of what would make our lives good. Historical, literary, and other interpretations are not usually connected with this sort of evaluative standard

But this first approximation needs to be revised. For we may regard the objects of our obsession or addiction as the important things in our lives, and yet admit that our lives are wasted, and what makes them so is what has assumed such importance in it. Alcoholics and drug addicts may think this way. This shows that more needs to be said, so I propose a reformulation. Suppose we have accurate self-knowledge about what is important in our lives. There are two possibilities. The simple one is that what we regard as important conforms to our ideals. The more complicated one is that we judge something to be important and yet recognize that it violates our ideals. In this judgment, importance and ideals of good lives are still connected; the judgment is still evaluative, but the evaluation is adverse. It could be adverse, however, only because there are ideals of which it falls short. The possibilities of addiction and obsession in the lives of people with self-knowledge establish that we can harm ourselves knowingly. And this does not undermine the connection I insist on between judgments of importance and our ideals of good lives.

If this connection is recognized, it will be seen that such ideals infuse self-knowledge; they make it evaluative through and through.[3] In their light, our characters are formed, dispositions are curtailed or fostered, and the respective importance of our wants is decided. And we can also see why if we are engaged in making our lives good we would be deeply concerned with knowing the truths about ourselves and with acting in accordance with them: the truths concern what we are, what we want to be, how the two differ, and action is directed at getting from one to the other. Self-knowledge is a virtue, a good way of being for everyone in civilized conditions, because it is necessary to living a good life, whatever form it takes.[4]

Implicit in my discussion is a distinction between three levels of self-knowledge, and it needs to be made explicit. The first level involves knowledge of our wants; the second, knowledge of the respective importance of our wants; and the third, knowledge of the ideals by which the respective importance of our wants is decided. Complete self-knowledge involves all three levels. On all levels, the descriptive, practical, and the interpretive aspects of self-knowledge are intermingled.

If we act to satisfy a want by considering only the immediate effects of our actions, if we do not attend to their long-term character-building consequences, we move by and large on the first level. The more our decisions involve considerations arising on the second and third levels, the more fully self-directed we are, the more likely we are to act reasonably, and thus to contribute to what we think of as good lives.

Self-Knowledge and Ignorance of Oneself

I have been concentrating on the reasons why if we want good lives we should aim to have self-knowledge. I shall reverse this perspective now and discuss the lack of self-knowledge: ignorance of oneself. This may be self-inflicted or not. If not, it is blindness to oneself.[5] If it is self-inflicted, it is self-deception. Crucial to both is the distinction between the three levels of self-knowledge. Bearing that distinction in mind, let us first consider blindness to oneself.

We cannot be completely blind to ourselves, for being human, we have wants and we cannot help knowing at least some of them. It is possible, however, to care very little about our wants. The cases we have to consider are not ones in which people train themselves to disregard their wants, for these involve deliberation, and blindness to oneself docs not. But some people naturally care very little about their wants for two main reasons. One is that their circumstances are comfortable and their wants are weak. There are people with dull appetites, no passions, who have not been fired by a deep concern for anything. Their lives are permeated with languid insipidity. The genteel resigned middle-aged characters of Chekhov, the ones his young girls dread to grow into, illustrate what I have in mind. Such people are harmless, but we are disinclined to give them credit for it, since they barely occupy their lives, and harmlessness comes, we suspect, from lack of energy.

The other reason that may lead people not to care about their wants is that, while they have them as everyone else, they regard them as unimportant. They are so concerned with something else that they do not care about themselves. Again, it is not that they have made a decision to sacrifice their own concerns at some altar; the idea of sacrifice would not occur to them, because they lack a sufficient sense of importance about their own wants. Heroes and villains are ruled by such devotion or obsession. They are on a quest and it dominates their lives. Captain Ahab, Lenin, Simone Weil, Savonarola, Joan of Arc, and Patrick White's Voss are examples of lives lived in this way. The overwhelming impressions is that of being tortured and driven; there is little balance, calmness, or peace in such lives.

It may be said against this that the lives I am criticizing conform to the model of good lives I have been describing. People on quests have wants, they judge some of them important, and their judgments are made in the light of ideals they consciously accept. Such people are conducting their own experiments in living. In objecting to them, it may be said, I am foisting one style of life upon unwilling recipients. Why should a good life involve a harmonious satisfaction of balanced wants rather than the single-minded pursuit of one want dictated by a passionately held ideal?

This is a crucial question and it ought to be clearly answered. The people I have been criticizing, the heroes and villains, are fanatics. They may be admirable or abominable, but mainly, they are driven by total dedication to an ideal. Their lack of self-knowledge consists in blindness to the existence of alternatives for themselves. They have no doubts, because they are unacquainted with the discipline of subjecting their own ideals to fundamental questioning. They have learned from their moral tradition, but they have not learned enough, for they have not understood the attraction of ideals other than their own. They lack the tolerant wisdom that only civilized minds possess.

It will be asked: Why does a good life require deep appreciation of ideals other than our own? Why is it not enough to have one, be passionately attached to it, and let it guide our lives? It is not enough for two reasons. One is that the ideal held in this manner could not have been reasonably adopted. Reasonable choice is based on considering the alternatives, but the lives of fanatics do not allow for that. The other is that fanatics ignore their own fallibility, the possibility that the ideal they so passionately pursue may be chimerical. Stalinists, Nazis, Puritans, inquisitors, conquistadors, flagellants, men of God or the sword, and the fundamentalists and the orthodox of many persuasions, have experienced, on occasion, the scales dropping from their eyes. This knowledge should curb the fanatics' passions. And fallibility characterizes not merely the ideals, but also the passions. It is remarkable how many heroes and villains are led to embark of their quest by an exaggerated sense of their own corruption. One

pitfall self-knowledge helps to avoid is seeing ourselves too in-
dulgently. The other, less common, error, is to see ourselves too
severely. Self-knowledge helps us to see ourselves as others would.
From that point of view, neither merits nor faults loom so large.

The other form of ignorance of oneself is self-deception.[6] We
may fail to know some things about ourselves, because we deliberately deceive ourselves. Self-deceptions seems paradoxical: it
clearly occurs, but it is not obvious how it could. If we deceive
others, we willfully lead them to believe something that we know
to be otherwise. But in the case of self-deception, the deceiver and
the deceived are the same. How can we both know that something
is so and be deceived about it being so?

The paradox disappears if we view it through the different
aspects and levels of self-knowledge. If self-knowledge were only
descriptive and if it occurred on the simplest level only, then self-
deception would indeed be paradoxical. If I know descriptively
something about myself, then I do know a fact about myself. I
may forget it, I may even make myself forget it; but if I have it, I
do know it, and so cannot be deceived. However, self-knowledge
is also interpretive and it occurs on two more complicated levels
besides that of knowing what we want. Self-deception is readily
explainable once it is placed in the context of our concern with
weighing the importance of our wants. It involves the deliberate
refusal to reflect carefully.

Consider a flatterer with some self-knowledge. He knows that
he tends to tell others what they want to hear. Because he does it
well, he is liked by his superficial acquaintances, and he wants to
be liked. It is important to him to have as little stress and unpleasantness in his everyday contacts as possible, to be greeted with
smiles rather than scowls. On the other hand, he knows that
flattery involves him in frequent lying. Often, his acquaintances
want to be reassured that their faults are not excessive, and the
flatterer obliges them. He realizes this about himself, and he does
not like it. He wants both to please and to be honest, and sometimes he succeeds, sometimes not. And so when his recently di-
vorced older colleague, who has so obviously fallen for the very
young and very pretty secretary, asks him with a solemn expression on his face to have a drink with him, because there is
something important he wants his advice about, our flatterer
knows that he is in a predicament. Let us follow the different lines
his reflection may take.

If self-knowledge guides him, he will ask himself: Is being
honest more or less important than being liked to the kind of

person I want to be? If the former, he will tell his colleague not to be a fool; if the latter, he will praise his youthful appearance and adventurous spirit. He, then, faces the relevant wants, weighs their respective importance, and makes his decision in the light of his ideals for himself. His ideals may or may not be defensible, but that is another question.

But suppose that self-deception prevails, how will he reflect then? He may say: honesty is more important to me than being liked. I do not want to be a flatterer, but this case is special. My colleague does need reassurance very badly; who can tell whether the infatuation may not bloom into a happy relationship; why should I spoil it for him; it does not matter what I say, for he wants a sympathetic ear, not advice. The mechanism of this self-deceiving reflection is to introduce dubious considerations, so that the scale of importance will favor what he finds easy to do and not what he thinks he ought to do. Doubt is artifically fanned so that what may possibly be a relevant fact is falsely supposed to have an actual bearing on the case. The self-deceiver elevates what could be a reason into an argument for doing what he knows he should not: he sways his own judgment by giving undue weight to marginal matters.

Or he may say: my colleague's need is immediate; he wants reassurance; I can give it, so I shall. Honesty, flattery, and being one kind of a person rather than another are remote considerations. I can do something, he may say, here and now; the future is unpredictable, my judgment is fallible. And so he deceives himself by ignoring the long-term character-building effect of his action. The fault here lies with the failure to reflect, while in the previous case, the fault was to reflect, but badly.

In each case, the means of correction are available and self-deceivers could use them, but they do not. Why? What is it that influences them? It is the immediate situation. The present satisfaction of a want provides a much more tangible gain than possible future benefits derivable from a slow accretion of episodes. The temptation to favor our present over our future selves is constant. The mechanism for minimizing in our own eyes the significance of succumbing to this temptation is self-deception. And it works by ignoring or misinterpreting the significance of our actions.

There is, therefore, a conflict underlying self-deception. But it is not the paradoxical one between us both knowing and not knowing something. Rather, it is a conflict between appraising the significance of an action from the points of view of our present and future selves. When the conflict is seen in this way, it becomes obvious why self-deception is a vice. It prevents us from improving ourselves by shaping our present selves to approximate more closely our better future selves. And since those selves are necessary for good lives, self-deceivers jeopardize their own chances of achieving them.

It may be objected to my criticisms of both forms of ignorance of oneself that we may actually benefit from them. For if we succeed in ignoring some destructive fact about ourselves, a fact we cannot alter, then we may be better off than if we adopted the realistic, but hopeless, attitude self-knowledge would dictate. Is it obvious, for instance, that the carefully nurtured false hope of a dying person is harmful?

My answer is a reminder of the context in which the pursuit of good lives is viewed. I am assuming that civilized conditions prevail and the various forms of hardship and impediment have been overcome. There are, of course, many things against which we should try to protect ourselves and many hardships that make good lives impossible. The false hope of a dying man belongs among these. I am concerned with another question: What should we live *for* when our lives go smoothly?

The search for good lives can be interpreted both negatively, as the attempt to avoid misery, and positively, as the attempt to approximate our ideals. Ignorance of oneself may indeed make us less miserable, but it will not make it easier for us to come closer to our ideals. Ignorance of oneself may be beneficial in primitive life-diminishing situations, but it is harmful in civilized contexts where self-direction is possible. Self-knowledge is a virtue, because it is necessary to making our lives good in civilized contexts.

Self-Knowlege and Its Context

We have seen that self-knowledge requires an awareness of our own psychological states and activities. This awareness is partly cognitive, because it involves description and interpretation. But it is also practical, because it guides how we go about satisfying our wants and exercising our capacities. Both the interpretive and action-guiding aspects of self-knowledge are morally evaluative, because their aim is to make good lives for ourselves. And ignorance of ourselves, the vice corresponding to the virtue of self-knowledge, is harmful, because it prevents us from satisfying our wants in accordance with our ideals.

I shall close this discussion of self-knowledge by considering the context in which it is exercised. Our normal situation is that we are born into a moral tradition and our education in it begins shortly after birth. By adolescence, we are saturated with the moral views of our tradition. We learn from it which of our wants are morally permissible to satisfy, how we may go about satisfying them, and how and to what ends we may exercise such capacities as we have. For each of us, our moral tradition provides the framework and the guidance for the lives we lead. But the fit between the tradition and individual lives guided by it is imperfect. The tradition is much richer; it provides many more ideals than we can realize in a lifetime. So we must choose among them. Nor is it always obvious what our wants and capacities are; consequently, it is often unclear whether or how ideals apply to our own cases. Also, there is a reciprocal process between our growing awareness of what we want and the opportunities provided by the tradition for realizing it. We find out what we want partly by considering the possibilities open to us, but many of these possibilities are defined by traditional ideals. One main function of self-knowledge is to overcome the imperfect fit between individual lives and the traditional guidance of ideals; it is to help develop our individuality by giving form to such inchoate, unarticulated wants and capacities as we may have. Self-knowledge helps us not by revealing what we are independently of the ideals that have and are forming us, but by reasonably guiding the way in which we are being formed by them.

The further our wants are from being physiological, the less clear it is what would satisfy them. We want love, enjoyment, respect, security, and an interesting life, and we want to avoid pain, hostility, contempt, fear, and boredom. But each of these objects is quite general: by wanting them we have not yet decided which of a vast array of satisfactions possible in our moral tradition we actually seek. Is my wanting to be loved, at this stage of my life, a longing for parental or sexual love; is it that I want it from my friends, spouse, colleagues, children, or students? To get clear about these, and countless other wants, is to understand specific instances as manifestations of my deeper, more general dispositions. And to understand the unspecific dispositions in the background is to come to know what particular episodes do and do not instantiate it. In reaching this understanding, however, I am engaged in a constant traffic with the traditional ideas which, in my context, influence the specific episodes that could fall under the heading of the dispositions. I am trying to find out what my range of relevant possibilities is and what possibilities, within that range, would satisfy the wants I have. But the wants become articulated and specified in terms of the possible satisfactions provided by my moral tradition. Self-knowledge helps to overcome the imperfect fit between tradition and individual lives by finding the traditional ideas that would suit us, given what we know about our characters and circumstances.

The search for this fit requires an imaginative effort. Its objects are our own future states of being and acting. They are imagined from the inside, from the point of view of ourselves as agents experiencing them. We try to imagine how we would feel about being in that state and act accordingly; we try to discern whether these states and activities would provide the anticipated satisfactions; we try to understand what life according to the imagined ideas would be like. And this leads us to the topic of the next chapter: moral sensitivity, the third virtue of self-direction.

8

Moral Sensitivity

The Central Question of Morality

Self-control and self-knowledge establish the possibilities and limitations of self-direction, so that we can proceed to transform ourselves from what we are to what our ideals of good lives prescribe we should be. For this transformation to occur, we must be alive to yet unrealized possibilities to ways of being and acting that we aspire to, but have not yet achieved. Moral sensitivity, the third virtue of self-direction, is this reflective, imaginative, and emotional awareness.

Moral sensitivity is fundamental to being a self-directed moral agent. However, there is a widespread mistake about moral agency that permeates much of contemporary thinking about morality. The origin of this mistake is Kant's view that the central question of morality is what ought I to do.[1] This gives choice a pivotal role, for choice is what we face when the question has to be answered. Since what is chosen is an action, the contemporary view of morality is action-oriented. And since actions are directed toward others, the contemporary moral emphasis is on altruism and impartiality as the morally praiseworthy ways of treating others. Morality is thus supposed to be activist and social. It is a sensible public-spirited enterprise in which responsible members of society will participate, because they realize that reason requires it. Such contemporary moral theorists as Kantians, utilitarians, and contractarians disagree, of course, about many things, but they agree that choice intending to lead to action contributing to the welfare of others is the central concern of morality. This view of morality has become an orthodoxy. As a result, challenge to it seems to be a challenge to morality itself. If morality does not have as its central concern the choice of altruistic action, then, the orthodox want to know, what is morality about?

I think that morality is about what sort of person we ought to be. The important moral concern is with the individual, not with society; with being, rather than acting, in a certain way; with reflection, and not with action; with making ourselves good, rather than with doing what is right.[2]

Now it must be emphasized that I am not opposing social concern and right action; only an immoralist would do that. What I am suggesting is that a morally good person will feel social concern and will do what is right as a matter of course. So the kind of people we are is a more fundamental, and thus a more important consideration than how we act. If it is seen that actions follow from our characters, then choice will loom less important and character more so. The trouble with the contemporary orthodoxy is that it leads us to suppose that we must choose to be moral agents, and only if that all-important choice is made can the rest follow. Thus choice is the supposed foundation of morality.

However, this is not so. Almost everybody is a moral agent and nobody has made such a choice. As we have seen, the fact is that we are born into a tradition and by adolescence we are deeply immersed in the moral views of our tradition and its values. Of course, we can come to reject our upbringing. But nobody starts with a decision to accept or to reject it, and if someone does come to reject it eventually, it is, short of suicide, for another tradition. We cannot leave behind traditions. The idea that choice lies at the foundation of morality is mistaken, because it ignores the fundamental role of tradition and education in morality.

My account of moral sensitivity is intended to displace choice for these deeper influences. The proper characterization of moral conflicts requires understanding the kinds of tensions that exist in sensitive moral agents. I shall begin, then, by contrasting two views of moral predicaments.

Moral Predicaments

In *Existentialism*[3] Sartre described a young man in France during the Second World War who had to choose between his country and his mother. Choosing one meant having to make his way to England to join the Free French forces; choosing the other required him to stay at home and support his aging mother. Patriotism pulled him one way, filial obligation the other.

We are supposed to perceive this choice as radical. The young man had to pick one, for if he had done nothing, he would in effect have chosen to stay and thus opt for his mother. The conflict was absolute, without the possibility of compromise or evasion, it called for a commitment, and the situation was so contrived that no higher principle or value could be appealed to in choosing. The choice concerned fundamental values. Sartre believed that such choices constitute the foundation of morality and they are arbitrary. The human situation, he thought, is that we can choose with this knowledge or evade it by one form of bad faith or another.

This way of looking at moral choices is obviously inadequate. For the mere fact that the young man found himself having to choose between his country and his mother showed that he was committed to both. His problem was not to make an arbitrary decision about which commitment he should accept, but to weigh the hold on himself of commitments he had already made. Morality enters into such situations long before choice. Thus arbitrary choices cannot be the foundation of morality. Indeed, choices cannot be entirely arbitrary, because what calls for a choice is prior commitment to both of the incompatible alternatives. The romantic agony of existentialist heroes does not tell us about the relation between morality and choice. But it requires us to go deeper into Sartre's case, if we are to understand it.

Consider some of the ways in which the young man may have regarded his mother and his country. The key to his commitment to his mother may have been some combination of gratitude for her love; pity for the once strong figure who is now a weak shadow of her former self; the obligation he was feeling, because he believed that members of a family must stand together in time of need; similarly his commitment may have been due to generosity, honor, charity, or religious piety. Also, less nobly, he may have felt committed to avoid shame, guilt, divine punishment, social disapproval, gain stature in his community, impress his future father-in-law, or bargain with God.

The idea of joining the Free French forces may have been prompted by equally varied considerations. He may have loved his land, felt ennobled by its culture, hated the enemy, wanted to follow his friends, been attracted by adventure, coveted military honors, hoped to do better than his father, tried to get out of a halfhearted engagement, be on his own, and so on and on.

Of course, it very rarely happens that we are motivated by only one consideration. In the usual course of events, motives are mixed and we are by no means aware of all the forces pushing us one way and another. To a very large extent, thinking about what to do involves trying to become aware of the considerations inclining us in different directions and in trying to sort out the elements composing our mixed motives. The moral task facing Sartre's young man was not to make an arbitrary decision, but to reflect and come to understand his deeper commitments. If he had achieved this understanding, what he ought to have done would have become much clearer.

If we think of Sartre's case, while bearing in mind the considerations just adduced, we must be struck by its great implausibility. For we are invited to believe that this young man was motivated only by two unmixed feelings, they exercised precisely equal attraction for him, and that this situation is typical of moral conflicts. I suppose such unmixed and equally balanced motives could coexist in human beings. But only a gross violation of common sense could lead us to regard such exceptional cases as typical. Tragedy and, I fear, melodrama may be made of such stuff, but our moral lives are normally less dramatic and more complicated.

Now contrast Sartre's case with Henry James's portrayal of Strether's predicament in *The Ambassadors*. Strether was the trusted friend of the leading family of the Massachusetts manufacturing town, Woollett. He was a shrewd and perceptive man, a Yankee through and through. He was the next thing to being engaged to Mrs. Newsome, the unquestioned head of the first family of Woollett; and his life, occupation, and financial affairs were all bound up with the Newsome family. Mrs. Newsome dispatched Strether to Paris on the mission of bringing home her only son, Chad. Nobody in Woollett really knew what Chad was doing in Paris. They did not want to know, because they suspected him of immorality. Strether was to put an end to that, exercise his moral authority, and recall Chad to his responsibilities.

Strether was prepared to find an errant young man, judge him firmly, appeal to his better nature, and take him home. But he did not find what he thought he would. He found a Chad who appeared to have changed for the better. From the good-natured youth of Woollett, he seemed to have been transformed into a civilized man of the world; he had become a gracious, discriminating, sensitive man.

Strether was understandably confused. He was intelligent and perceptive enough to entertain the possibility that Chad had greatly improved; but if so, not in a way that Woollett could have appreciated. Strether had come to apply the standards of Woollett and he found them inapplicable. With much help, Strether gradually came to understand Chad; but as he was going through this process, so he was leaving Woollett and its standards behind. And although he tried, he could not make Woollett understand what he had come to understand.

Now Chad was not very important for James, nor is he for me. What matters is that Strether's struggle to perceive Chad accurately required Strether to change his moral vision, and this fundamentally changed Strether. He had come to Paris as a man of Woollett and he prepared to leave Paris, at the close of the book, as a larger-souled man. He had grown, because his moral possibilities were enlarged. He had discovered a way of being that he thought was better than what he had known before.

The discovery had nothing to do with facts. Chad, for instance, was immoral, Strether eventually found out, in the eyes of Woollett. But this no longer mattered. For Strether no longer saw the facts as Woollett saw them. On the contrary, he came to judge Woollett and Mrs. Newsome in the light of his changed vision and deeper understanding of moral possibilities.

Strether made no significant choices, he decided very little, and he had no moral epiphany. True, he ended up advising Chad not to go home; he came to see that he could not marry Mrs. Newsome, and life at Woollett had become impossible for him. These changes would have been unthinkable when he had arrived in Paris. But they were expected and flowed naturally from his altered character. Strether's choices and decisions were not significant in themselves; they derived their significance from being the natural outcome of something much deeper. The man Strether had become could not have chosen or decided otherwise. His actions followed with a kind of inevitability from the way he was. This is the kind of necessity Iris Murdoch has in mind in describing moral change. "Moral change and moral achievement are slow, we [can not] . . . suddenly alter outselves since we cannot suddenly alter what we see and ergo what we desire and are compelled by. In a way, explicit choice seems now less important: less decisive (since much of the 'decision' lies elsewhere) and less obviously something to be 'cultivated'. If I attend properly I will have no choices and this is the ultimate condition to aim at. . . . The ideal situation . . . is . . . a kind of 'necessity.'"[4] Thus for Strether, as for us, the decision is not about choosing to do this or that, but about being the kind of person who is alive to moral possibilities. This aliveness is necessary for self-direction, and it is what I mean by moral sensitivity. James's Strether and not Sartre's young man is the case in point.

Moral Growth

Imagine a composer setting down the score of a symphony. He writes note after note. Each note acquires significance from its place in the symphony. The symphony itself is the public result of a private creative effort: a long imaginative process involving the selection of melodies, variations, and instruments. It is informed by the tradition, the composer's own precepts, his more or less clear conception of what the finished product should be, practical considerations about orchestration, the skill of musicians, the receptivity of the likely audience, and so on. The symphony, of course, *is* made of notes. But it is the symphony, not the notes, that matters.

A moral action is like a note. The life of a person is the symphony from which the action acquires significance. As a symphony, so also a life can be appreciated only by understanding the tradition forming its background, the practical options available to the person living it, and the private world of which the actions are manifestations. The same actions have vastly different moral significance. To concentrate on actions is to miss their significance.

The composer can be said to choose each note: no one forces him and he may always use one rather than another. But to say this is to emphasize the wrong thing. For if it goes well, the choice of notes is dictated by the tradition, by his own precepts and conceptions, and by practical considerations. The emphasis on choice in morality is similarly misleading. Most actions most of the time follow from the character of the agent. People normally do just the sort of thing they would do. Choosing an action is rarely and only exceptionally a conscious process of deliberation. We act as a matter of course, given the past, our ideals, our perception of the situation, and the practical exigencies. This is Iris Murdoch's necessity, and this is why concentration on choice obscures the real texture of moral life. To appreciate that texture, we must start with how we see the situation in which we are to act. Sensitive perception is the crux of the matter.

Consider some terms of our moral vocabulary connoting moral approval: forthright, unassuming, generous, faithful, honorable, considerate, trustworthy, modest, courageous, honest, pure, and conscientious; and some further terms of condemnation: corrupt, cruel, treacherous, envious, petty, hypocritical, selfish, greedy, cowardly, overbearing, obsequious, and arrogant.

Sensitivity to moral situations depends, in the first instance, on the moral vocabulary available to us. It reflects the required and variable conventions of our tradition. Every society has such a vocabulary and the lists of terms culled from different societies, historical periods, and intellectual epochs contain by and large the same items. But this is not to say that the significance of the terms is also the same. This is true of many other types of terms as well. I suppose most languages have words for *family, stranger, peace, religion,* and *manhood;* but what these words suggest, their emotional force and cultural connotations vary, of course, from context to context. Understanding another culture or period involves understanding not just the surface, but also the deeper meaning such words have. And so it is with the moral vocabulary. *Courage* and *cowardice,* for instance, were moral terms in Alexandrian Macedonia, Roosevelt's Washington, the Weimar Republic, and Stalin's Russia. But their significance was vastly different. The moral vocabulary we have available for our uses thus acquires significance partly from the moral tradition.

However, the moral tradition contributes only a part; another part is added by moral agents. The personal significance of the moral vocabulary depends on the understanding we may acquire of it. Moral education is little more than teaching children to match moral terms with the appropriate occasions for their employment. If children learn that they apply to everyone, including themselves, one phase of their moral education is complete. They are now saturated with the conventional morality of their society. Many people stop here, but others grow in their appreciation of the significance of their moral vocabulary.

One aspect of this growth involves understanding that conventional morality is only the form of morality we happen to be born into. What counts as courage, honor, modesty, or generosity in one way of life need not so count in another. Appreciating the endless variations possible on the theme provided by a particular moral term is to have an outward, comparative dimension to our moral understanding. Courage may be understood to involve physical bravery, the willingness to incur unpopularity, the quiet determination to continue as we have in a world gone mad, opposition to misguided authority, or risking our well-being for principle. To be alive to these possibilities requires disciplined imagination and informed intelligence. This is what liberal education should impart and thus make its recipients better.

Conventional morality will inculcate habits and the outward, comparative dimension of moral understanding will open up possibilities. But we need something more to give personal significance to moral idioms. Outward comparison without an inward appreciation leads to that facile relativism many social scientists put in the way of moral understanding. Its purveyors are so impressed by the apparent diversity of options that they fail to perceive their common ground in a shared humanity. The inward

dimension of moral sensitivity leads us to see how different forms
are forms of the same thing. It leads us to attend properly, as Iris
Murdoch would say. The vehicle of this proper attendance is
personal experience reflectively transformed from its immediacy,
and imaginative identification achieved by sympathetically thinking and feeling as we suppose another to do. This is what makes
us see that what made Robinson Crusoe create for himself a
miniature civilization; what enabled Montaigne to maintain his
private self uncompromised; what gave Spinoza the strength to
follow his own light; and what enables countless mothers, political
prisoners, and long-suffering patients to get through their difficult days is the same: courage.

The inwardly directed understanding of the significance of
moral terms, provides a perspective from which moral agents can
transform themselves and come to a more accurate appreciation
of others. Strether's struggle to see Chad accurately helps us to
understand this. Strether had to make up his mind about Chad.
The easy part was to recognize that the morality of Woollett was
not the morality of Paris, yet they were both moralities. This was a
question of comparative appreciation, and Strether's intelligence
stood him in good stead here. His serious difficulties began when
it occurred to him that the improvement in Chad was in part at
least due to having left behind the morality of Woollett for that of
Paris. He faced the possibility that the morality of Paris was better.
Chad was the living testimony that the vision of good lives Paris
offered may have been superior to Woollett's. That Strether enter-
tained this possibility was an indication of his growth in sensitivity,
which proved illuminating about Chad and also about Strether
himself.

As far as Chad was concerned, Strether's understanding improved. He came to see that where Woollett was common, indis-
criminate, and vulgar, Chad had become civilized, refined, and
discriminating, one to whom standards or excellence had become
second nature. Thus new possibilities opened up for Strether. His
growth in the inward dimension made him see these alternatives
as real possibilities; not just as something foreigners might do, but
as possibilities for himself. And this imaginative capacity led him
to his most serious difficulty: to form a view about how these
possibilities should affect him.

So the question of how to see Chad receded, and the question of
how Strether should change, if at all, came to the fore. This was
really the fundamental question, for Strether's response to Chad,
and to everything else, depended on an inward appreciation of

the significance of the moral vocabulary in which were couched the possibilities he considered making his own.

This kind of understanding must be fought for. Conventional morality and breadth can be taught, but inward appreciation cannot be. It requires the constant imaginative effort to try to see moral situations as a person would who approximated more closely than we presently can the ideals to which we aspire. This imaginative effort is one driving force of self-direction. But we are driven by it both outwardly and inwardly, and although they are inseparable from a practical point of view, they are different all the same.

Strether asked: had Chad been *corrupted* or *refined?* These moral terms had one meaning in Woollett and another in Paris. Understanding this took outward, comparative understanding; employing one rather than another to Chad and especially to himself in the light of this understanding was a sign of inward growth. It had required reflection on human possibilities, and on his own and Chad's possibilities, and coming to a conclusion about the most fitting term. The employment of the term, of course, called for appropriate action. If Chad was corrupted, Strether should have made him go home; if he was refined, he ought to have been encouraged to stay.

Part of the inward aspect was the realization that the term Strether found fitting depended on what he thought of as corruption and refinement. The mere fact that he hesitated showed that he was becoming aware of new moral possibilities for himself. And that he came to see Chad this way rather than that, indicated that he himself had changed. For he had passed from the simple view of corruption and refinement, through a realization that they take many different forms, to an appreciation that behind these forms there was, after all, a common element. It was corruption, if it was an exercise in the clever manipulation of distinctions; it was refinement, if it led to a closer approximation of the ideal to which Chad aspired. But that Strether was capable of thought and judgment of this sort was an improvement in Strether. It was due to his having achieved greater moral sensitivity and, thus, greater self-direction.

Moral terms, then, gain significance from their conventional and linguistic context and from such outward and inward appreciation as individual moral agents can give them in their own lives. The better we appreciate the significance of our moral vocabulary, the keener is our sensitivity to the moral situations characterized by them. My claim is that one crucial moral task is to perceive accurately the situation in which we are called upon to act. And accurate perception depends on the growth of our appreciation of the available moral vocabulary. This is the task of moral sensitivity.

The Nature of Moral Vocabulary

It would be convenient at this point to have a definition of the terms of moral vocabulary involved in moral sensitivity. However, I cannot give it, I doubt that it could be given, and I think that we can do without it. To appreciate the difficulty, consider what a comparable definition of legal, aesthetic, engineering, or medical terms would be. One can give examples, and this I have done. One can rely on the usage of experts, and I have indicated that this too can be done by observing how people with moral sensitivity employ them. These considerations, however, will not help to decide how to add to the list of moral terms, or how to contest the inclusion of items on the list. I can go some way toward helping to decide, but, in the end, decision depends on an intelligent and sensitive discussion of contested cases.

To begin with, the terms are *moral.* They are intended to indicate concern for human welfare; with their help, judgments of good and evil can be expressed. Part of the reason why a definition is neither available nor needed is that this territory shades into others. Morality shares with jurisprudence such terms as *justice, fairness, impartiality; charity, humility,* and *faithfulness* are as religious as they are moral; *purity, solemnity,* and *sensitivity* are on the borderline between moral and aesthetic considerations; *politeness, propriety,* and *dignity* are claimed by both morality and social customs, manners, and mores; *politics, commerce, psychology,* and *education* claim yet other terms. All in all, I doubt that there is a moral term with an exclusively moral use.

The terms involved in moral sensitivity are *specific* rather than general. General moral terms are, for instance, *good, right, obligation,* and *duty.* If situations are described in such general terms, we remain uninformed about the personalities of the agents or the nature of their conduct. These general terms are abstract so we need specific ones to give content to them. But the terms involved in moral sensitivity are not entirely specific either. For they themselves may be used in many different forms. Thus their specificity consists in being more specific than the most general moral terms, such as *right* or *good.* But since interest in morality is both general and specific, some degree of generality is inevitable. Concentration on the sort of moral terms I have listed seems to me to maintain the right balance between generality and specificity.

These moral terms describe human *character traits:* dispositions to conduct ourselves in certain ways. When an action is described by the adverbial form of a moral term, the intention is to identify it as an episode instantiating a disposition. To behave courageously is to exercise courage. Of course, not every instance of courage exemplifies the disposition and dispositions do not inevitably issue in instantiating episodes. A person can act uncharacteristically, but to do so calls for explanation; that an honest person acts honestly, does not. These character traits are virtues and vices. In the Aristotelian tradition they are placed at the center of moral philosophy. And I agree that moral thinking should recognize the central moral importance of these character traits. They form us and prompt the actions that are manifestations of these deeper structures.[5]

Moral terms are *interpretive* rather than descriptive. This is a difficult contrast to draw, as we have seen in discussing self-knowledge, and I am not supposing that a sharp distinction can be defended. Yet there is a kind of argument about interpretation that is different from descriptive arguments and it is the kind involved in disagreements about the application of moral terms. These are arguments about the significance of agreed upon facts, not about the facts themselves. They typically occur when there is agreement about the purpose of an interpretation, but there is disagreement about the importance of the elements upon which the interpretation is to be based. These disagreements hinge on what is taken to be central rather than marginal, novel rather than banal, surprising rather than routine, revealing rather than obscure. These are some of the considerations influencing the assignment of moral terms. The interpretive disputes need not be public, for moral agents may be arguing with themselves.

Moral terms are *morally evaluative;* thus they form a subclass of interpretations. Historical interpretations of wars, treaties, revolutions, anthropological interpretations of the significance of rituals and observances, and interpretations of a text by literary critics need not carry with them a moral evaluation. But if a moral term has been applied to characterize a situation, then the person applying it is committed to a corresponding moral evaluation. If we describe Socrates's drinking the hemlock as honorable, we are thereby committed to a favorable moral judgment.

Lastly, moral terms are *action-guiding.* This is not to say that if we characterize a situation by a term, then we are committed to acting in a certain way. We frequently evaluate situations without any possibility of doing anything. Historical and fictional events are the clearest cases in point. But even in actual and present situations, where we could conceivably act according to the moral term assigned, we often do not, because it would be inappropriate. Yet moral terms *are* action-guiding, because *if* we are called upon to act in a situation, moral terms guide the way in which we ought to act. If a man asking for help is properly characterized as a conniving scoundrel, we are guided one way; if he is the victim of injustice, in another.

This is an important characteristic of moral terms, for it shows why it is mistaken to regard the question of what ought I to do as central to morality. If I am satisfied by my characterization of a situation in terms of a particular moral term, then what I ought to do is usually clear. The action, then, need not be chosen, for we have already instructed ourselves about what we ought to do. If I perceive the man asking for help as a victim of injustice, and I can help, that is what I recognize as being what I ought to do. Of course, problems remain. For knowing what I ought to do does not tell me how I ought to do it, and how much of it, at what cost to myself ought I to do it. But moral terms do guide us to the kind of action we should perform.

The terms involved in moral sensitivity, then, are specific, rather than general; refer to virtues and vices instantiated in moral action; interpretive, rather than descriptive; morally evaluative; and action-guiding. Moral terms have a central importance in morality, for to characterize a situation by a moral term is to understand it in a certain way and to recognize what sort of response we are called upon to make. The question of what ought I to do has a straightforward answer once the situation has been understood to come under the provenance of a moral term. The selection of terms, therefore, is a far more important and problematic matter in morality than the choice of action.

The Selection of Moral Terms

Moral sensitivity involves the selection of moral terms for the appraisal of appropriate situations. Their selection depends on the facts of the case and on reflection. Let us discuss them in terms of Strether's situation. The facts concerned both Strether and Chad. Strether's mission was to bring Chad home, because that is where Chad ought to be. He had had his fling and now he should assume his responsibilities, or so Woollett and Strether believed. The fact about Chad was that he had changed, and Strether saw that. He was more refined, more thoughtful, more discriminating than he had been when he left Woollett. The problem for Strether was to decide what to make of these changes. This called for moral sensitivity.

Strether had to make up his mind about the moral significance of the changes in Chad, and this led to complications. The complications could have been avoided if Strether had been able to convince himself that the changes were irrelevant to his task of persuading Chad to go home. But he could not do this: he sensed that there was more to it than bringing the moral vision of Woollett to the present situation. And so the first crack appeared in the hitherto united front presented by Strether and Woollett. What made Strether's task complicated was that the conventions by which he was accustomed to evaluate the significance of the facts had been called into question. Making a decision, therefore, required both appraising the significance of the facts and of the conventions by which their significance was to be judged.

What Strether had asked himself was whether he should see the change in Chad as a sign of corruption, a loss of the simple certitudes of Woollett, a culpable displacement of duty in favor of frivolous sophistication, or, as a sign of growth, an enhanced awareness of the possibilities of life, a deepening of civilization. He was reflecting on the moral terms by which Chad could be described accurately. And the importance of Strether's reflection, for my purposes, is the inward aspect concerning the question of what sort of person should Strether be. Should he have continued to see the world as Woollett saw it, or should he have shared the new vision his encounters with Chad and Paris suggested?

We have seen that the outward and inward aspects of moral sensitivity lead us to reflect in this way. Strether's encounter with Chad had enlarged him. He had learned that the perspective of Woollett is not the only one. And as Strether reflected, so he acquired greater moral sensitivity. He came to believe that moral possibilities were better realized in the worldlier vision that Chad had acquired than by the older one first Chad and now he had left behind. Woollett constricted, it functioned by exclusion, it curtailed imagination and growth; the new view afforded a more generous vision, it encouraged a liberality of spirit.

As Strether came to share this new moral vision, so the moral terms through which he appraised the world and Chad were realigned. There was no drastic change, only a subtle shift. Corruption, from Woollett's point of view; refinement, from the new perspective. Woollett expressed itself in terms of duty, responsibility, obligation, commercial success, and prudence, in brief, the Protestant Ethic. Chad's conduct seemed strange, and probably much worse, if seen in that light. Strether shifted his vision; he made room for the moral importance of the appreciation of nuances, manners, fineness of perception, tolerance of idiosyncrasies, the celebration of individual differences, and the enjoyment of mainly aesthetic pleasures. He had not abandoned the language of duty, but relegated it to a lesser place. Strether remained an intelligent, shrewd, and morally fastidious person. But these qualities came to be exercised in the framework of an altered vision.

From both old and new visions, judgments and actions followed. In the eyes of Woollett, Chad was blameworthy, he ought to be made to go home, and Strether's duty was to use his influence to that end. From the new perspective, Chad was praiseworthy, he ought to stay, and Strether's duty was to help him to do so. To see this as a conflict of unpleasant choices, a zero-sum game, as our pundits would call it, is to be blind to the background visions and moral terms from which the judgments and actions follow with such inevitability.

Speaking negatively, the recognition of the role moral sensitivity plays should alert us to the error of seeing choice and action as central to morality. Speaking positively, it reveals yet another requirement of the attempt to live good lives. Strether was creating a better self. Growth in the outward and inward dimensions of moral sensitivity is crucial to this, for improving ourselves is possible only by contrasting our moral vision and the terms in which it is couched with other visions and other ways of expressing them.

This should be qualified in three ways. First, as James told it, Strether was transformed by changing his old view. However, moral growth need not have this result. We may be strengthened in our old view as a result of contrasting it with alternatives. Moral sensitivity is needed not to change ourselves, but to remain open to the possibility of doing so, if it is warranted.

Second, the changes we bring about in ourselves may be for the worse. Moral sensitivity can be misused. It is by no means clear, for instance, that if we leave behind James's point of view, then Strether was indeed made better by exchanging the forthrightness of Woollett for the aestheticism of Paris. However, our concern here is not with judging him, but with understanding how we can achieve self-direction.

Third, it would be a bad misunderstanding to represent Strether as having faced a choice between two conflicting visions and the moral terms suited to them. To think so is to resurrect the error I have been criticizing for placing choice at the foundation of morality. The transformation of Strether through heightened moral sensitivity depended on the discovery of new moral possibilities. But they may be new in two ways. One is the kind of novelty that, for instance, Kantians may find in Homeric morality. It is a radically different alternative. The other is to discover hitherto unknown possibilities in our own view. In this way, Christians may come to a better understanding of humility by appreciating that it does not involve public self-denigration, but realizing, privately perhaps, the insignificance of one's concerns when viewed in a cosmic context.

Now Strether's discovery was of the second kind. He did not face a choice between refinement and corruption. He discovered that his previous understanding of what these idioms expressed was shallow. He did not choose his new deeper understanding; he was open and it came, because he reflected on the complexities inherent in the moral tradition which was already his own. His discovery was not like a tone-deaf person suddenly acquiring an appreciation of music. Rather, it was like a musically inclined person coming to appreciate through a lot of listening the pattern of a difficult composition.

Moral Sensitivity and Self-Direction

In stressing the importance of moral sensitivity to self-direction, and thus to good lives, I have been arguing against the mistaken emphasis on choice in much contemporary thinking about morality. Self-direction is not decisiveness in making choices; nor is morality primarily about choices. I have been arguing for a deeper view. According to it, before the question of choice can arise, we must form some understanding of the moral situations we face. Our choices are normally straightforward consequences of the understanding we have reached. So one task of self-direction, and one primary concern of morality, is to arrive at an accurate understanding. This understanding is an interplay between our moral tradition and our individual characters and circumstances. The tradition provides the moral vocabulary in terms of which our understanding must be expressed. But we must grow in our appreciation of the outward and inward significance of the moral terms at our disposal, if we are to go beyond the simple-minded matching of the conventions we have been taught and the situations we encounter. Growth in our appreciation of moral possibilities, limitations, and complexities determines the accuracy of our understanding. Moral sensitivity is a virtue of self-direction, because it is toward it that this kind of growth aims. The more sensitive we are, the more accurate will be our understanding. However, no matter how good or bad our understanding is, it exerts a decisive influence on the choices we come to make.

Moral sensitivity guides self-direction in two ways. First, by helping us toward seeing moral situations accurately. Second, by being instrumental in forming our characters. For the significance of how we understand moral situations is not merely the immediate choices we make, but also the formation of habits to see moral situations in terms of some particular possibilities and not others. The primary purpose of self-direction is not to make those choices that the person we aspire to be would make. Rather, its primary purpose is to make us into the person we aspire to be, so that we naturally make the choices such a person would make. And we become what we aspire to be by cultivating our moral understanding; moral sensitivity is what enables us to do so.

9

Wisdom

A First Approximation

Wisdom is like love, intelligence, and decency in that it is a good thing to have and the more we have of it the better we are. The opposite of wisdom is foolishness, universally recognized to be a defect. Wisdom is a virtue intimately connected with self-direction. The more wisdom we have the more likely it is that we shall succeed in living good lives. And the contrary, of course, is also true: the more foolish we are, the less likely we are to realize our aspirations. The possession of wisdom shows itself in reliable, sound, reasonable, in a word, good judgment; through it, we bring our knowledge to bear on our actions. Thus to understand wisdom, we have to understand its connection with knowledge, action, and judgment.

As a preliminary illustration, I shall borrow a list of people who had more wisdom than their aptly contrasted counterparts.

In the gallery here proposed there will be a new arrangement of portraits. . . . Among men of faith we shall find Luther and Knox occupying less space, and Emerson . . . rather more. Among literary folk we shall find ourselves in the tradition of Sophocles and Goethe and Arnold and Eliot rather than that of Baudelaire and Swinburne and Verlaine; and we shall give George Eliot a re-reading before dismissing her for George Sand. Among philosophers we shall not choose rationalists only; for some rationalists, like Tom Paine, have lacked the rational temper, while some empiricists, like Hume, have had it. Plato will be there, and St. Thomas, and Spinoza, and Butler, and . . . Henry Sidgwick. There will be open spaces where Rousseau, Schopenhauer, and Nietzsche once hung, and Kierkegaard will be packed and crated for permanent storage.[1]

Let us now explore what qualifies people for a place in this illustrious company.

Wisdom and Knowledge

To understand wisdom, we have to understand what kind of knowledge is connected with it. I shall approach this by considering Tolstoy's Ivan Ilyich who lacked it.[2] Ivan Ilyich was "a capable, cheerful, good-natured and sociable fellow, though strict in the performance of what he considered as his duty; and he considered as his duty whatever was so considered by those in authority over him." He spent his life as an official "smoothly, pleasantly and correctly." But he had a recurrent pain, and it grew worse.

> Suddenly he felt the old familiar, dull, gnawing pain, the same obstinate, steady, serious pain. . . . His heart sank, his brain felt dazed. . . . A cold chill came over him, his breathing ceased, and he heard only the throbbing of his heart. . . . Ivan Ilyich saw that he was dying, and he was in continual despair. In the depth of his heart he knew he was dying but, so far from growing used to the idea, he simply did not and could not grasp it. The example of a syllogism which he had learned in Kiezewetter's Logic: "Caius is a man, men are mortal, therefore Caius is mortal," had seemed to him all his life to be true as applied to Caius . . . Caius was certainly mortal, and it was right for him to die; but for me, little Vanya, Ivan Ilyich, with all my thoughts and emotions—it is a different matter altogether. It cannot be that I ought to die. That would be too terrible.

There is a sense in which Ivan Ilyich knew that he will die, but in another, he did not know.

The kind of knowledge relevant to wisdom is what Ivan Ilyich did not have his death. What did he lack? Well, it was not information; the trouble was not his ignorance of actuarial statistics. The knowledge necessary for wisdom is not descriptive. Nor is it knowing how to do some particular task; Ivan Ilyich did not lack cleverness, skill, or expertise. He had the worldliness needed to get along in life well, but worldliness is not enough. To be good at finding means to one's ends is useless, and may actually be harmful, if the ends themselves are not good.

The beginning of the answer is that the knowledge involved in wisdom concerns means to good ends or ideals. The knowledge of means is relatively simple. It comes to knowing what actions to perform, provided we know that our ideals are good. The complicated matter is knowledge of good ideals. What kind of knowledge is this?

It is a kind of interpretive knowledge. In descriptive knowledge

we know facts; in interpretive knowledge we know the significance of the descriptively known facts. To know that the house
burned down, because faulty wiring caused a short circuit and the
resulting sparks ignited the dry wood ceiling, is to have descriptive
knowledge. To know that we should have realized the danger,
taken preventive measures, had not done so, and we were, therefore, negligent, is to have interpretive knowledge. Agreement in
matters of descriptive knowledge is compatible with disagreement
in matters of interpretive knowledge. In fact, there can be genuine dispute about interpretation only if there is agreement about
the relevant description. History, literary criticism, medical diag-
nosis, jurisprudence, and the formulation of military, diplomatic,
or political strategy are some of the domains in which interpretive
knowledge is important.

The interpretive knowledge involved in wisdom is concerned
with three matters. The first is the "massive central core of human
thinking which has no history—or none in recorded histories of
thought; these are the categories and concepts which, in their
most fundamental character, change not at all. Obviously, these
are not the specialities of the most refined thinking. They are the
commonplaces of the least refined thinking; and yet the indispensable core of the conceptual equipment of the most sophisti-
cated human beings."[3] These "commonplaces of the least refined
thinking" are basic beliefs about human experience. They concern
the physiological, psychological, and social conditions of human
welfare discussed in chapter 2. They set limits to human possibility; individual variations and differences occur within these
limits. Basic beliefs are universal: Every sane, normal, and mature
person is committed to them. But this commitment does not entail
consciousness. We are committed to basic beliefs in the sense that
we think and act as if they were true. If challenged, we may
express them or affirm our commitment to them, but these beliefs
are so obvious that we usually go through life without having any
need or opportunity to testify to our acceptance of them.

The reason for the universality of basic beliefs is that they are
unavoidable. We have no choice about holding them. They do not
depend on persuasion, on gathering evidence, or on getting from
a state of neutrality to a state of commitment. Willingness plays no
role in our coming to accept them. We can certainly say, for
instance, that we do not believe that we have bodies. But saying is
not disbelieving, for our actions betray our continued commitment to the belief. And other things we say, to our physicians, for
instance, clearly contradict our denials.

Basic beliefs are universal and unavoidable, because, as we have seen, they are based on human nature. It is simply a fact about us that we perceive in certain sense modalities; that we have certain mental capacities; that we are capable of certain kinds of interaction with other people; and that these interactions must involve cooperation, communication, some device for resolving conflicts, and so on. Thus the interpretive knowledge involved in wisdom is supplied one set of its yet-to-be interpreted facts by basic beliefs. They are the products of the most elementary form of descriptive knowledge. These facts are believed to hold by all mature and normal human beings, and we believe them simply because we are human. Although in this domain "there are no new truths to be discovered, there are old truths to be rediscovered."[4] One of the tasks of the interpretive knowledge involved in wisdom is the rediscovery, when needed, of these old truths.

The second task of interpretive knowledge is the recognition of the required and variable conventions of our moral tradition. This is knowledge of the limits our moral tradition prohibits transgressing; of the appropriate employment of the moral vocabulary; of the rules that guide casual impersonal dealings; of the rights and duties of various roles, offices, and positions; of the differences between the obligatory and the supererogatory, of the moral and the nonmoral; of the public and the private, and so on. Some of these involve controversial questions, because in a moral tradition there is bound to be change and disagreement. But if the required conventions do indeed articulate universal and unavoidable requirements of human welfare, then the controversies cannot reasonably concern them. Part of wisdom is to know which conventions are required and which are variable; and to know that what makes them so is the presence or absence of a connection with the basic requirements of human welfare.

The third task of interpretive knowledge is to connect basic beliefs and the conventions of the moral tradition with our characters and circumstances. This requires going beyond the descriptive knowledge everybody has, and even beyond the interpretive knowledge of the significance of basic beliefs and conventions. Wisdom also requires us to see the past, present, and future events of our own lives in the light of the significance of basic beliefs and conventions. It is to strike and maintain a balance between the requirements of our individuality, on the one hand, and those of our tradition and common humanity, on the other. This is the difficult task of simultaneously cultivating the respects

in which we differ from others and controlling them in the light
of traditional and human limitations. Success in this endeavor
depends both on the possession of the other three virtues of self-
direction and on our ideals. For unless we had self-control, we
could not guide our conduct in the light of human, traditional,
and individual possibilities as represented by our ideals, and the
corresponding limitations on them. If we had no self-knowledge,
we would not know how to control our conduct, because we would
not know what our individual ideals and limitations were. And if
we had no moral sensitivity, we would not know which of our
individual and traditional possibilities conform to the ideals of our
conceptions of good lives. So, in the interpretive knowledge
wisdom requires all virtues of self-direction play a role.

Ivan Ilyich lacked this knowledge. He despaired as he was
dying, because he realized that he lacked it.

> His mental sufferings were due to the fact that in the night . . . the
> thought had suddenly come into his head: "What if in reality my
> whole life has been wrong?" It occurred to him that what had ap-
> peared utterly impossible before—that he had not lived his life as he
> should have done—might after all be true. . . . "But if that is so,' he
> said to himself, 'and I am leaving this life with the consciousness that I
> have lost all that was given to me and there's no putting it right—what
> then?'

Well, then his life had been wasted, because he failed to realize
that death sets a limit to it, and so he must find the things
important to him, and not waste time with trifles. The significance
of death is not only that it puts an end to our projects, but also that
these projects should be selected and pursued in the light of the
knowledge that this will happen. And this, Ivan Ilyich did not do.

Death is only one example of the conditions we must take into
account. Another is the changing seasons of life. Youth, maturity,
and old age set standards of appropriateness by altering physiological and psychological capacities. If our ideals fit one of these
phases only, we are bound to be badly guided by them when the
inevitable changes occur, bringing in their wake the inappropriateness of the ideals. And then there is the unavoidable
tension between balancing the short against the long-term significance of satisfying or frustrating wants. If we live only in the
present, our future will be bad; but if we care about the future
only, our lives will be without satisfaction, for the future is always

ahead. Ideals, therefore, must balance present satisfactions and hopes for the future; otherwise we are bound to deprive ourselves of the satisfactions we hope to have.

What wise people know, therefore, is what to put in the balance and how to maintain it, so that, given the human situation, they are likely to live good lives. This knowledge is within everyone's reach. But it is difficult to achieve, because it takes self-control, enabling us to modify our wants in accordance with our ideals; self-knowledge, for knowing what our wants and ideals are; moral sensitivity, for appreciating what life according to various ideals would be like. Speaking popularly, we can say of those who have all this that they know what's what; and speaking to echo Arnold's homage to Sophocles, we can say that they see life steadily and see it as a whole.

Wisdom and Action

Recognizing the significance of the limitations and possibilities inherent in human nature, moral tradition, and our characters is only part of wisdom. Wisdom ought also to show in the conduct of those who have it. But it is not clear how it shows. Contrast courage with wisdom. We can tell that people are courageous if they habitually act courageously in the appropriate circumstances. But what actions give evidence of wisdom? If we look for examples, we are liable to be misled. If people are reputed to have acted wisely, we expect them to have acted carefully, cautiously, judiciously. And while, of course, it is usually good to act in these ways, what stands revealed is prudence, not wisdom. The reference of *wise* in wise action is not straightforwardly connected with wisdom. There is a difficulty here and we can find our way out of it by reflecting on what Aristotle said about wisdom.

Aristotle distinguished between theoretical and practical wisdom.[5] Theoretical wisdom is an intellectual matter having primarily to do with knowledge. Practical wisdom is mainly action-guiding, and although it too involves knowledge, it is not the same as the kind involved in theoretical wisdom. The knowledge required for theoretical wisdom is metaphysical: It is of first principles, of fundamental truths about reality. On the other hand, the knowledge involved in practical wisdom is of means to ends.

So what I mean by wisdom is not quite Aristotle's theoretical wisdom, nor is it exactly his practical wisdom. It is not theoretical wisdom, because I think of wisdom as action-guiding and not involving metaphysical knowledge. The reason for denying that wisdom involves metaphysical knowledge is that the latter, if it exists, is esoteric, accessible only to a very few, while wisdom can be possessed by anyone willing to make the arduous effort to gain it—an effort different from the one required for becoming a philosopher.

The reason for not identifying practical wisdom with wisdom is that wisdom involves knowledge of reasonable ideals, not merely of means to achieving them. Thus, wisdom can contribute more to living good lives than the prudence of practically wise people does. This can be seen in Ivan Ilyich's life; he, or someone like him, had prudence and yet conspicuously lacked wisdom. So wisdom is not the same as Aristotle's theoretical or practical wisdom.

There is yet another ancient conception of wisdom from which I want to dissociate my account: the Socratic. The wisdom of Socrates consisted in realizing his own ignorance. Many of the early dialogues can be read as warning of the harm involved in the failure to realize that we lack metaphysical knowledge; Socrates, of course, did not claim to have had it. He claimed, as I understand him, that the extent to which we have it, is the extent to which we can live good lives. Socrates might have explained his intentions to Aristotle as an attempt to demonstrate how far short of wisdom do Aristotle's yet to be described practically wise people fall. The wisdom of Socrates is negative.

Now as I think of wisdom it involves knowing something positive. For to realize the significance of human nature, moral tradition, and our individuality for living good lives is to know something where ignorance is costly. I also think of wisdom as partly theoretical, although what makes it so is not metaphysical knowledge, and partly practical, for wisdom *is* action-guiding. We shall understand better how wisdom is action-guiding, if we reflect further on the knowledge involved in it.

There are two traditions of thinking about this knowledge. One claims the allegiance of Plato, Aquinas, Descartes, and their disciples.[6] The other has the support of Protagoras and Montaigne, and it has achieved its first formulation by the insufficiently appreciated Charron in *De la Sagesse*. "Augustine's rethinking of the meaning of wisdom illustrates [the two traditions]. . . . [H]e alters its meaning by splitting it into two parts, distinguishing the knowledge of divine things from human things and limiting the object of wisdom to the divine. Knowledge of human things is *scientia*. Wisdom is . . . *sapientia* . . . an intellectual cognition of eternal things."[7]

Both traditions think of the knowledge involved in wisdom as providing a perspective on the human situation. For the first, metaphysical, tradition, the perspective is *sub specie aeternitatis;* it views human affairs from the perspective of eternal things, God, or the unchanging rational order of reality. For the second, humanistic, tradition, the perspective is *sub specie humanitatis;* a view of the human situation from the vantage point of humanity. For the first, the possession of wisdom consists in understanding and willing the rational order of reality. For the second, wisdom is to arrange human affairs for the benefit of humanity in the midst of an indifferent reality. The distinction between the two traditions is not absolute. The metaphysical view is compatible with love of humanity; nevertheless, this love is secondary, and it must be informed by knowledge of eternal things. Similarly, the humanistic view is not indifferent to impersonal knowledge of reality; indeed, science is one of the glories of this tradition. All the same, it insists that the human point of view is unavoidable for humans. It should not go as far as the mistaken Protagorean relativism believing that man is the measure of all things, but it should recognize that we are the measurers of all things.[8]

My understanding of wisdom is humanistic. The theoretical aspect of it is knowledge *sub specie humanitatis*. More specifically, it is interpretive knowledge of the human significance of the natural, traditional, and individual limitations and possibilities for living good lives. How, then, is wisdom, thus understood, action-guiding?

It is action-guiding negatively: by issuing warnings of what not to do if we want to have good lives.[9] Wisdom is corrective. It reminds the unwise of the relevance their own descriptive knowledge has for their pursuits. The proper occasions for such reminders are those frequent lapses in which we are attracted by ideals whose achievement is impossible due to human or personal limitations. Wisdom guides action in two ways: by differentiating between what is possible and impossible for anyone, and by drawing the same distinction for us, in our particular context. Wisdom licenses the possible and warns against the impossible. It identifies both the ideals to which we may reasonably commit ourselves in pursuit of good lives and ideals incompatible with them.

Ivan Ilyich lived a foolish life, because he lacked the corrective of wisdom. He knew, descriptively, that he will die, but he did not realize the limitations this imposed on him. The lack of realization allowed him to be preoccupied with trivial pursuits and he failed to concentrate his attention on finding out what was important in his life. And so Ivan Ilyich wasted his life, but at the end he became tragic. The tragedy was that by the time he came to see his life steadily and see it as a whole, it was too late to do anything about it. (Tolstoy intimates otherwise, but I find this quite unconvincing.) Ivan Ilyich is emblematic of the human situation, because his case shows that we do not get a second chance to put right the shortcomings of a wasted live. Wisdom is corrective, because it guards against this happening by reminding us of what is significant and trivial in our lives.

For Ivan Ilyich to have been wise would, among other things, have been to realize the significance of the Caius-syllogism before he was dying. If he had realized it, it would have affected his life by altering his commitments to ideals. It would have forced him to think about his priorities in view of the limitations mortality forces on our projects. Mortality is only one of the commonplaces of whose significance wisdom is a reminder. Other limitations are imposed by other aspects of human nature, our moral tradition, and our individual situation. To be wise is to be alive to these limitations on self-direction, and to be foolish is to be blind to them.

Thinking of wisdom as corrective runs the risk of what I shall call the *Polonius-syndrome*. Most characters in *Hamlet* are not what they seem and Polonius is one of them. He seems like a foolish old man, and yet he speak what are perhaps the wisest lines in the play when he advises Laertes about how he should live (act 1, scene 3). In reciting to his respectful but impatient son these precepts, Polonius stands in a long tradition of wisdom-literature. All the major religions have texts encapsulating pieces of advice; and folk-wisdom, in the form of proverbs, is full of them. Yet they are frequently embarrassing by being nothing but clichés. The reason why Polonius seems foolish in that scene is that he appears to be mouthing platitudes. To avoid the Polonius-syndrome, we must ask: how are the reminders offered by wise people different from platitudes?

The same sentence can be a wise reminder and a platitude. What distinguishes them is the spirit in which they are offered. *I shall die* was a platitude in Ivan Ilyich's mouth before he was actually dying; and if he had recovered and gone on living, but with an appreciation of his mortality, then *I shall die* would have become a wise reminder. Similarly, Polonius said: "to thine own self be true . . ." and so on. Whether we take this as a sign of wisdom depends on whether Polonius was repeating the tedious message his father gave him on a no less awkward occasion, or whether Polonius was giving the hard-earned results of his own reflections. We have to know about Polonius to decide how to take what he said. What transforms a platitude into a wise reminder is the utterer's recognition that it expresses an enduring truth about the human situation.

It may be asked, however, what point there could be to wise reminders. To the foolish, they will seem fatuous, and for the wise they will be gilding the lily. The answer is that these reminders are likely to find fertile soil in the very large majority that is neither foolish nor wise. Most of us are a mixture of some degree of the two. In cool moments, we see wisdom as a good thing and foolishness as bad, because we want to have the good lives to which wisdom contributes and from which foolishness detracts. We cannot be given interpretive knowledge of the significance of these reminders; we must come to the realization alone. But we can be offered, by ourselves or by others, the reminders whose significance we need to realize. This gives point to expressing the fruits of wisdom.

Wisdom and Good Judgment

We have seen that the knowledge involved in wisdom is interpretive and action-guiding. Its objects are ideals and the means to them. The means are actions whose performance is called for by commitments to ideals of good lives. Wisdom guides these commitments by eliminating ideals whose pursuit goes counter to human, traditional, and individual limitations and possibilities. The sign of wisdom is good judgment, and that is what we need now to discuss.

Since wisdom is corrective, it is exercised only when correction is needed, and that happens when things do not go smoothly. Therefore, the context in which the sign of wisdom, good judgment, is to be sought is where we must make decisions about hard cases. To understand hard cases, consider first an easy one. Take a young man, unencumbered by family obligations, who possesses considerable talent as a painter; he knows it, he passionately wants to be a painter, and he has imposed on himself the hard discipline required for the development of technique. But life is not easy for him, because he is poor. Suppose, then, that he is offered a lucrative but time-consuming teaching job. His decision is easy: he should not accept it. Continuing with the hard work is far more important for him than easing his poverty. Wisdom or good judgment are hardly engaged here, for his course of action is clearly indicated by his ideal and commitments.

Hard cases occur when a decision is called for and it is unclear what ideals should guide us. The unclarity is not due to the absence of ideals, but to jurisdictional conflict among them. We do not know which ideal has provenance over the case, because it can reasonably be regarded as falling under several. It is in such cases that good judgment is needed and its possession shows. My example will be Leonard Woolf, as he viewed his life with Virginia Woolf.

Leonard was committed to political life: he was active both theoretically and practically. He was at work on his *magnum opus*, *Principia Politica*, and he was an indefatigable committeeman. Simultaneously, he and Virginia founded and ran a publishing house, and we know now that they made history by publishing important new works. And, then, there was Virginia, her writing, and her recurrent mental illness. She was vulnerable, difficult, and, of course, promised greatness. She lived in constant dread of another breakdown; she had to be guarded, cajoled, protected, and nursed when ill. She had a sharp intellect, great sensitivity, and a good deal of malice. She could not and should not have been deceived, pitied, or patronized. All in all, it was very difficult for Leonard. He had to contend with politics, publishing, and Virginia. His life involved one hard decision after another, and it is instructive how he coped.

His days were an endless succession of competing tasks, each with a claim on his allegiances, and his life would have been impossible if he had not had a way of judging their respective importance. But he did. Virginia came first, and politics and publishing had to compete for what was left. However, if this had been all, he would have transformed a hard case into an easy one. Most of the time Virginia was well and working, and she did not need him; while his writing and political activities made constant demands on him, as did the need to earn a living and serve his authors through publishing. So, although his priorities were clear, he continually had to monitor the competing tasks facing him to judge whether a particular occasion called for the assertion of the priorities. Was Virginia just in a bad mood or was it the first sign of depression? Did the call to an urgent meeting signal a political crisis or was it just the questionable judgment of the man charge?

Was his own work on *Principia Politica* in the same class as the predecessors' to whom the title alludes or was it a second-rate treatise not meriting a high priority?

Day in and day out he had to thread his way through these problems and make judgments about what he should do. That Virginia came first did not help in deciding whether a situation was a crisis, and if it was, how far he should go in neglecting his other commitments in the course of doing his share to resolve the crisis. What made it possible for Leonard to exercise good judgment was firm self-direction. He was able to weigh the short and long-range effects of particular actions, because he had self-control; he knew what he wanted and he knew the respective importance of his ideals, because he had self-knowledge; he was able to perceive accurately the moral situations he faced, because he had moral sensitivity.

A sceptic may grant that Leonard's judgment did indeed follow from the his self-direction and go on to ask why we should think that his judgment was good. The answer is to look at the judgments he made and consider whether contrary judgments would have been reasonable. If we do so, Leonard will prove to have been right and the sceptical doubts misplaced. Clearly, it was right for him to suppose that Virginia had the makings of a great writer, that to keep her going depended on him, and that it was more important than politics or publishing. The point, of course, is not that Virginia and her books were more important than politics and publishing, but that Leonard's contributions to Virginia's welfare were more important than his contributions to politics and publishing. Virginia's work will endure; *Principia Politica* will not; Leonard's committee work was not indispensable; and literature would have survived without the Hogarth Press. Leonard saw all this, he judged reasonably in the midst of a very difficult life, and that is why we are right to celebrate him.

Good judgment, then, is a sign of wisdom. Wisdom is to arrange our lives so as to satisfy wants that accord with our ideals, while paying due regard to human and traditional limitations and possibilities in general, and to our own limitations and possibilities in particular. My discussion of wisdom is intended to clarify how these limitations and possibilities can be known and how knowledge of them can guide action.

Wisdom, however, cannot be taught. Fools can learn to say all the things the wise say, and to say them on the same occasions. But the wise are prompted to say what they do, because they recognize the significance of limitations and possibilities, because they are guided in their actions by their significance, and because they are able to exercise good judgment in hard cases, while the fools are mouthing clichés. It takes time to acquire wisdom and we must do it by ourselves. The most the wise can do in the way of teaching others is to remind them of the facts whose significance they should realize, if they want to have good lives. But the realization must be theirs.

The acquisition of wisdom takes time, because to order our commitments requires appreciation of ideals, of the context in which they are pursued, and of limitations and possibilities. One who has attained these is self-directed. Growth in wisdom and self-direction go hand in hand. They are tasks for a lifetime, hence the connection between wisdom and old age. We can be old and foolish, but the wise are likely to be old, simply because such growth takes a long time.

Can wisdom be lost? Only in a peculiar sense. Once we achieve the knowledge necessary for wisdom, we have it, unless we are incapacitated. But wisdom is to be exercised in action and judgment. These have a context and the context may drastically change. If the change is cataclysmic, wisdom is lost in the sense that we do not know how to exercise it. The destruction of old cultures provides melancholic illustrations. The fall of Rome, the European takeover of China, the secularization of the West, and the election of Hitler may have seemed such cataclysmic events to a wise Roman, Chinese, Christian, or German. They have no more lost their wisdom than the last few surviving speakers of a language have lost their language, yet something has been lost.

Since wisdom is connected with old age and its exercise requires a nonrevolutionary context, the suspicion may grow that wisdom supports a reactionary attitude. This suspicion is misplaced. Wisdom curtails experiments in living only in the sense of warning against forseeable failure. It is true that those who lack it may feel wisdom only as the dead hand of tradition. But, then, they are unwise.

The Virtues of Self-Direction

My discussion of the virtues of self-direction is now complete. If we possess self-control, self-knowledge, moral sensitivity, and wisdom, then one requirement of good lives is met, for the virtues regulate the conduct of self-directed people. I need to say something now about how they regulate conduct.

Human conduct is initiated by multifarious wants whose object is to obtain satisfactions. Having wants and seeking their satisfaction is a natural process. In the course of evolution, this natural process has become complicated. The wants are not only physiological, but also psychological, social, aesthetic, moral, and intellectual; not only immediate, but also long-term; not all are beneficial to satisfy or harmful to frustrate; not all concern ourselves; not all are compatible; not all can be satisfied. Satisfactions are similarly complicated, because the same wants frequently have many different satisfactions; it is unclear what may satisfy some wants; the satisfactions of wants compete with each other both synchronically and diachronically; and we are frequently mistaken about something being a satisfaction. For many wants and their satisfactions, the simple connection represented by an itch and a scratch has disappeared. This has advantages and disadvantages.

By far the greatest advantage is that we have been able to assume some control over the complex system into which nature has made us. Provided the wants prompted by the basic requirements of human nature are satisfied, there is some free play about the rest. This is made possible by there being more wants than we can satisfy and more satisfactions than we can seek. So we can take control of ourselves by selecting the wants to be satisfied and the satisfactions to be sought. True, the wants and satisfactions still come from our nature, but they come in such abundance, and so much less life-threateningly, that we can exercise considerable discretion in selecting among them. Self-direction is the process whereby this discretion is exercised. And the virtues of self-direction are something like the forms the process takes. The practical question facing us about the conduct of our lives is what we should do about our manifold wants and the multitude of potential satisfactions, if we want our lives to be good. We are forced to select among our wants and satisfactions, and the virtues make our selections as reasonable as possible in the circumstances.

Through self-control, we can consciously and deliberately alter some of our own psychological states and thereby alter the causal process that results in our decision to do or not to do something. Through self-knowledge, we become aware of our wants, of their importance, and of the ideals in the light of which their importance is judged. Through moral sensitivity, we acquire understanding of the personal significance of the moral vocabulary of our tradition. And through wisdom we recognize the limitations and possibilities set by human nature, our moral tradition, and our characters and circumstances.

Self-direction is a cognitive process. It results in actions aimed at satisfying or frustrating our wants. The actions follow from the complex process of judging the wants in the light of our commitments to ideals. The judgment depends on whether the satisfaction of the wants would conform to or violate our commitments. And the justification of the judgment is that strengthening or weakening the dispositions instantiated by the contemplated actions would bring us closer to our ideals. Of course, this justification requires that the ideals themselves be justified, but we have seen in chapter 5 how that is done.

Self-direction is a conscious process. For we must be aware of our wants, commitments, and ideals in order to be able to monitor them. Consciousness is necessary, because this monitoring is difficult. It requires agility to move from one level of surveying ourselves to another. On the simplest level, we have wants. Some of them are insistent enough, so there is no special difficulty in being aware of them. But not all wants speak with a loud voice; some are inarticulate; some concern the distant future; some have disturbing emotional undercurrents; some are confused longings for impossible goals, like wishing the past to be different, or undoing present unpleasantness in fantasy, or hoping for wildly unrealistic future developments. Consciousness is needed, because we must not only know the wants we have but also whether to satisfy the ones we know we have. And that knowledge comes from being clear about our commitments and applying them to wants. Wants are judged in the light of commitments and they can be so judged only if we are conscious of them. So if they are to be effective in guiding the satisfaction of wants, we must keep our ideals before our minds as well.

Self-direction involves deliberate efforts, because it erects a barrier between what we recognize as a want and its satisfaction. The temptation to favor present over future self is constant. And there is much that can be said for giving in to it. Commitments to ideals rarely crumble because of single violations; dispositions are not made or broken by isolated episodes; if long-term goals are always preferred to immediate satisfaction, then there will be no satisfaction at all; if we are always suspicious of our wants, we shall be hopelessly divided within ourselves and be reduced to neurotic impotence or to overcivilized, moralistic, dithering inaction.

But these doubts are misplaced. They derive from the failure to realize that in self-direction we weigh the conflicting claims of our own wants; we are not frustrating our wants, but planning the most reasonable way of satisfying them. Doing that frequently involves frustration, but frustration is the unavoidable by-product, not the goal, of the process. And the alternative to this kind of frustration is not satisfaction, but more frustration.

Self-direction is inner-directed. This can be taken to mean that it is motivated by considerations having to do with our inner lies and also that its objects are our inner lives. I mean by inner-directedness both the motivation and the object. Self-direction is motivated by our concern with being in charge of our own lives. The natural and traditional contexts in which we live influence, but do not determine this process. They influence it by limiting it. Human nature and moral tradition provide the possibilities among which we can choose, and the options we have for realizing them. The motivation for self-direction is the satisfaction of our wants within the constraints imposed by these external factors. Its aim is to answer the question of what we should to with ourselves within the natural and traditional limits imposed on us. And the objects toward which we are directed are ourselves, because we shall answer this question by judging our wants in the light of our ideals.

Self-direction is not only a cognitive process, but also an emotive and imaginative one. The good lives we seek through it are meant to be emotionally satisfying, for we want to like our lives, be pleased by them, and have good feelings about how they are unfolding, and before we can reasonably embark on the attempt to make a life our own, we must imagine what it would be like to achieve it. The emotive and imaginative components of self-direction are not just piecemeal attitudes toward particular aspects of our lives, but also responses to the whole pattern of them. The virtues are enlisted in the establishment of these patterns, the ideals are components of them, and the system of our commitments determine their structure.

10

Good Lives and Happiness

Introduction

The central idea I have been developing is that good lives depend on doing what we reasonably want to do. This depends on self-direction, and self-direction, in turn, requires the development of the four virtues and commitment to appropriate ideals. Success in this endeavor, however, is not sufficient for good lives, because circumstances over which we have no control may prevent us from achieving them. But if we are self-directed and if our circumstances are favorable, then we shall find our lives good, because we are succeeding in satisfying our important wants.

The goodness of lives is a matter of degree, because the satisfactions we achieve can be more or less. Insofar as the hoped for satisfactions depend on us, we can make our lives better by improving our self-direction. But since satisfactions also depend on circumstances we cannot influence, how good our lives are is, to some extent, a matter of luck. It is part of wisdom to distinguish between what we can and cannot alter, and to concentrate self-direction on the domain where we may prevail.

Assume that we find our lives good. There are two large questions remaining. One is whether finding them so is a guarantee that they are so. I shall argue that our favorable judgment is necessary but not sufficient to guarantee the goodness of our lives. How our judgment should be strengthened by appealing to independent grounds is the topic of the final chapter. The other outstanding question is whether the lives we find good are also happy. I shall consider this now. It will soon become obvious that these two questions are closely connected.

A Simple View of Happiness

Of the many senses of happiness, I shall concentrate on one: the attitude we may have toward our whole lives. I shall begin with a simple view of this kind of happiness and then go on to refine it by noticing the complexities implicit in it. There are striking similarities between happy and good lives. The similarities, however, do not go far enough to permit their identification. To understand their connection, therefore, we have to note both the respects in which they are alike and those in which they differ.

According to the simple view,[1] if we are happy, we are satisfied with our lives. We should like them to continue in the same way. If asked, we would say that things are going well for us. Our most important wants are being satisfied. We are doing and having most of what we really want. We frequently experience joy, contentment, and pleasure. We are not divided about our lives, for, on the whole, they are as we want them to be. We are not often beset by fundamental inner conflicts. We are not given to depression, anxiety, or frustration. We do not contemplate fundamental changes in the way we live: we have no serious regrets about the important decisions we have taken; nor are we lastingly resentful, envious, guilty, ashamed, or jealous.

Happiness has two aspects: one is an attitude, the other is a collection of episodes contributing to forming the attitude. The episodes are experiences of satisfaction derived from what we do and have. The attitude is satisfaction with our lives as a whole. What we have need not be material goods. They may be talents, personal relationships, the respect of others, worldly success, or a private sense of well-being. Nor should our activities be thought of merely as publicly observable conduct. Reflectiveness, aesthetic appreciation, feelingfulness, and quiet amusement are dispositions reflected in private activities, yet they are conducive to happiness.

The attitudinal aspect of happiness is more than a succession of satisfying episodes. For the attitude requires that the significance of the episodes be appraised in terms of our whole lives. This appraisal need not involve conscious reflection, although it frequently does. It may simply be an unspoken feeling of approval of our lives and a sense that particular episodes fit well into it. The episodes may be goals achieved, obstacles overcome, experiences enjoyed, or just the seamless continuation of the approved patterns of our lives.

Without many such episodes, however, the attitude cannot be reasonable. But the connection between satisfying episodes and an attitude of satisfaction with our lives is not simply that if we do and have what we want, then we are happy. It is certainly true that happiness is incompatible with complete frustration. However, it is a mistake to suppose that the satisfaction of our wants assures happiness.

To begin with, some wants are important and lasting, while others are trivial and transitory. Wanting the waiter to hurry up with my lunch is not in a class with Hamlet's passion. All of us can tolerate unsatisfied minor wants, and they only exceptionally stand in the way of happiness. So we must concentrate on people who have all they seriously want. But suppose that they seriously want only one thing; they pursue it single-mindedly, at the exclusion of everything else, and while they get it, their souls shrivel. Rich misers, successful avengers, and triumphant climbers of life's greasy poles often find themselves empty, once their obsessions are satisfied. Or people may want only what they do not have, and when they get it, like Don Juan, they no longer want it. Yet others are mistaken in thinking that what they want will satisfy them. The glittering sophistication of an inner circle may pale once the outsider is accepted. Having what we want, therefore, is no guarantee of happiness.

Nor should it be supposed that doing all that we seriously want leads to happiness. Of course, not being able to do anything we really want makes happiness impossible. But doing what we seriously want is not sufficient for it, because we may want to do something with the full realization that it will not make us happy. We may want to commit suicide; do our duty at great cost to ourselves; choose the happiness of our children, parents, or lovers over our own; or continue with a deadly routine out of fear, resignation, or lack of imagination. Moreover, it would be similarly mistaken to assume that doing all that we seriously want is necessary for happiness. For happy people can tolerate frustrated wants. The cost of happiness is frequently to leave some important wants unsatisfied. Life forces us to choose. Happiness is connected with the capacity to prevent frustration from spoiling what we have. So we must reject the simple view of happiness.

Happiness as Satisfaction with Our Lives

In place of the simple view, I offer the suggestion that happiness, like good lives, requires that we should be satisfied with many of the important things we do and have. Doing and having what we want figure as formal notions in this suggestion. The advantage of this is that we can say what happiness consists in without having to specify all the particular possessions and activities conducive to it. Happiness essentially involves satisfaction, but there is no particular satisfaction indispensable to happiness, nor a dissatisfaction inevitably prohibiting it.

The satisfaction of important wants involves the episodic aspect of happiness. Happiness, however, has an attitudinal aspect as well. This is also connected with satisfaction, but its objects are the overall patterns of our lives. The connection between these two aspects can be approached through the notion of importance. Happiness requires the satisfaction of many important wants. What they are depends on the hierarchy of our commitments; the importance of a want is determined by where the commitment to satisfying it stands in the hierarchy.

We should distinguish between specific and general wants and also between specific and general satisfactions.[2] A specific want is about doing or having some particular things; a general want is about having lives in which many of our important specific wants are satisfied. A specific satisfaction is obtained from the fulfillment of specific wants; general satisfaction consists in having satisfied the general want. Thus we have many specific wants and satisfactions, but only one general want and satisfaction.

Specific wants and satisfactions belong in the context of the episodic aspect of happiness. Their objects are particular activities and possessions. The general want and satisfaction occur in the context of the attitudinal aspect of happiness. Their objects are our complete lives. General satisfaction logically depends on specific satisfactions and the general want necessarily involves specific wants. The precise nature of their logical connection, however, cannot be established, for it is impossible to specify in general terms what particular wants, how many of them, with what frequency, and to what extent must be satisfied, so that we could reasonably judge that we are satisfied with our lives. The only justifiable general claim that can be made is that we can be happy only if our general want is satisfied.

This has important implications. First, we are extremely unlikely to have happy lives without having more or less clearly formed views about the forms our lives should take. If seekers of haphazard satisfactions can truly claim to have enjoyed a great many of them, they still cannot be said to have happy lives, for their satisfactions may be of unimportant wants or of only a few important wants. Wisdom teaches us that one condition of life is that we must select among satisfactions. The clearer we are about the intended forms of our lives, the more reasonable selection may contribute to our happiness; and similarly the less self-direction there is, the poorer are the chances of achieving happy lives. Therefore, happiness, like good lives, involves the reasonable pursuit of specific satisfactions. If human nature were otherwise, the control of reason would not be required. I am not denying that lack of self-direction is compatible with many episodic satisfactions; I am denying that these have more than the remotest chance of adding up to happy lives.

Episodic happiness is a temporary result of specific satisfactions. A demanding task well done, sexual gratification, the experience of a work of art, and the sight of cavorting puppies may produce it. Lasting happiness comes from the general satisfaction involving our complete lives. We cannot be lastingly happy, unless we are frequently episodically happy. But we can be episodically happy and yet not be lastingly happy, for specific satisfactions may not endure.

A further difference between episodic and lasting happiness is their asymmetry with respect to explanation. That certain kinds of activities or possessions make us episodically happy is just a fact about us. We are the sorts who take delight in puppies, but not in pigeons. If we inquire further, we are asking about the causal antecedents that have made us what we are. It is otherwise with being lastingly happy. If we are asked why our lives make us lastingly happy, in addition to causal antecedents, there are also reasons we can give. We can tell about our ideals, the forms our self-direction have taken, and the progress we have made in shaping ourselves. And when we encounter such reasons, we can argue about them. The explanation of why we are episodically happy about something is causal; the explanation of why we are lastingly happy with our lives involves both causes and reasons. Happy lives can be arrived at reasonably, partly because reasons can be weighed. So being lastingly happy is more than just frequently feeling happy; the additional element is self-direction.

Another implication is about pleasure and pain. We can put up with a great deal of pain and still have lastingly happy lives. In the first place, physical or psychological suffering may be episodic and such episodes may be outweighed by others in the long run. Furthermore, even if we are frequently in pain, we may enjoy lasting happiness, provided many of our important wants are satisfied.

The connection between happiness and pleasure, of course, informs the history of this subject. It is an obvious point that if pleasure is taken to mean all forms of satisfaction, then happiness is necessarily connected with it. But this is just a misleadingly expressed truism. On the other hand, if pleasure is regarded as a specific physical sensation, then it is clearly false that happiness is necessarily connected with it. For there are many forms of satisfaction—aesthetic appreciation, parental love, or being given our due—which have nothing to do with this physical sensation. A life without any pleasure, in this second sense, probably cannot be lastingly happy. But it is a mistake to suppose that the physical sensation of pleasure is part of every episode of specific satisfaction.[3]

Happiness comes in degrees. The extent to which we are happy depends, first of all, on the satisfaction of our important specific wants. These satisfactions are partly quantitative, having to do with number and frequency, and partly qualitative, depending on the intensity of specific satisfactions. But the degree to which we are happy also depends on the kind of specific wants we regard as important. We differ about this and so it is not to be expected that when different people are correctly described as being lastingly, as opposed to episodically, happy, then it is reasonable to make quantitative or qualitative comparisons between them. The cluster of specific satisfactions Falstaff, Saint Theresa, Disraeli, Picasso, and Montaigne regarded as important were different, to put it mildly. Each was happy to a degree, and even if we could ascertain that they were happy to the same degree—whatever the *same* could mean here—it would be fatuous to suppose that they were comparable. For lasting happiness is an attitude, and the objects of it, our lives, differ from person to person. I labor this point, because cruder forms of utilitarianism and decision theory rest on the supposition that a common measure can be found for comparing the extent to which different people approximate happiness.[4]

Reasonable people want to be as happy as possible. But this does not mean that all reasonable people want the same thing, nor that whatever they want is wanted by them unconditionally. Happiness differs from person to person, because specific wants and satisfactions differ. And the pursuit of happiness is not unconditional, because we may come to believe that our important specific wants are incompatible, harmful, or injurious to those we love; or that the requirements of our family, country, or profession take precedence over the satisfaction of our wants. So, while it is reasonable to want to be happy, this does not mean that happiness is the only or the most important aim reasonable people can have.

A fourth implication is that the nearly universally applauded activity: the pursuit of lasting happiness, is liable to serious misunderstanding. Lasting happiness cannot be pursued the way a

Nobel Prize, a political office, or the title of grandmaster of chess can be pursued. This kind of happiness involves an attitude, and we cannot pursue an attitude directly. We can pursue the object in whose presence the attitude is appropriate. In the case of lasting happiness, this object is the life we would find satisfactory. If it is achieved, then lasting happiness comes to us as a by-product. Therefore, the best policy we can follow in order to achieve lasting happiness is to forget all about it and try to honor the commitments our ideals dictate.[5] If we have selected our ideals well, and if we have acted on our commitments to them, we have done all we can toward achieving lasting happiness. And if our ideals are faulty, or if we lack the required virtues of self-direction, then, apart from improving our ideals or ourselves, there is nothing we can do to achieve lasting happiness.

We can say, then, that if we are satisfied with our lives, because we have successfully directed ourselves to satisfy our important wants in accordance with our ideals, and if we are fortunate in our circumstances, then we are likely to be lastingly happy.

Happiness and good lives both involve the satisfaction of many of our important specific wants. Since this depends on successful self-direction, happiness and good lives are alike in requiring that too. These considerable similarities, however, are not sufficient for identifying happy and good lives. The basic reason for this is that the satisfaction of wants, essential to good lives, need not involve episodes of feeling happy, necessary for happiness. The wants whose satisfaction we rationally seek may concern doing hard, unpleasant, altruistic, impersonal, dutiful, self-sacrificial, heroic, self-denying, and occasionally even self-destructive things. And none of these is usually conducive to feeling episodically happy.

Put more precisely, good lives are neither necessary nor sufficient for happiness. They are not necessary, because it is possible, although extremely unlikely, that we can be lastingly happy without self-direction. It is conceivable, for instance, that lastingly happy lives consist entirely of a long succession of pleasurable episodes that we enjoy without much reflection in an idyllic context. This possibility requires us to have no harmful wants; no conflict between our important wants; no serious weaknesses in our characters; no external obstacles to overcome; no need to defend ourselves against hostile or aggressive interference; and no political, social, or economic unrest in the society where we happen to live. But the existence of Paradise or the Garden of Eden, which this possibility requires, is a fiction. Some of us are no doubt more fortunate in our circumstances than others, but the human situation is that, in any case we can realistically entertain, the road to lasting happiness is through having good lives. Normally, although not necessarily, self-direction is a requirement for lasting happiness. And the more self-directed we are, other things being favorable, the more likely it is that we shall be lastingly happy.

Yet good lives are not sufficient for lasting happiness either, because they may take forms in which happiness is repudiated or regarded as unimportant. Mothers, nuns, and social reformers may consciously prefer the happiness of others to their own. They may do so out of love or because they feel that they have no right to either episodic or lasting happiness when multitudes live in abject misery. No doubt, the motivation for such a life of service may be flawed. Guilt, self-deception, a deep sense of personal inadequacy, or hope for reward in an afterlife may prompt it. But it can also be inspired by love and justice. In such cases, we conclude that our own happiness is less important than the happiness or the alleviation of the misery of others. Lives of this sort can surely be good and yet not happy.

Or take lives involving the exploration of the limits of human or individual possibilities. I am thinking of people like Marco Polo who, impelled by curiosity and adventure, went beyond the limits of the known world; and of arctic explorers, astronauts, test pilots, and stuntmen who risk their lives daily to test their capacity to function under extreme physical conditions. Adventure and risk are valued higher by such people than the pursuit of happiness. Yet it would be indefensible to claim that they cannot have good lives.

These examples show that good lives need not be lastingly happy, because successful self-direction and favorable external conditions do not guarantee it. Yet we seek lasting happiness. The best chance of achieving it is to live good lives by becoming self-directed.

Internal and External Views of Good Lives

Happiness requires that we should be satisfied with our lives, as we regard them overall. The source of happiness is that we are enjoying the satisfaction of many of our important specific wants. And, if we are fortunate enough to possess this general satisfaction, we also find our lives good. But is this sufficient? After all, finding our lives good involves a judgment, and judgments can be reasonable or unreasonable, appropriate or inappropriate, or justified or unjustified. Can we be mistaken in judging the goodness of our lives, or does the sincerity of our favorable judgment guarantee that the judgment is correct? The internal and external views give different answers to this question. I shall eventually argue that the correct answer is a combination of them, but my present purpose is to show the weaknesses of both views.[6]

According to the internal view, if we sincerely believe that our lives are good, because our important wants are being satisfied, then there is nothing further that can or needs to be said in the way of justification. The external view requires more. Sincere belief about the goodness of our lives is necessary but not sufficient for it being reasonable to regard our lives as good, because we may be mistaken. The external view calls for going beyond what we believe about our lives and ascertaining the correctness of our beliefs. Thus the external view rests on the possibility that this can be done, while the internal view depends on the repudiation of this possibility.

One traditional argument for the external view derives from the perfectionist interpretation of the naturalistic conception of human nature, as we have seen in chapter 2. Its fundamental idea is that given human nature, it is possible to formulate an ideal way of life, a summum bonum for all human beings. The goodness of a life, then, depends on how closely this ideal is being approximated. Perfectionists, like many Platonists, Aristotelians, Thomists, and Marxists, differ among themselves about what the canonical ideal is, but they agree that there is one. And they agree also that what makes the ideal they favor canonical is that it leads to the approximation of the summum bonum.

There is a metaphysical dimension to perfectionism. For underlying the belief that there is only one good life for human beings is the supposition that the good life depends on living in harmony with the scheme of things. Thus the explanation and justification of the ideal is that it alone expresses the correct view of the nature of reality and our place in it. It is a considerable embarrassment to perfectionists that they disagree in their metaphysics. But I shall put this problem to one side, for my objections to perfectionism are independent of the particular metaphysics its defenders favor and also of the particular interpretation of the summum bonum that goes with it. It is the very idea of there being a summum bonum that I reject.

One early formulation of perfectionism is Aristotle's. "For man

. . . the life according to reason is the best and pleasantest, since reason more than anything else *is* man. This life therefore is also the happiest."[7] A possible interpretation of this is that the summum bonum is the life according to reason; progress consists in approximating it and perfection is its attainment. Given the nature of reality, rational life is the only beneficial form of life for us.

The claim that we are perfectible assumes that human nature dictates a certain ideal toward which we naturally strive. But this ideal can be interpreted positively, to involve the pursuit of the summum bonum, or negatively, to prompt the avoidance of what is harmful for us. I think that the negative interpretation is correct. There are certain things that all human beings do naturally want to avoid, because they are harmful. These are the violation of the minimum conditions for living good lives set by the physiological, psychological, and social requirements of human welfare. Of course, we may be prepared to accept the violation of these requirements in exceptional circumstances. But this acceptance is highly unusual and calls for explanation. Normally we do strive to avoid being harmed in these ways, and doing so is dictated by human nature.

However, the avoidance of harm cannot be interpreted as perfecting ourselves. Harm avoided can do no more than guarantee that the pursuit of good lives can proceed unimpeded. If our lives are secure, if we are free from injury, pain, and incapacity, and if there is no undue restriction on satisfying our wants, there is still the all-important question of what we are going to do with ourselves. So the thesis of human perfectibility is necessarily connected with the positive interpretation, with there being a summum bonum. And the assumption on which it rests is that just as there are harmful things we naturally want to avoid, so also there are ideals we naturally pursue. The issue, then, is: are there ideals that all reasonable human beings always pursue and is this pursuit essential to good lives?

An affirmative answer requires showing what these ideals are. The most frequently offered candidate is happiness. As we have seen, the claim that all of us always pursue happiness becomes an old and mistaken thesis. The objection to it is not merely that there are a few counterexamples, but rather that human conduct routinely contradicts the generalization. There are many people who consciously and reasonably give up happiness for other ideals. They do it for social justice, like Orwell; or to pursue intellectual passion, like Nietzsche; or for a cause they believe in, like various freedom fighters; or to carry on with their art, like Van Gogh. Surely, many people spend their lives pursuing perfectly reasonable ideals whose achievement has very little to do with happiness. So it is a mistake to suppose that all human beings always pursue happiness.

But what about other ideals? Well, pleasure is not such an ideal, for puritans, fanatics, and ascetics repudiate it; power is renounced by many artists and scholars; romantics and fundamentalists of various sorts scorn reason; many think that beauty is a dispensable frivolity, wealth the root of all evil, the esteem of others worthless, and truth an illusion. We must conclude, I think, that while people do seek to realize ideals, ideals are so numerous and varied that none of them can be said to be a universal requirement for all good lives.

This version of the claim that humanity is perfectible would be true only if there were a fixed number of ideals whose pursuit would satisfy all of us. In contrast, we can seek good lives by being self-directed even if the number of ideals is indefinite. Self-direction is open-ended; the pursuit of perfection is not. Self-direction presupposes that while part of human nature is constant and universal, other parts can be and are being transformed. Thus self-direction commits one, negatively, to the rejection of the kind of perfectionism I have been criticizing, and positively, to a pluralistic view of ideals.

My view of good lives is that it is a requirement of human welfare that there be diversity within a moral tradition. It is a condition of good lives that a moral tradition should embody a multiplicity of equally important and yet irreducibly different ideals, conventions, and ways of life, and so it is a condition to exclude the idea of a summum bonum, the idea that there is a best, highest, or ideal way of life. Diversity within a moral tradition is not a necessary evil, produced perhaps by human blindness about the summum bonum, but a requirement of human welfare.

The fundamental reason for this is that if there were a summum bonum, human life would be instrumental to a predetermined end. The goodness of a life would be proportionate to the degree this end has been approximated, and evil would be deviation form it. But there is no such end. It would have to come from an external authority that ordained an ideal for us. No good reason exists for supposing that there is an external authority, and even less that it has provided a single ideal of a good life for all of humanity.

According to my view of good lives, common wants and capacities provide the starting point for all of us. The first steps we take beyond them are guided by the various moral conventions into which we are born. But good lives involve more than the satisfaction of common wants and conventional conduct. They involve a creative forging of an amalgam of some of our wants and capacities and of the conventions, ideals, and practices prevailing in our moral tradition. Good lives differ, because they essentially depend on going beyond the natural and conventional aspects of our lives that we share with others. This transcendence is an affirmation of individuality, an effort in self-creation.

None of this would be desirable if there were a summum bonum. For, then, trying to live good lives would require forcing ourselves to conform to the predetermined pattern that is the blueprint for all good lives. This would require the repression of individuality and the deliberate cultivation of just those aspects of our nature that we share with others and that conform to the blueprint.

However, the aspects of our nature that we share with others include benign and vicious characteristics, rational and irrational tendencies, the capacities for selfishness and altruism, stupidity and intelligence, and love and aggression. If good lives depended on the realization of common human potentialities, then perfectionism would involve us in the development of many irrational and immoral tendencies. From the fact that human nature potentially is in certain ways it does not follow that it ought to be in those ways. In fact, trying to live good lives must include repressing some human potentialities. The question of which parts of our complex nature we should curb or foster is crucially relevant to good lives, but it cannot be settled by reference to human nature, for it is our nature that prompts the question.

Defenders of the internal view see this problem clearly. Their position follows from what they take to be the impossibility of finding external grounds for believing that our lives are good. Human nature does not provide such grounds and there is no reason for supposing that transcendental grounds are available. According to them, the best policy for us is to make a decision about how we want to live. The decision is a leap in the dark; without it, we shall waste our lives; while taking it holds out the possibility of lives that we may find good. If our decisions led to such lives, they have been justified to the fullest extent possible. This justification, however, is internal, for it is based on how we ourselves regard our lives. To hope for more is an illusion. The internal view is held by emotivists, many egoists, voluntarists, and existentialists.

The central difficulty with the internal view is that it overlooks two crucial considerations; one about human nature, and the other about moral tradition. Defenders of the internal view are correct in supposing that we cannot infer from human nature what lives are good. What they fail to see is that we can infer from human nature what lives cannot be good. There are certain conditions all lives must meet, if they are to be reasonably regarded as good; these conditions follow from human nature. Meeting them does not guarantee good lives but failing to meet them guarantees bad lives. These conditions are independent of what anyone believes, because they are external constraints on all human lives.

The other consideration overlooked by defenders of the internal view is that human beings do not approach the task of self-direction anew. In trying to decide how we should live, we can learn from the examples of those who lived before us. There are many real and fictional lives recorded in our moral tradition. We may find some admirable and inspiring and we may try to shape our lives so as to approximate them. Therefore, our decisions about how we should live need not be leaps in the dark. They may be deeply reflective adoptions of traditional ideals. There is room for external justification here, because we can decide how well we approximate the ideals we have chosen, and also because the ideals themselves are capable of rational appraisal through their presuppositions.

Thus, as I shall argue in the next chapter, we can and should go beyond the internal view. The external view is needed, because we may be mistaken about the goodness of our lives. We may believe that we are satisfied with them and be wrong. Since satisfaction is something we all seek, it is in everyone's interest to eliminate errors. Hence, the external view is not an arbitrarily imposed requirement, but part of the care reasonable people will take to assure that they live as close to their ideals as possible.

The difficulties of the external and internal views set the stage for the alternative I propose to defend. In the next chapter, I shall argue for the possibility of external justification, and thus I oppose the internal view. But, in opposition to the external view, I shall sever the connection between external justification and the metaphysics that traditionally supported it.

11

Good Lives and Justification

The Insufficiency of Internal Justification

Human judgments are fallible, and there is no reason to suppose that judgments about the goodness of our own lives are exempt. If this is so, there must be some grounds on which the cognitive credentials of such judgments can be evaluated, for otherwise we could not rely on them. These grounds can be external or internal. External grounds require the possibility of appealing to some considerations independent of the lives being judged; internal grounds are features of the lives themselves. I have argued that the appeal to one traditional external ground, to the summum bonum, is unjustifiable. Yet I think there are external grounds. The purpose of this chapter is to show what they are and how the reasonableness of judgments about the goodness of our own lives can be established with reference to them.

As a first step, I shall argue that a purely internal justification is insufficient for deciding whether such judgments are reasonable. We may sincerely believe that our lives are good, on the ground that our important specific wants are being satisfied, and yet we may be mistaken. Now, of course, we do have a very special authority in deciding whether or not we are enjoying some specific satisfactions. There may be exceptional circumstances in which our authority can be justifiably overruled, but the case I intend to make does not depend on these. The possibility I want to concentrate on is that we may be mistaken in our judgments that the specific satisfactions we are enjoying actually add up to a good life. The mistake is not about specific satisfactions, but about the overall satisfaction with the totality of our lives.

The temporal perspective is crucial to this possibility. We can view our lives retrospectively, as a biographer may do. Or we may plan for the future and construct scenarios about how we should like our lives to go; this is the adolescent outlook. But I want to consider thinking about our lives midstream, the way most people think about them. And, by hypothesis, the lives we are thinking about in this manner have a well-ordered structure of commitments and we believe that through them our important specific wants are being satisfied. Thus we are mature, self-directed, and we sincerely believe that our lives are going well. Given this, how can we be mistaken about them?

We can be mistaken if due to inherent defects our lives cannot continue to yield the satisfactions they have been yielding. The reason why this type of mistake may occur is that the causes of potential dissatisfactions are obscured from us. We have no pressing reason to suspect their presence, because things are going well for us and the portents of such danger signals as there are may be minimized by the satisfactions we presently enjoy. There are countless ways in which we may come to make this kind of mistake, but I shall mention only four: hidden incoherence, unrecognized impoverishment, lack of realism, and the incapacity to adjust to foreseeable changes.

Hidden incoherence is due to commitments to conflicting ideals. This occurs when the attempt to approximate one ideal we hold is incompatible with the attempt to approximate another. And it is hidden, because the incompatibility has not yet become evident due to luck or lack of reflection. If we have a fierce commitment to independence, we shall not be long satisfied in a tightly organized institution requiring obedience, such as an army or a monastic order. Things may go well for us for a while, and we may reasonably believe that we are satisfied with our lives, but this cannot last. The satisfaction will eventually be destroyed.

Unrecognized impoverishment occurs when we are committed to a too meager set of ideals. If a life has no place in it for some love, beauty, imagination, discipline, and playfulness, to mention some examples, it is extremely unlikely to be satisfactory. Of course, we may still be satisfied with it. A slightly differently placed Robinson Crusoe, without Friday and liberation, may have lived out his life lacking personal relationships and love. It is conceivable that he may have come to terms with his solitary lot and have developed a kind of resigned equilibrium. He may have said to himself that, given his circumstances, he was satisfied with his life. The satisfaction, however, did not come from the presence of many good things in his life, but from having succeeded in making the most of what his misfortune left him. He could have readily specified what would make his life better.

However, having a meager set of ideals is a defect only if we could have a richer one and lack it. We want certain physical and psychological satisfactions; circumstances may stand in their way, and we can still make do. But if we ourselves create the circumstances in which we are deprived of satisfactions, then occurs the defect I am describing. Of course, we can, do, and sometimes ought to make choices leading to lives less satisfying than they could be. But that is not the situation I have in mind. I am thinking of people who aim to have satisfying lives, no external obstacles stand in the way, and, through lack of reflection or through misguided reflection, they allow an important part of themselves to lie fallow.

The symptoms of this self-imposed deprivation are the uncultivated capacity to love, often manifesting itself in an inability to express affection; an undeveloped sense of beauty, leading to a vulgar knowingness of the price of everything and the value of nothing; lack of playfulness, producing stolid people without a sense of humor; untrained discipline, making serious engagement in any endeavor impossible; and the lack of imaginative life, resulting in dreariness and boredom. The effect of all this is to create a life that stands in the way of satisfactions.

Lack of realism is another internal defect; it makes lives futile. This may be disguised from us for quite some time, but eventually it leads to lives wasted in their own terms. Futility results from an unrealistic appraisal of the suitability of a way of life to our characters and circumstances. One way this can come about is by committing ourselves to ideals whose approximation requires talents or temperament we lack. Clumsy people should not try to be artisans; irritable and irascible people will fail as teachers of young children; people needing a great deal of solitude should not have large families; physical cowards will be poor war correspondents; and righteous, dogmatic people will do badly as negotiators. Furthermore, although a way of life may be right for us, it can be unsuitable to our social or historical contexts. In another age and in another country, General MacArthur would not have had to wait until old age to encounter a task equal to his talent, and he would not have been treated with proper democratic suspicion and distrust.

Finally, there is the internal defect of rigidity. A life may fail through being incapable of adjustment to inevitable changes. The cult of youth and the abhorrence of old age breed much frustration. We all wrinkle, sag, droop, lose resiliency, tire more easily, and have diminishing capacities. Lives whose ideals suit only one period of a normal human life are bound to be unsatisfactory, no matter how well things go for us during the period suited to the ideals.

In all the cases I have described, lives are defective in their own terms. They have been capable of satisfying many of our important specific wants, but they will not continue to do so. The defects are obscured from us, because we have not reflected sufficiently about the future. Therefore, if we want to continue to enjoy satisfactions, we shall want to eliminate hidden incoherence, unrecognized impoverishment, too meager or unrealistic ideals, and rigidity. However, since we may not be aware of the presence of these obstacles to our continued satisfaction, we may believe that we are justifiably satisfied with our lives overall, and be mistaken. For this reason, a purely internal justification is not sufficient to render reasonable the judgment that our lives are good. If we want to improve our chances of living such a life, we shall seek external justification to remove possible mistakes from our judgments.

External Justification

External justification consists in testing our sincere judgments about the goodness of our lives by appealing to certain grounds. These grounds allow us to evaluate the goodness of lives regardless of the forms they take, because they constitute external standards that exist independently of any particular form of life. They are universal, for all lives, always, everywhere must be favorably judged on these grounds, if their goodness is to be reasonably maintained. But these ground are merely prima facie, not necessary, because they can be appealed to in evaluating only lives intended to be good. Normally, we all want to have good lives, because we want to satisfy our important specific wants. Yet there may occur circumstances in which we cease to want them. Love, a sense of justice, overwhelming adversity, the disintegration of a moral tradition may lead people to give up wanting good lives for themselves. If this happens, it is inappropriate to judge their lives on these grounds. So my claim is that human lives can be good only if they are favorably judged on these external, universal, and prima facie grounds.

What, then, are these grounds? The first one is that the wants created by the physiological, psychological, and social conditions, discussed in chapter 2, must be at least minimally satisfied. Unless this happens, people die or they are seriously damaged. Exactly what items and how much of them should be included in a complete list of these minimal satisfactions is a scientific question to which I do not know the precise answer. The important point for my purposes is that no life can be good if the satisfactions in it fall below the minimum required by human nature.

My claim is compatible with the undeniable fact that some people deprive themselves even of minimal satisfactions. Parents may starve themselves to death to save their children from a similar fate. In doing so, they nobly sacrifice their own chances for good lives for the sake of others. But such cases strengthen, rather than weaken, the necessary link between minimal satisfactions and good lives.

The second ground is that we must observe the required conventions of the moral tradition of our society, as well as the variable conventions that give form to the required ones and establish social cohension. As I have argued in chapter 3, this requirement is contingent on the conventions actually protecting the welfare of people living in the society. Provided they do so, observing them is in everybody's interest, for they establish one condition for the pursuit of good lives.

Many conventions governing the institutions and practices of a society are intended to guarantee that this general interest is served. If the conventions accomplish this, conformity to them benefits us. If they fail to accomplish it, it is in our interest to improve them. Each deviation from a generally beneficial convention contributes to social instability, because injuring someone's interest is likely to weaken the structure of conventions. Therefore, it is in the interest of each member of a society who, on balance, benefits from it, to protect the conventions governing the existing institutions and practices.

The fundamental reason for this ground of evaluation is that conformity to conventions aids self-direction, and the more self-direction there is, the better are the chances for good lives. The difficulty is that we need both self-direction and the benefits society can provide. Yet the price of these benefits is to consent to some curtailment of self-direction. The benefits society can provide must be balanced against this constraint. The principle obviously must be to maximize self-direction and minimize constraint. But it is not easy to achieve an optimal balance, and even if it is achieved in one context, the balance will have to be re-established in changing circumstances.

The justification I am offering for conformity to beneficial conventions is prudential. Since we all want to have good lives, and since having it depends on self-direction, society should be arranged to reduce interference with self-direction as much as possible. That I am offering a prudential justification needs emphasis, because it is widely supposed that a moral justification is available.[1] Thus appeal is made to natural or human rights, respect for others, the categorical imperative, the greatest happiness for the greatest number, the Golden Rule, loving one's neighbor, and the like. I doubt that moral justification at this fundamental level can avoid begging the questions; for the question about the morality of the standard appealed to can always be legitimately raised and it cannot be answered by appealing to the same standard. If I am wrong about this and moral justification of basic moral standards is possible, then the prudential justification I am offering is strengthened; whereas if I am right, and moral justification at this level is not available, the prudential justification still stands.[2]

The third ground for favorably evaluating lives is that we must sincerely believe that we are satisfied with them. But such beliefs must be held on the ground that our important specific wants are being satisfied. I have argued in the previous section of this chapter that holding the belief on this ground is not sufficient to establish its reasonability. I shall now argue that it is necessary. What is necessary is both that the belief be sincerely held and that it be held on this ground.

Holding the belief does not require that it be expressed either publicly or privately. We may not even be conscious of it. We hold the belief in the sense that if asked whether we are satisfied with our lives, we would answer affirmatively. And if others were to observe our conduct, it would be reasonable for them to infer that we like our way of life; we do not look for basic changes; we are satisfied with our work; we enjoy our marriage; and we are not deeply frustrated on their account.

But we may hold this belief with or without appropriate grounds, and a reasonable evaluation requires appropriate grounds. This condition is not always met, because satisfaction with our lives may be based on carefully nurtured self-deception, on taking perverse delight in our own frustrations, due to feelings of guilt or shame, or on having been so crushed by circumstances that satisfaction is produced by the spectacle of our own deterioration and fast approaching death. The belief is reasonably grounded if it is based on what we take to be the satisfactions of our important specific wants. Of course, the belief may still be false, and that is why this ground is only necessary and not sufficient to establish the reasonability of the belief that our lives are good.

It may be objected, however, that our lives may be good even if we believe them to be otherwise, and so favorable evaluation on this ground is not even necessary. In good lives our important specific wants are reasonably satisfied. The objection rests on the supposition that this could happen even if we believe that they are not being satisfied. But our beliefs about our wants and satisfactions have a special authority, because the wants and satisfactions are experienced by us and by no one else. We are, therefore, uniquely well-placed to form beliefs about them. If we come to believe that our important specific wants are not being satisfied, we do so, provided we are reasonable, either on the ground that we have failed in self-direction, or because we are frustrated by our circumstances. Given our unique authority, there is a presumption in favor of this belief. And it is hard to know what could defeat the presumption. Thus, if we believe that our lives are not good, our judgments should be accepted, unless it can be shown that we are mistaken about our wants, satisfactions, or self-direction.

My general point is that our reasonable beliefs about the overall satisfaction with our lives have a crucial bearing on the evaluation of the judgment that our lives are good. If we are dissatisfied with our lives, on appropriate grounds, our lives are not good, for their goodness depends on the satisfaction of our important specific wants, and we know best about them. On the other hand, if we are satisfied with our lives, on appropriate grounds, they may still not be good, because we may be mistaken about their capacity to continue to be satisfying.

The fourth ground of evaluation concerns the appropriateness of our ideals. They are appropriate, if we have at least a chance of living a satisfying life if we pursue them.[3] Ideals could fail to be appropriate by containing false presuppositions, as we have seen in chapter 5. I shall not repeat the discussion of how the truth or falsehood of presuppositions can be established. It will suffice to say here that good lives are impossible without appropriate ideals. For we aim to satisfy our wants in accordance with ideals, and if the ideals are inappropriate, our wants are bound to be frustrated. Since good lives require the satisfaction of important specific wants, they also require appropriate ideals.

The fifth ground is the possession of the virtues of self-direction. Having them makes our lives much more likely to be good than otherwise. But the possession of these virtues is a matter of degree. The present requirement is that they should be significant features of our characters. They should be so important as to render seriously inadequate any psychological profile of us which fails to give them a central place.

If we pass this requirement, we have ourselves firmly in control, because we have decided which of our wants we aim to satisfy, and we have organized our commitments accordingly. We know our wants, ideals, and commitments. We are sensitive moral agents, and so we have considerable skill in interpreting the situations we encounter in terms of the moral vocabulary available to us. Thus, when we are called upon to respond, we are likely to do so on the basis of an accurate appraisal of what confronts us and what we should do about it. And wisdom enables us to know and observe the limits within which we must act, and judge accordingly.

To be this sort of a person is to have a fine character. It enables us to avoid or surmount obstacles that may injure the lives of those who lack them. Cataclysmic misfortune may still deprive us of good lives, but lesser adversity will not. And such fine characters are not self-centered. If people possessing them are indeed wise, then they know that a stable social order and intimate personal relationships are necessary for good lives. So they will care about love and justice, not merely because they make their lives better, although, of course, they do, but because they are among their ideals.

But having the four virtues of self-direction as central features of our characters is only a prima facie ground of justification, because good lives are possible even without fine characters. This possibility depends on great good fortune throughout a life. It must be free from adversity, from personal weakness, and from significant challenges; it must run its course smoothly, proceeding from success to success, and the appreciation of other people must by and large coincide with the agent's satisfaction with the life. But since such great good fortune is rarely to be found in human lives, possession of the four virtues of self-direction is a requirement of good lives.

Yet it would be a mistake to conclude that if we meet these requirements, then we shall have good lives, provided nothing cataclysmic happens. For, while we shall be guided by appropriate ideals, we may develop doubts about them, and doubtful ideals will lead to doubtful satisfactions.

This brings us to the sixth ground of justification. Our ideals come to us from three sources: our moral tradition, personal experience, or we create them ourselves. The most important of these is the moral tradition, for it is rich in varied ideals, while personal experiences of good lives that we would wish to direct ourselves to live are rare, and the ability to create appropriate ideals is even rarer. Suppose, then, that we adopt ideals from our moral tradition and make such adjustments in them as necessary to fit our own context and characters. Could we not safeguard in this way against doubtful ideals?

Clearly one great advantage of fashioning ourselves in conformity to traditional ideals is that they are tried and true. So they are unlikely to be inherently faulty, and if we do indeed conform to the other requirements of good lives, then we shall eliminate faults from the process of adjusting ideals to suit our characters and circumstances. Why not say, then, that if we meet the other requirements and live according to appropriately adjusted traditional ideals, our lives will be good? Before embracing this conclusion, we need to consider our attitudes to ideals a little further.

From the fact that we adopt suitable traditional ideals, it does not follow that there are no other ideals equally suitable. Suppose that we are aware of this. Our situation is that we have chosen, we know that we have chosen well, and our lives are actually unfolding as we planned them. Yet, we may still have doubts. We may say to ourselves that we have chosen well, but not as well as we might have. We have opted for the life of a scholar, but we could have opted for being a statesman or an artist; we have married the person we loved and we have a fine life together, but there are other people, other kinds of marriages, and perhaps, there is much to be said for remaining single. These are not idle doubts, but serious questions about the success of self-direction. The issue is not whether we have succeeded or failed. I am assuming that we have succeeded. The question is whether having succeeded at one life is as good as it would have been to succeed at lives we chose not to live. What would remove these doubts?

In answer, I shall make use of Nietzsche's suggestive notion of eternal recurrence, but I do not claim to be faithful to his obscure intentions.[4] The idea is that our lives would be free from the sort of doubts I have just described if we would wish them to go on without essential changes. And if we were asked to perform a Faustian thought-experiment, in which we could start again and do things differently if we wished, we would make the same important decisions as we made before. Wishing for eternal recurrence suggests that the lives that have thus proved themselves are free from serious doubts. Of course, reflective people cannot help wondering about their lives in this way. But the wonderings are introspective musings, not symptoms of dissatisfaction.

Thus we are led to the last ground of justification: happiness. For it is a truth about human beings that if their lives satisfy the requirements established by the previous grounds of justification, then they will be happy with their lives as a whole. Consider, in a summary way, what is involved in lives satisfying these requirements. At the most basic level, physiological, psychological, and social wants are at least minimally satisfied. Beyond this, the agents live in a morally healthy society where the required and the appropriate variable conventions are generally respected both by themselves and by others. Going further, the agents sincerely believe that they are satisfied with the overall pattern of their lives. And this belief is based on the satisfactions they derive from living according to ideals whose appropriateness has been established. If, in addition, they can be truly said to have fine characters, because the four virtues of self-direction significantly influence their conduct, and if, upon surveying their past and present opportunities, they can truthfully wish for no serious changes in their lives, then, it seems to me, it is reasonable for them to claim, and for others to agree, that they have happy lives. These, then, are the external grounds upon which judgments about the goodness of lives can be justified.

Conclusion

It may be objected that the account I have given of good lives is incomplete and the justification of them is inconclusive, because I have failed to specify the relevant ideals. This doubt rests on the expectation that the ideals ought to be specified. I think that this expectation is misplaced and the doubt is unjustified. The account of good lives must be incomplete and the justification must be inconclusive, and it is good that they are so.

The account of good lives must be incomplete, because good lives are self-directed and self-direction is incompatible with the expected completion. Completion is possible only if there are metaphysically ordained ideals or if there are ideals imprinted on human nature. But metaphysicaly ordained ideals are fictions. Nor are there ideals imprinted on human nature, for our nature is partly open and it is compatible with a large number of ideals that could give us good lives. Human nature restricts our possibilities, but it does not determine them. The account of good lives must be incomplete, because our possibilities are numerous and the metaphysics underlying attempts to curtail them lacks rational warrant. The expectation of completion is produced by the familiar and misplaced longing for the summum bonum with universal authority. The existence of such an authority would render self-direction impossible, and, consequently, it would make good lives impossible. This is why the incompleteness of my account is not only inevitable, but good.

From this consideration it follows that if I had set myself the task of trying to specify the ideals good lives must have, I would have undermined the point of my enterprise. Its point is that good lives depend on self-direction, and self-direction cannot be done by others for us. The task of philosophers here is not to direct others, but to explain what is involved in directing ourselves. "[P]hilosophy can no more show a man what he should attach importance to than geometry can show a man where he should stand."[5] Just as the virtues we need cannot be developed by others for us, so the ideals that should guide us cannot be either. It is true that ideals exist independently of individual human beings, but ideals function as ideals only if we make them our own by adapting to our characters and circumstances and by committing ourselves to them.

The justification of ideals is not like the justification of descriptions. Descriptions are either true or false, although it may be difficult to tell which they are. Ideals are different, partly because human lives, can be rendered good by many different ideals. Particular ideals present desirable ways of shaping our future selves insofar as we can. In this realm, "there are many truths, but no truth."[6] The false notion that there is one good life for each of us assumes that there exists the same pattern of ideals for all of us, and making a good life consists in finding it. But there is no such pattern.

Yet it does not follow that all ideals are equally acceptable. We can criticize them, partly because ideals have factual components and human nature has tangible needs. Ideals of good lives, therefore, must be realistic. They must take account of human nature and of the moral tradition in which we live, and they must foster the reasonable satisfaction of our important specific wants. In arguing this way, I have accepted the view that

[m]oral philosophy is the examination of the most important of all human activities, and . . . two things are required of it. The examination should be realistic. Human nature . . . has certain discoverable

attributes, and these should be suitably considered in any discussion of morality. Secondly, since an ethical system cannot but commend an ideal, it should commend a worthy ideal. Ethics should not be merely an analysis of ordinary mediocre conduct, it should be a hypothesis about good conduct and about how this can be achieved. How can we make ourselves better? is a question moral philosophers should attempt to answer.[7]

The answer I have given and endeavored to defend is that we shall make ourselves better if we succeed in satisfying our important specific wants reasonably. Thinking of good lives in this way creates a presumption in favor of self-direction and against interference. The significance of this is that what I take to be natural, and thus not in need of justification, is doing what we want. It is interference with self-direction that requires justification. Of course, such interference can be justified. But, my point is, that is what needs to be justified. The presumption against interference stands in the way of coercing us, in the name of some notion of the common good, to live lives whose ideals we are forced to accept by some authority whose credentials are always poorer than our own.

All appeals to the common good more or less coercively impose ideals on us. The only goods are those individuals find as such. The common good is a defensible conception only if it means the establishment of conditions in which individuals can pursue their ideals with as little interference as possible. Any reasonable alternative to this kind of coercion must be able to answer the question of what we can do to make our lives good, if we are free from illegitimate interference. I hope to have gone some way toward answering it in this book.

The answer relies on ideals drawn from the Western moral tradition, but they have application to human lives everywhere in civilized circumstances. These ideals do not exist in isolation from each other, nor from the context surrounding them. Their importance can be appreciated only in juxtaposition with competing ideals; they exist in a state of tension. In closing, I shall describe some of these tensions which form the background to my way of thinking.

The first tension is between a view of human nature embodied in the natural law tradition deriving from Aristotle[8] and the liberal view of human beings as malleable.[9] According to Aristotle, human nature is fixed and in essential respects closed. Our function follows from our nature; the good life consists in the exercise of this function; and this establishes the only form a good life can take. At the opposite pole is the liberal idea that human nature is open and hence changeable. Good lives are projects of self-transformation, whose aim is to make ourselves better. We are perfectible only because our nature is malleable. Consequently, there is no inherent function that we have and there is no preordained pattern of the good life.

My view is that human nature is partly open and partly closed. Aristotelians are right in thinking that we are made better by developing certain virtues and that what they are follows from human nature. Human nature is not indefinitely malleable. Nevertheless, it is not completely closed either, because there are many ideals that may reasonably inspire self-direction. We can and do change ourselves, sometimes for the better, sometimes not. However, the scope for this change is limited by the fixed aspect of human nature.

The second tension is about justification. It is caused by the conflict between the classical rationlist view and a thoroughgoing relativist one.[10] For classical rationalists, the aim of justification is certainty. It can be achieved by deduction proceeding from well-established first principles. The task of metaphysics is to prove the first principles and of logic to guide us to certain conclusions. Our knowledge of human nature comes from metaphysics and rational views about the good life are deductive consequences of it. Relativists are right in rejecting this neat system. The history of philosophy has failed to yield well-established first principles, the ideal of certainty is chimerical, and logic is as open to revision as any other heuristic device. But it does not follow from the failure of classical rationalism that the distinction between reasonable and unreasonable views disappears. The alternative to classical rationalism need not be relativism.

My view of justification is another alternative. All views are fallible, but not all views are equally reasonable. Given our fallible view of human nature, we can still defend conclusions about it on the grounds that we have good reasons to accept them and no reason to doubt them. But the conclusions are negative. They are capable of establishing only that some candidates for good lives are unreasonable, because there are some condition any good life must fulfill and the unreasonable candidates cannot do so. Justification, therefore, proceeds by the elimination of failures, not by the specification of the best. This, of course, goes hand in hand with my view that there is not a best.[11]

The third tension is between individual freedom and moral

tradition. Freedom is a necessary condition of good lives, for it is what makes self-direction possible. But so is moral tradition. It receives its sanction from being the repository of the accumulated experiences of mankind. Without moral tradition, each of us would have to start self-direction anew, and thus fail to benefit from the achievements and failures of those who had gone before us. Society institutionalizes moral tradition, and it is another necessary condition of good lives. Therefore, the question is not whether we should have freedom or tradition, but how much freedom and how much tradition ought there to be.[12]

My answer is part of what I said about self-direction. The proper sphere of moral tradition is the preservation and cultivation of ideals and the proper sphere of freedom is our acceptance or rejection of them. Moral tradition provides the options and freedom allows us to deliberate about them. Of course, both freedom and tradition can be abused. Tradition can be rigid and coercive and freedom can be destructive of the conditions required for its own existence. How to avoid these dangers is one of the main problems of political thought, and I have said little about it. However, the guiding principle must surely be that the resolution of conflicts of this sort should aim at safeguarding the conditions in which we can live self-directed lives.

The fourth tension is between living selfish lives in which we care only about ourselves and living selfless lives devoted to the service of others. Selfishness is a vice. But selfless lives of service also have their pitfalls. For we can be of service to others only if we respect their ideals of good lives and if understand that they must achieve them themselves. It is easy to see that service in uncivilized conditions means removing the obstacles to self-direction. But it is not at all easy to know what service we can perform for self-directed people. We must know them well, be their friend, love them. Intimacy is required for that, and it takes a long time to achieve.

Self-direction strikes a balance between selfishness and selflessness. In living good lives, we must care about ourselves, because we must satisfy our wants, accept appropriate ideals, make our commitments, and develop our virtues. But our objects need not be ourselves. Good lives require caring for others, as well as for ourselves. In this book, I have aimed to show how we can care for ourselves reasonably.

Notes

Chapter 1. An Approach to Good Lives

1. All quotations are from chap. 5, John Stuart Mill, *Autobiography* (Indianapolis, Ind.: Bobbs-Merrill, 1957).

2. See W. D. Joske, "Philosophy and the Meaning of Life," *Australasian Journal of Philosophy* 52 (1974): 93–104.

3. Thomas Nagel, "The Absurd," in *Mortal Questions* (Cambridge: Cambridge University Press, 1979), pp. 11–23.

4. Ibid., p. 13.

5. Ibid.

6. Baruch de Spinoza, "Ethics," in *The Collected Works of Spinoza*, Vol. 1, ed. and trans. Edwin Curley (Princeton: Princeton University Press, 1985), pt. 3, prop. 7.

7. Richard Taylor, "The Meaning of Life," in *Good and Evil* (New York: Macmillan, 1970), chap. 18.

8. Taylor, *Good and Evil*, p. 260.

9. My discussion of Taylor is indebted to David Wiggins's "Truth, Invention, and the Meaning of Life," *Proceedings of the British Academy* 62 (1976): 331–78.

10. The achievement of this coherence is one of the main concerns of Richard Wollheim's *The Thread of Life* (Cambridge: Harvard University Press, 1984). One of the ways in which my account differs from Wollheim's is his acceptance of, and my rejection of, psychoanalytic explanation.

11. Wiggins, "Truth," pp. 348–49.

Chapter 2. The Limits of Self-Direction: Human Nature

1. These facts are well described by H. L. A. Hart in *The Concept of Law* (Oxford: Clarendon Press, 1961), chap. 9.

2. W. H. Walsh argues for this view in "The Constancy of Human Nature," *Contemporary British Philosophy*, 4th Ser., ed. Hywel D. Lewis (London: Allen & Unwin, 1976), pp. 274–91.

3. Bernard Gert in *The Moral Rules* (New York: Harper, 1973) gives a fine account of the evils that makes lives bad. He says little about goods, but his list of evils can easily be reformulated to make a list of goods.

4. The main contemporary opponent of this account is Richard M. Hare; see *The Language of Morals* (Oxford: Clarendon Press, 1952), *Freedom and Reason* (Oxford: Clarendon Press, 1963), and *Moral Thinking* (Oxford: Clarendon Press, 1981).

5. My account has close affinities with John Rawls's account of primary goods in *A Theory of Justice* (Cambridge: Harvard University Press, 1971) and Alan Gewirth's account of necessary goods in *Reason and Morality* (Chicago: University

of Chicago Press, 1978). Each goes on to attempt to derive rights from these goods; in this, however, I part company from them.

6. See, e.g., Peter Winch, "Human Nature," in *The Proper Study*, The Royal Institute Lectures (London: Macmillan, 1971), ed. G. N. A. Vesey, pp. 1–13.

7. See, e.g., Richard Rorty's *Philosophy and the Mirror of Nature* (Princeton: Princeton University Press, 1979) and *Consequences of Pragmatism* (Minneapolis: University of Minnesota Press, 1982).

8. See, e.g., Henry B. Veatch, *Human Rights* (Baton Rouge: University of Louisiana Press, 1985).

9. In this, I differ from Thomas Nagel's *The View from Nowhere* (New York: Oxford University Press, 1986), in which he argues that good lives require the combination of the *sub specie aeternitatis* perspective with our own.

Chapter 3. The Context of Self-Direction: Moral Tradition

1. Stuart Hampshire's *Morality and Conflict* (Cambridge: Harvard University Press, 1983) and Alasdair MacIntyre's *After Virtue* (Notre Dame Ind.: University of Notre Dame Press, 1981) have strongly influenced my account.

2. David Hume, *Enquiry Concerning Human Understanding and Concerning the Principles of Morals*, ed. L. A. Selby-Bigge, 2d. ed. (Oxford: Clarendon Press, 1902), sec. 5, pt. 1.

3. See Michael Oakeshott, "On the Civil Condition," in *On Human Conduct* (Oxford: Clarendon Press, 1975).

4. For a general account of tradition from a sociological perspective, see Edward Shils, *Tradition* (Chicago: University of Chicago Press, 1981).

5. Erving Goffman perceptively describes these rituals, cues, and ceremonies in many works. See, e.g., *The Presentation of Self in Everyday Life* (New York: Doubleday, 1959) and *Interaction Ritual* (New York: Pantheon, 1957).

6. Mill, *Autobiography*, chap. 5.

Chapter 4. Self-Direction

1. Isaiah Berlin, *Four Essays on Liberty* (Oxford: Oxford University Press, 1969), p. 131.

2. See *The Complete Essays of Montaigne*, trans. Donald M. Frame (Stanford: Stanford University Press, 1958); the numbers in parentheses in my text refer to the pages of this edition.

3. For this information, I am indebted to Donald M. Frame's *Montaigne: A Biography* (San Francisco: North Point Press, 1984).

4. William B. Yeats, "The Second Coming," in *The Collected Poems of W. B. Yeats* (London: Macmillan, 1982).

5. Frame, *Montaigne*, p. 289.

Chapter 5. Ideals and Commitments

1. Aristotle, *Eudemian Ethics*, in *The Complete Works of Aristotle*, vol. 2, ed. Jonathan Barnes, 1214b, trans. J. Solomon, Bollingen Series 71 (Princeton: Princeton University Press).

2. Plato, *The Republic,* in *The Dialogues of Plato,* vol. 1, trans. Benjamin Jowett (New York: Randon House, 1937), pp. 359–61.

3. My interpretation of ideals makes them essentially contestable. For the origin of this notion, see W. B. Gallie, *Philosophy and the Historical Understanding* (London: Chatto & Windus, 1964), chap. 8. I develop this notion, under the name of perennial arguments, in *The Nature of Philosophy* (Oxford: Blackwell; Totowa, N.J.: Rowman and Littlefield, 1980), pt. 2.

4. I am indebted to Iris Murdoch's "Vision and Choice in Morality," in *Christian Ethics and Contemporary Philosophy,* ed. Ian Ramsey (New York: Macmillan, 1966), and "The Idea of Perfection," in *Sovereignty of Good* (London: Routledge, 1970).

5. Of course, this is a large topic. The contemporary works that influenced my view most are: Berlin, *Four Essays on Liberty,* Michael Oakeshott, *Rationalism in Politics and Other Essays* (London: Methuen, 1962), and Karl R. Popper, *The Open Society and Its Enemies* (London: Routledge, 1945).

6. Charles Taylor "Responsibility for Self," in *The Identities of Persons,* ed. Ametie O. Rorty (Berkeley: University of California Press, 1976), pp. 281–99 has illuminatingly discussed in terms of being a strong evaluator what I mean by being guided by ideals.

7. Robert Bolt, *A Man for All Seasons* (New York: Random House, 1965).

8. Ibid. p. xiii.

9. My discussion owes much to Hampshire's "Morality and Pessimism" in *Morality and Conflict.*

10. Hume, *Enquiry,* p. 209.

Chapter 6. Self-Control

1. Hume, *Enquiry,* p. 225.

2. Murdoch, *Sovereignty of Good,* pp. 99–100.

3. My discussion of these strategies is indebted to John Watkins's "Three Views Concerning Human Freedom," in *Nature and Conduct,* ed. R. S. Peters (London: Macmillan, 1975), pp. 200–228.

4. My thinking about this strategy is deeply influenced by Stuart Hampshire's *Thought and Action* (London: Chatto & Windus, 1960); *Freedom of the Individual* (Princeton: Princeton University Press, 1975), exp. ed.; and "Spinoza and the Idea of Freedom," in *Freedom and Mind* (Oxford: Clarendon Press, 1972).

5. The formulation of this account is influenced by Frithjof Bergmann's *On Being Free* (Notre Dame, Ind.: University of Notre Dame Press, 1977). Henry G. Frankfurt in "Freedom of the Will and the Concept of a Person," *Journal of Philosophy* 68 (1971): 5–20 and Wallace I. Matson in *Sentience* (Berkeley: University of California Press, 1976) develop accounts similar to my own.

6. I am indebted for this discussion of natural endowments to Bernard Williams's "Moral Luck," *Proceedings of the Aristotelian Society,* suppl. vol. 50 (1976): 115–135.

7. My position on this point is close to Taylor's in "Responsibility for Self," in *The Identities of Persons,* pp. 281–99.

Chapter 7. Self-Knowledge

1. My argument in this section is indebted to David W. Hamlyn's "Self-Knowledge," in *Perception, Learning and the Self* (London: Routledge, 1983).

2. The role of interpretation in self-knowledge is illuminatingly discussed by Wollheim in *The Thread of Life*, particularly in chap. 6, "The Examined Life." Perhaps I should note that I settled on the title of my book before I read Wollheim.

3. See Charles Taylor, "What is Human Agency?" in *Human Agency and Language: Philosophical Papers* (Cambridge: Cambridge University Press, 1985).

4. For a general view, very close to my own, of the place of self-knowledge in self-directed lives, see David L. Norton's *Personal Destinies* (Princeton: Princeton University Press, 1976).

5. Iris Murdoch, in her novels and also in some of her philosophical writings, discusses with great sensitivity the varieties and pitfalls of ignorance of oneself. Of the novels, I particular recommend *The Nice and the Good* (London: Chatto & Windus, 1968) and *The Black Prince* (New York: Viking, 1973); see also the philosophical essay "The Sovereignty of Good Over Other Concepts" in *The Sovereignty of Good*.

6. The literature on self-deception is immense. For a good bibliography and a selection of recent articles, see M. W. Martin, *Self-Deception and Self-Understanding* (Lawrence: University of Kansas Press, 1985).

Chapter 8. Moral Sensitivity

1. Immanuel Kant, *The Critique of Pure Reason*, trans. Norman Kemp Smith (London: Macmillan, 1953), A 800–801 and A 805. In this sense, both contemporary utilitarians and contractarians are Kantians. Some representative works are: Richard B. Brandt's *A Theory of the Right and the Good* (Oxford: Clarendon Press, 1979), Gewirth's *Reason and Morality*, Hare's *The Language of Morals, Freedom and Reason* and *Moral Thinking*, Rawls's *A Theory of Justice*.

2. In arguing this way, I join a growing group of writers who reject the Kantian concentration on choice and right action: Philippa Foot, *Virtues and Vices* (Berkeley: University of California Press, 1978), Hampshire, *Morality and Conflict*, MacIntyre, *After Virtue*, Murdoch, *Sovereignty of Good*, Williams, *Moral Luck*, Norton, *Personal Destinies*, and Edmund Pincoffs, *Quandaries and Virtues* (Lawrence: University of Kansas Press, 1986).

3. Jean-Paul Sartre, *Existentialism and Human Emotions*, trans. Bernard Frechtman (New York: Philosophical Library, 1957), pp. 24–26.

4. Murdoch, *Sovereignty of Good* pp. 39–40.

5. The position I am developing has come to be known as a virtue theory. A recent collection of papers illustrates this approach and provides a useful bibliography; see Robert B. Kruschwitz and R. C. Roberts, eds., *The Virtues* (Los Angeles: Wardsworth, 1987).

Chapter 9. Wisdom

1. Brand Blanshard, *Reason and Goodness* (London: Allen & Unwin, 1961), p. 446.

2. Leo Tolstoy, "The Death of Ivan Ilyich," *The Cossacks and Other Stories*, trans. R. Edwards (Harmondsworth: Penguin, 1974).

3. Peter F. Strawson, *Individuals* (Garden City, N.Y.: Doubleday, 1963), p. xiv.

4. Ibid., p. xiv.

5. Aristotle, *Nicomachean Ethics*, bk. 6, trans. W. D. Ross, rev. J. O. Urmson, in *Complete Works*, vol. 2.

6. This is well discussed by J. D. Collins in *The Lure of Wisdom* (Milwaukee, Wis.: Marquette University Press, 1962); the discussion of Descartes is especially valuable.

7. E. F. Rice, *The Renaissance Idea of Wisdom* (Cambridge: Harvard University Press, 1958), p. 4. This is an excellent study of Charron and his tradition.

8. The conflict between these two ways of thinking is the topic of Nagel's *The View from Nowhere*.

9. For this view of the virtues in general, see Foot, *Virtues and Vices*, and G. H. Von Wright, *Varieties of Goodness* (London: Routledge, 1963).

Chapter 10. Good Lives and Happiness

1. For an excellent discussion of the simple view and its shortcomings, see Ilham Dilham, *Morality and the Inner Life* (London: Macmillan, 1979).

2. A distinction similar to mine is between first-and second-order desires. See Frankfurt, "Freedom of the Will and the Concept of a Person," 5–20.

3. Elizabeth Telfer, *Happiness* (London: Macmillan, 1980) contains an extended discussion of this.

4. See, e.g., Nicholas Rescher, *Ethical Idealism* (Berkeley: University of California Press, 1987), chap. 3, and Max Black, "Making Intelligent Choices: How Useful Is Decision Theory?" *Dialectic* 39 (1985): 19–34.

5. A. MacBeath, *Experiments in Living* (London: Macmillan, 1952), lec. 14.

6. See Richard Kraut's "Two Conceptions of Happiness," *Philosophical Review* 88 (1979): 167–97. Kraut attempts to defend the subjective view.

7. Aristotle, *Nicomachean Ethics* 1178a, in *Complete Works*, vol. 2. A contemporary statement of Aristotelian perfectionism is Henry B. Veatch's *Rational Man* (Bloomington: University of Indiana Press, 1962). For a conflicting interpretation of Aristotle, see W. F. R. Hardie, *Aristotle's Ethical Theory* (Oxford: Clarendon, 1980), 2d ed., and John M. Cooper, *Reason and the Human Good in Aristotle* (Cambridge: Harvard University Press, 1975).

Chapter 11. Good Lives and Justification

1. Readers who have persevered this far may have noticed that there has been little discussion of the issues that preoccupy much of contemporary moral thought. The reason is that the controversies among utilitarians, Kantians, contractarians, and rights theorists seem to me to rest on the assumption I here question. For a systematic formulation of my doubts, see MacIntyre's *After Virtue*.

2. Thus I am in general agreement with Foot's "Morality as a System of Hypothetical Imperatives," *Virtues and Vices*.

3. Rescher, in *Ethical Idealism*, argues that impossible ideals may be reasonable. I am willing to accept this, provided those who pursue the ideals do not believe that they are impossible.

4. Friedrich Nietzsche, *Thus Spoke Zarathustra*, trans. R. J. Hollingdale (Harmondsworth: Penguin, 1961). The best interpretation of eternal occurence I know of is Alexander Nehamas's *Nietzsche: Life as Literature* (Cambridge: Harvard University Press, 1985), chap. 5.

5. Peter Winch, "Moral Integrity," in *Ethics and Action* (London: Routledge, 1972), p. 191.

6. Peter F. Strawson, "Social Morality and Individual Ideal," in *Freedom and Resentment* (London: Methuen, 1974), p. 29.

7. Murdoch, *Sovereignty of Good*, p. 78.

8. See, e.g., John Finnis, *Natural Law and Natural Rights* (Oxford: Clarendon, 1980) and Veatch, *Human Rights*.

9. John Passmore's *The Perfectibility of Man* (London: Duckworth, 1970) traces the history of this idea.

10. For the controversy, see Bryan R. Wilson, ed., *Rationality* (Oxford: Blackwell, 1970), Martin Hollis and Steven Lukes, eds., *Rationality and Relativism* (Oxford: Blackwell, 1982), and Michael Krausz and Jack W. Meiland, eds., *Relativism* (Notre Dame, Ind.: Notre Dame University Press, 1982).

11. This view of justification derives from Karl R. Popper's, sec, e.g., his *Conjectures and Refutations* (New York: Harper and Row, 1963) and *Objective Knowledge* (Oxford: Clarendon Press, 1972). I have developed this view in *A Justification of Rationality* (Albany: State University of New York Press, 1976).

12. The best discussion of this subject is Berlin's *Four Essays on Liberty*.

Works Cited

Aristotle. *Eudemian Ethics*. Translated by J. Solomon. In *The Complete Works of Aristotle*, vol. 2, edited by Jonathan Barnes. Bollingen Series 71. Princeton: Princeton University Press, 1984.

———. *Nicomachean Ethics*. Translated by W. D. Ross and revised by J. O. Urmson. In *The Complete Works of Aristotle*, vol. 2, edited by Jonathan Barnes. Bollingen Series 71. Princeton: Princeton University Press, 1984.

Bergmann, Frithjof. *On Being Free*. Notre Dame, Ind.: University of Notre Dame Press, 1977.

Berlin, Isaiah. *Four Essays on Liberty*. Oxford: Oxford University Press, 1969.

Black, Max. "Making Intelligent Choices: How Useful Is Decision Theory?" *Dialectic* 39 (1985): 19–34.

Blanshard, Brand. *Reason and Goodness*. London: Allen & Unwin, 1961.

Bolt, Robert. *A Man for All Seasons*. New York: Random House, 1965.

Brandt, Richard B. *A Theory of the Right and the Good*. Oxford: Clarendon Press, 1979.

Camus, Albert. "Caligula." in *Caligula and 3 Other Plays*. Translated by Stuart Gilbert. New York: Random House, 1958.

———. *The Myth of Sysiphus*. Translated by J. O'Brien. New York: Alfred A. Knopf, 1955.

———. *The Stranger*. Translated by Stuart Gilbert. New York: Alfred A. Knopf, 1946.

Charron, Pierre. "Wisdom." In *The "Wisdom: of Pierre Charron, an Original and Orthodox Code of Morality*. Translated and edited by Jean Charron. University of North Carolina Studies in the Romance Languages and Literatures, no. 34. Chapel Hill, 1961.

Collins, James D. *The Lure of Wisdom*. Milwaukee, Wis.: Marquette University Press, 1962.

Conrad, Joseph. *Lord Jim*. Harmondsworth: Penguin Books, 1957.

Cooper, John M. *Reason and the Human Good in Aristotle*. Cambridge: Harvard University Press, 1975.

Defoe, Daniel. *Robinson Crusoe*. New York: Charles Scribner's Sons, 1957.

Diderot, Denis. *Rameau's Nephew and Other Works*. Translated by Jacques Barzun and Ralph H. Bowen. Indianapolis, Ind.: Bobbs-Merrill, 1982.

Dilham, Ilham. *Morality and the Inner Life*. London: Macmillan, 1979.

Finnis, John. *Natural Law and Natural Rights*. Oxford: Clarendon Press, 1980.

Foot, Philippa. *Virtues and Vices*. Berkeley: University of California Press, 1978.

Frame, Donald M. *Montaigne: A Biography*. San Francisco: North Point Press, 1984.

Frankfurt, Henry G. "Freedom of the Will and the Concept of a Person." *Journal of Philosophy* 68 (1971): 5–20.

Gallie, W. B. *.Philosophy and the Historical Understanding.* London: Chatto & Windus, 1964.

Gert, Bernard. *The Moral Rules.* New York: Harper & Row, 1973.

Gewirth, Alan. *Reason and Morality.* Chicago: University of Chicago Press, 1978.

Goffman, Erving. *Interaction Ritual.* New York: Pantheon, 1957.

———. *The Presentation of Self in Everyday Life.* New York: Doubleday, 1959.

Hamlyn, David W. *Perception, Learning and the Self.* London: Routledge, 1983.

Hampshire, Stuart. *Freedom of Mind.* Oxford: Clarendon Press, 1972.

———. *Freedom of the Individual.* Princeton: Princeton University Press, 1975.

———. *Morality and Conflict.* Oxford: Blackwell, 1983.

———. *Thought and Action.* London: Chatto & Windus, 1960.

Hardie, W. F. R. *Aristotle's Ethical Theory,* 2d ed. Oxford: Clarendon Press, 1980.

Hare, Richard M. *Freedom and Reason.* Oxford: Clarendon Press, 1963.

———. *The Language of Morals.* Oxford: Clarendon Press, 1952.

———. *Moral Thinking.* Oxford: Clarendon Press, 1981.

Hart, H. L. A. *The Concept of Law.* Oxford: Clarendon Press, 1961.

Hollis, Martin, and Lukes, Steven, eds. *Rationality and Relativism,* Oxford: Blackwell, 1982.

Hume, David. *Enquiry Concerning Human Understanding and Concerning the Principles of Morals.* Edited by L. A. Selby-Bigge, 2d ed. Oxford: Clarendon Press, 1961.

James, Henry. *The Ambassadors.* Harmondsworth: Penguin Books, 1979.

Joske, W. D. "Philosophy and the Meaning of Life." *Australasian Journal of Philosophy* 52 (1974): 93–104.

Kant, Immanuel. *The Critique of Pure Reason.* Translated by Norman Kemp Smith. London: Macmillan, 1953.

Kekes, John. *A Justification of Rationality.* Albany: State University of New York Press, 1976.

———. *The Nature of Philosophy.* Oxford: Blackwell; Totowa, N.J.: Rowman and Littlefield, 1980.

Krausz, Michael, and Meiland, Jack W., eds., *Relativism.* Notre Dame, Ind.: Notre Dame University Press, 1982.

Kraut, Richard, "Two Conceptions of Happiness," *Philosophical Review* 88 (1979). 167–97.

Kruschwitz, Robert B., and Roberts, R. C., eds. *The Virtues.* Los Angeles: Wardsworth, 1987.

MacBeath, A. *Experiments in Living.* London: Macmillan, 1950.

MacIntyre, Alasdair. *After Virtue.* Notre Dame, Ind.: University of Notre Dame Press, 1981.

Martin, M. W., ed. *Self-Deception and Self-Understanding.* Lawrence: University of Kansas Press, 1985.

Matson, Wallace I. *Sentience.* Berkeley: University of California Press, 1976.

Melville, Herman. *Moby Dick or the White Whale.* Everymans Library. London: J. M. Dent, 1907.

Mill, John Stuart. *Autobiography.* Indianapolis, Ind.: Bobbs-Merrill, 1957.

Montaigne, Michel de. *The Complete Essays of Montaigne.* Translated by Donald M. Frame. Standord: Stanford University Press, 1958.

More, Thomas. *Utopia.* In *The Complete Works of St. Thomas More,* vol. 4, edited by Edward Surtz and J. H. Hexter. New Haven: Yale University Press, 1965.

Murdoch, Iris. *The Black Prince.* New York: Viking Press, 1973.

————. *The Nice and the Good.* London: Chatto & Windus, 1968.

————. *The Sovereignty of Good.* London: Routledge, 1970.

————. "Vision and Choice in Morality." In *Christian Ethics and Contemporary Philosophy,* edited by Ian Ramsey. New York: Macmillan, 1966.

Nagel, Thomas. *Mortal Questions.* Cambridge: Cambridge University Press, 1979.

————. *The View from Nowhere.* New York: Oxford University Press, 1986.

Nehamas, Alexander. *Neitzsche: Life as Literature,* Cambridge: Harvard University Press, 1985.

Nietzsche, Friedrich. *Thus Spoke Zarathustra.* Translated by R. J. Hollingdale. Harmondsworth: Penguin Books, 1961.

Norton, David L. *Personal Destinies.* Princeton: Princeton University Press, 1976.

Oakeshott, Michael. *On Human Conduct.* Oxford: Clarendon Press, 1975.

————. *Rationalism in Politics and Other Essays.* London: Methuen, 1962.

Orwell, George. *Nineteen Eighty Four.* Harmondsworth: Penguin Books, 1954.

Passmore, John. *The Perfectibility of Man.* London: Duckworth, 1970.

Pincoffs, Edmund. *Quandaries and Virtues.* Lawrence: University of Kansas Press, 1986.

Plato. *Phaedrus.* In *The Dialogues of Plato,* vol. 1, translated by Benjamin Jowett. New York: Random House, 1937.

————. *The Republic.* In *The Dialogues of Plato,* vol. 1, translated by Benjamin Jowett. New York: Random House, 1937.

Popper, Karl R. *Conjectures and Refutations.* New York: Harper & Row, 1963.

————. *Objective Knowledge.* Oxford: Clarendon Press, 1972.

————. *The Open Society and Its Enemies.* London: Routledge, 1945.

Rawls, John. *A Theory of Justice.* Cambridge: Harvard University Press, 1971.

Rescher, Nicholas. *Ethical Idealism.* Berkeley: University of California Press, 1987.

Rice, E. F. *The Renaissance Idea of Wisdom.* Cambridge: Harvard University Press, 1958.

Rorty, Richard. *Philosophy and the Mirror of Nature.* Princeton: Princeton University Press, 1979.

————. *Consequences of Pragmatism.* Minneapolis: University of Minnesota Press, 1982.

Sade, D. A. F., Marquis de. *The 120 Days of Sodom or The Romance of the School of Libertinage.* Translated by Pieralessandro Casavini. Paris: Olympia Press, 1957.

Sartre, Jean-Paul. *Existentialism and Human Emotions.* Translated by Bernard Frechtman. New York: Philosophical Library, 1957.

Shakespeare, William. *Hamlet, Prince of Denmark.* In *The Complete Works of William Shakespeare,* edited by W. J. Craig. London: Oxford University Press, 1954.

———. *King Lear.* In *The Complete Works of William Shakespeare,* edited by W. J. Craig. London: Oxford University Press, 1954.

———. *Othello, the Moor of Venice.* In *The Complete Works of William Shakespeare,* edited by W. J. Craig. London: Oxford University Press, 1954.

Shils, Edward. *Tradition.* Chicago: University of Chicago Press, 1981.

Sophocles. *Oedipus the King.* In *The Three Theban Plays,* translated by Robert Fagles. New York: Viking Press, 1982.

Spinoza, Baruch de. *Ethics.* In *The Collected Works of Spinoza,* vol. 1, edited and translated by Edwin Curley. Princeton: Princeton University Press, 1985.

Strawson, Peter F. *Freedom and Resentment.* London: Methuen, 1974.

———. *Individuals.* Garden City, N.Y.: Doubleday, 1963.

Taylor, Charles. "Responsibility for Self." In *The Identities of Persons,* edited by Amelie O. Rorty. Berkeley: University of California Press, 1976.

———. *Human Agency and Language: Philosophical Papers.* Cambridge: Cambridge University Press, 1985.

Taylor, Richard. *Good and Evil.* New York: Macmillan, 1970.

Telfer, Elizabeth. *Happiness.* London: Macmillan, 1980.

Tolstoy, Leo. *The Cossacks and Other Stories.* Harmondsworth: Penguin Books, 1974.

Turnbull, Colin. *The Mountain People.* London: Pan Books, 1980.

Veatch, Henry B. *Human Rights.* Baton Rouge: University of Louisiana Press, 1985.

———. *Rational Man.* Bloomington: University of Indiana Press, 1962.

Walsh, W. H. "The Constancy of Human Nature." In *Contemporary British Philosophy,* 4th ser, edited by Hywel D. Lewis. London: Allen & Unwin, 1976.

Watkins, John. "Three Views Concerning Human Freedom." In *Nature and Conduct,* edited by R. S. Peters. London: Macmillan, 1975.

White, Patrick. *Voss.* Harmondsworth: Penguin Books, 1960.

Wiggins, David. "Truth, Invention, and the Meaning of Life." *Proceedings of the British Academy* 62 (1976): 331–78.

Williams, Bernard. *Moral Luck.* Cambridge: Cambridge University Press, 1981.

Wilson, Bryan R., ed., *Rationality.* Oxford: Blackwell, 1970.

Winch, Peter. *Ethics and Action.* London: Routledge, 1972.

———. "Human Nature." In *The Proper Study,* The Royal Institute Lectures, edited by G. N. A. Vesey. London: Macmillan, 1971.

Wollheim, Richard. *The Thread of Life.* Cambridge: Harvard University Press, 1984.

Woolf, Leonard. *Principia Politica.* London: Hogarth Press, 1953.

Wright, Georg H. Von. *Varieties of Goodness.* London: Routledge, 1963.

Yeats, William B. *The Second Coming.* In *The Collected Poems of W. B. Yeats.* London: Macmillan, 1982.

Index

Absurdity, 23–25
Alexander, 71, 80
Aristotle, 9, 42, 77, 92, 150–51, 169–70, 185, 189 n.1 (chap. 5), 191 n.5 (chap. 9), 192 n.7 (chap. 10)
Arnold, Matthew, 145, 150

Bad lives, 22–25
Basic beliefs, 147–48
Bentham, Jeremy, 82
Bergmann, Fritjhof, 190
Berlin, Sir Isaiah, 62, 189 n.1 (chap. 4), 190 n.5 (chap. 5), 193 n.12
Black, Max, 11, 192 n.4 (chap. 10)
Blanshard, Brand, 191 n.1 (chap. 9)
Bolt, Robert, 89, 91, 190 n.7 (chap. 5)
Brandt, Richard, 191 n.1 (chap. 8)
Butler, Joseph, 145

Caligula, 98, 113
Camus, Albert, 23, 25, 90, 98, 113, 116
Celli, Roberto, 11
Chad, 132–33, 136–38, 140–43
Charron, Pierre de, 151
Choice, 105–8, 129–33, 142–43
Christianity, 60, 85
Commitments, 64–67, 75–76, 89–94, 132–33, 159–60
Conrad, Joseph, 90
Contractarianism, 10, 50, 129
Convention, 45–51, 54–58, 148–49
Cooper, John M., 192 n.7 (chap. 10)
Crusoe, Robinson, 136, 175

Decency, 55, 145
Descartes, René, 79, 151, 192 n.6 (chap. 9)
Dirty hands, 66–67

Egalitarianism, 42–43
Einstein, Albert, 24

Eliot, George, 145
Eliot, Thomas S., 145
Elitism, 42–43
Eudaimonism, 9

Facts and values, 36–39
Foot, Philippa, 191 n.2 (chap. 8), 192 n.9
Frame, Donald, 189 n.2 (chap. 4)
Frankfurt, Henry G., 190 n.5 (chap. 6), 192 n.2 (chap. 10)
Freedom, 97–113, 186–87
Friendship, 55

Gert, Bernard, 188 n.3 (chap. 2)
Gewirth, Alan, 188 n.5 (chap. 2), 191 n.1 (chap. 8)
Golden Rule, 50, 179
Good and evil, 37, 41, 44
Gould, Josiah, 11

Hamlet, 163
Hamlyn, David, 190 n.1 (chap. 7)
Hampshire, Stuart, 189 n.1 (chap. 3), 190 n.4 (chap. 6), 191 n.2 (chap. 8)
Happiness, 161–73, 183
Hare, Richard M., 188 n.4 (chap. 2), 191 n.1 (chap. 8)
Henry VIII (king of England), 89
Herodotus, 70
Hill, Thomas E., Sr., 11
Historicism, 31–36, 39–40
Hitler, Adolf, 157
Hope, 82–84
Human nature, 15, 31–44, 185–86
Hume, David, 49, 57, 92, 96, 97–99, 111, 113, 145, 189 n.2 (chap. 3), 190 n.1 (chap. 6)

Ideals, 20, 71–72, 77–94, 175–76, 181–85

Ignorance of oneself, 112–26
Ilyich, Ivan, 146–50, 152–53
Important necessary characteristics, 32–34
Individuality, 67–72, 75, 143–44
Internal causation, 99, 102–5
Internal vs. external view, 168–73
Interpretation, 117–22, 139, 146–50
Intimacy, 55, 56, 187

James, Henry, 132–33, 142
Judgment, 145, 154–57, 159
Justification, 58–61, 88–89, 174–87

Kant, Immanuel, 82, 129, 191 n.1 (chap. 8)
Kantianism, 10, 49–50, 129–30
Kolenda, Konstantin, 11

La Boetia, Etienne de, 63, 65, 70, 75
Lenin, Vladimir I., 85, 123
Locke, John, 85
Love, 55, 144

McFall, Lynne, 11
MacIntyre, Alasdair, 189 n.1 (chap. 3), 191 n.2 (chap. 8), 192 n.1 (chap. 11)
Matson, Wallace I., 11, 190 n.5 (chap. 6)
Mill, John Stuart, 20–22, 23, 24, 29, 42, 60, 120, 188 n.1 (chap. 1), 189 n.6 (chap. 3)
Moderate naturalism, 39–44
Montaigne, Michel de, 9, 62–76, 79, 113, 136, 151, 166, 189 n.2 (chap. 4)
Moral growth, 133–38
Moral sensitivity, 76, 129–44, 158
Moral tradition, 45–61, 67–72, 143–44, 178–79, 186–87
Moral vocabulary, 93, 134–43
More, Saint Thomas, 89–94
Murdoch, Iris, 97, 133, 134, 136, 190 n.4 (chap. 5), 191 n.5 (chap. 7), 193 n.7

Nagel, Thomas, 23–24, 188 n.3 (chap. 1), 189 n.9, 192 n.8
Naturalism, 31–36, 43–44
Natural necessity, 97–105
Nietzsche, Friedrich, 79, 145, 170, 182, 192 n.4 (chap. 11)
Norton, David, 11, 191 n.4 (chap. 7)

Oakeshott, Michael, 189 n.3 (chap. 3), 190 n.5 (chap. 5)
Oedipus, 90, 100
Orwell, George, 60, 170

Perfectionism, 169–72
Plato, 24, 42, 70, 77, 82, 85, 101, 145, 151, 190 n.2 (chap. 5)
Pleasure, 18–19, 165–66
Polonius-syndrome, 153–54
Popper, Karl R., 190 n.5 (chap. 5), 193 n.11
Presuppositions, 84–89
Principles, 49–51
Public service vs. private life, 64–67

Rawls, John, 50, 188 n.5 (chap. 2), 191 n.1 (chap. 8)
Realism, 176
Reflection, 16–17, 96, 103
Relativism, 41–42, 58–61, 186
Rescher, Nicholas, 11, 192 n.4 (chap. 10)
Responsibility, 108–11
Rights theories, 10

Sartre, Jean-Paul, 130–33, 191 n.3 (chap. 8)
Satisfaction, 18–20, 27, 36–39, 54–58, 158–60, 163–68, 177–78, 179–80
Schopenhauer, Arthur, 25, 26, 145
Self-control, 76, 95–113, 158
Self-deception, 124–26
Self-direction, 18, 20, 25–30, 45, 55, 62–76, 129, 143–44, 157–60
Self-knowledge, 74, 76, 114–28, 158
Simple will, 25–30
Socrates, 71, 77, 80, 85, 113, 139, 151
Sophocles, 24, 145, 150
Spinoza, Baruch de, 24, 25, 26, 79, 80, 82–85, 99–102, 111, 136, 145, 188 n.6
Stoicism, 101, 111
Strawson, Sir Peter, 191 n.3 (chap. 9), 192 n.6 (chap. 11)
Strether, 132–33, 136–38, 140–43
Sub specie aeternitatis, 23–24, 86, 152
Sub specie humanitatis, 44, 152
Summum bonum, 43–44, 169–72
Sysiphus, 25–27

Taylor, Charles, 190 n.6 (chap. 5), 191 n.3 (chap. 7)
Taylor, Richard, 25–27, 188 nn. 7, 8, and 9
Theresa, Saint, 79, 166
Thomas Aquinas, Saint, 145, 151
Tolstoy, Leo, 146, 191 n.2 (chap. 9)

Utilitarianism, 10, 50, 129

Veatch, Henry B., 189 n.8, 192 n.7 (chap. 10), 193 n.8
Virtues, 20, 95–96, 157–60, 180–81
Virtue theory, 9

Wants, 18–19, 25–30, 158–60, 163–68
Weil, Simone, 79, 123
Wiggins, David, 188 n.11
Williams, Bernard, 190 n.6 (chap. 6), 191 n.2 (chap. 8)
Winch, Peter, 189 n.6 (chap. 2), 192 n.5 (chap. 11)
Wisdom, 76, 145–60
Wollheim, Richard, 188 n.10, 191 n.2 (chap. 7)
Woolf, Leonard and Virginia, 155–56

Yeats, William B., 69, 189 n.4 (chap. 4)